POPULAR WOODWORKING'S
ARTS & CRAFTS
FURNITURE PROJECTS

POPULAR WOODWORKING BOOKS
CINCINNATI, OHIO
www.popularwoodworking.com

READ THIS IMPORTANT SAFETY NOTICE

To prevent accidents, keep safety in mind while you work. Use the safety guards installed on power equipment. When working on power equipment, keep fingers away from saw blades, wear safety goggles to prevent injuries from flying wood chips and sawdust, wear hearing protection and consider installing a dust vacuum to reduce the amount of airborne sawdust in your woodshop. Don't wear loose clothing, or jewelry when working on power equipment. Tie back long hair to prevent it from getting caught in your equipment. People who are sensitive to certain chemicals should check the chemical content of any product before using it. The authors and editors who compiled this book have tried to make the contents as accurate and correct as possible. Plans, illustrations, photographs and text have been carefully checked. All instructions, plans and projects should be carefully read, studied and understood before beginning construction. Due to the variability of local conditions, construction materials, skill levels, etc., neither the author nor *Popular Woodworking* Books assumes any responsibility for any accidents, injuries, damages or other losses incurred resulting from the material presented in this book. Prices listed for supplies and equipment were current at the time of publication and are subject to change.

Popular Woodworking's Arts & Crafts Furniture Projects. Copyright © 2008 by Popular Woodworking Books. Printed and bound in China. All rights reserved. No part of this book may be reproduced in any form or by any electronic or mechanical means including information storage and retrieval systems without permission in writing from the publisher, except by a reviewer, who may quote brief passages in a review. Published by Popular Woodworking Books, an imprint of F+W Publications, Inc., 4700 East Galbraith Road, Cincinnati, Ohio, 45236. First edition.

Distributed in Canada by Fraser Direct
100 Armstrong Avenue
Georgetown, Ontario L7G 5S4
Canada

Distributed in the U.K. and Europe by David & Charles
Brunel House
Newton Abbot
Devon TQ12 4PU
England
Tel: (+44) 1626 323200
Fax: (+44) 1626 323319
E-mail: postmaster@davidandcharles.co.uk

Distributed in Australia by Capricorn Link
P.O. Box 704
Windsor, NSW 2756
Australia

Visit our website at www.popularwoodworking.com or our corporate website at www.fwpublications.com for information on more resources for woodworkers and other publications.

Other fine Popular Woodworking Books are available from your local bookstore or direct from the publisher.

12   11   10   09   08   5   4   3   2   1

Library of Congress Cataloging-in-Publication Data

Popular woodworking's arts & crafts furniture projects.
    p. cm.
  Includes index.
  ISBN-10: 1-55870-846-4 (pbk. : alk. paper)
  ISBN-13: 978-1-55870-846-4 (pbk. : alk. paper)
1. Furniture making--Amateurs' manuals. 2. Furniture--Styles--Amateurs' manuals. 3. Arts and crafts movement--Amateurs' manuals. I. Popular woodworking. II. Title: Arts & crafts furniture projects.
  TT194.P665 2008
  684.1--dc22
                                                    2007034903

Editor: *David Thiel*
Designer: *Brian Roeth*
Production Coordinator: *Mark Griffin*
Photographer: *Al Parrish and individual authors*
Illustrator: *John Hutchinson*

F+W PUBLICATIONS, INC.

METRIC CONVERSION CHART

to convert	to	multiply by
Inches	Centimeters	2.54
Centimeters	Inches	0.4
Feet	Centimeters	30.5
Centimeters	Feet	0.03
Yards	Meters	0.9
Meters	Yards	1.1

ABOUT THE AUTHORS

Robert W. Lang
Bob is senior editor for *Popular Woodworking* magazine and is also the author of five books focusing on arts and crafts furniture and related architectural details.

Christopher Schwarz
Chris is editor of *Popular Woodworking* magazine, a contributing editor to *The Fine Tool Journal* and teaches traditional woodworking techniques. He has two DVDs produced by Lie-Nielsen Toolworks on nearly forgotten hand tools and on blending hand tools and power tools.

Steve Shanesy
Steve served as editor of *Popular Woodworking* magazine for nine years, before being named publisher of the magazine, a position he continues to hold.

Jim Stack
Jim is senior editor of *Popular Woodworking* books and is the author of eight woodworking books. As a result, he's tired and will answer no more questions.

Jim Stuard
Jim is a former editor for *Popular Woodworking* magazine and is currently enjoying his two children and creating fly-fishing videos for the internet.

David Thiel
David is executive editor for Popular Woodworking books, and served as an editor for *Popular Woodworking* magazine for eleven years. He is also the host of the DIY Network program DIY Tools and Techniques.

Kara (Gebhart) Uhl
Kara served as managing editor for *Popular Woodworking* for four years, learning woodworking skills along the way. She is currently managing editor for *Writer's Digest* magazine.

CONTENTS

INTRODUCTION

Arts & Crafts furniture stirs different emotions in every person. Interestingly to many people who grew up shortly after the first "movement" (ending around 1920) much of this furniture is remembered as clunky, dark and often relegated to a porch or basement. Happily, for a much larger audience, the simple lines, solid construction and homey esthetics of Arts & Crafts furniture strike a more harmonious chord.

From a woodworking point of view Arts & Crafts furniture serves as an excellent learning medium for furniture building. Arts & Crafts furniture offers a reasonably short learning curve requiring only a few basic joinery techniques that can be easily mastered. Along with Shaker furniture, Arts & Crafts furniture lets the craftsman build a quality piece of furniture in a reasonable amount of time and provides a very successful and satisfying experience.

Beyond the simple joinery and lines, the wood used in Arts & Crafts furniture (quarter-sawn white oak, mahogany and even ebony details) provide a beautiful finished appearance and a particularly satisfying detail for lovers of wood for itself.

As a category Arts & Crafts furniture is frequently identified with a single manufacturer, Gustav Stickley. Because of this, many woodworkers (and non-woodworkers) have a single image of the furniture style in their mind. Quite the opposite, there are many different manufacturers (discussed in detail in the history chapter of this book) offering very individual and varied styling, all encompassed in the larger category of Arts & Crafts. If Stickley isn't to your taste, perhaps Roycroft or Greene & Greene will appeal.

We're happy to offer this collection of Arts & Crafts furniture projects (on both the book and the extra articles and projects included on the CD-ROM) as both a skill-building tool for woodworking, and as a collection of furniture projects that the *Popular Woodworking* staff considers to be some of most visually appealing pieces of furniture ever created. We hope you'll enjoy building and living with these projects as much as we have.

David Thiel
Executive Editor, Popular Woodworking Books

THE HISTORY OF
ARTS & CRAFTS FURNITURE

by Christopher Schwarz

Arts & Crafts furniture was the product of a brief but fruitful social movement in the United States at the turn of the 20th century. For a short moment in history, the American people declared they didn't want frilly, highly carved, machine-made stuff. They wanted furniture and decorative objects that were made by hand, with simple straight lines and honest construction.

Furniture makers and philosophers gave the American people what they demanded (though sometimes they created it using machines) until consumers' attention turned to World War I. Though the Arts & Crafts period lasted less than 20 years, its societal and stylistic impact is still felt today by scholars, home decorators and woodworkers.

My first encounter with the Arts & Crafts movement occurred more than a decade ago in a foggy field outside Pickens, South Carolina. A friend and I had awoken before dawn that day to attend a farmers' market that promised fresh produce, Mennonite baked goods and the occasional piece of furniture pulled from a barn or an attic. As we left the truck, carrying flashlights and heading into the fog, we ran into four men toting shotguns. It was going to be a dangerous day ... but not because of the gun-wielding locals. I was facing the precipice of a deep hole from which few ever emerge: I was about to become a hard-core collector of all things Arts & Crafts.

The farmer's market was chockfull of men trading guns,

Gustav Stickley

military memorabilia, tools and other junk — which is the stuff we were looking for. One old guy had a truck that was almost completely covered in rust, except for the worn wooden gates on the sides that kept the stuff on his flatbed from spilling off the truck and onto the highway. This morning he had a few old dressers, some rusted metal things of unknown origin or use and one rocker. The back of the rocker was covered by an ugly blanket and its runners were soaked with dew, but the minute I glimpsed the outline of the first Arts & Crafts piece I had ever seen, I was hooked. I learned later that the rocker was an old copy of a low-slung L.& J.G. Stickley piece, but all I knew back then was that it was only $30 and so it was going to be mine. I took it home, and my fiancee allowed it to occupy a corner of the office. A few weeks later, I bought a huge Arts & Crafts settee that concealed a massive iron bed frame. It was stuffed with the original horsehair and had been owned by the first African American doctor in Rome, Georgia. And it was only $125. So it, too, became mine.

For the next few years, I spent every spare dime of my disposable income on Arts & Crafts furniture, books, pottery and metalwork. I went to lectures at the Grove Park Inn in Asheville, North Carolina. I spent hours poring over the reprints of manufacturers' catalogs that were just then becoming widely available. And I learned everything I could about how Arts & Crafts furniture was made: mortise and tenon, quadrilinear post construction, wedged and keyed through-tenons.

Of course, by 1993 it seemed the whole world was doing the same thing. And the newcomers had a lot more money. Soon, the pieces of furniture I wanted were selling at auction for prices that rivaled my yearly salary as a writer. Then, one day, I heard about a woodworking class at the University of Kentucky. The class focused on hand tools and traditional joints. At that moment, I knew I would become a woodworker.

The professor spent a lot of time teaching me and my classmates how to cut a mortise-and-tenon joint with a backsaw and a chisel. I cut mine as fast as I could in a piece of poplar. "Lynn," I asked, "could you show me how to cut a wedged through-tenon?" My instructor looked at me kind of funny. He built high-end modern stuff with lots of plywood and lots of bent laminations, "Why would you want to learn such an old-fashioned joint?" he asked. I didn't tell him why, because I certainly didn't need one more person interested in the Arts & Crafts movement. But he showed me how to do it with hand tools. Then he showed me how to use a hollow chisel mortiser, and I was hooked.

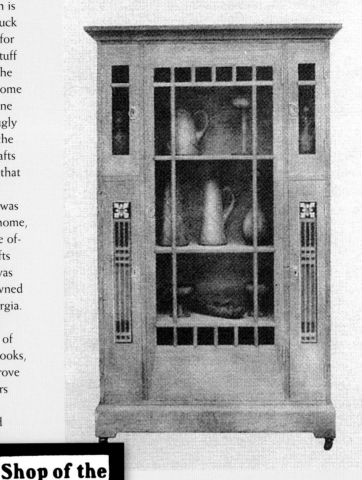

Item #326, China cabinet, from 1906 Shop for the Crafters at Cincinnati catalog.

TOO EXPENSIVE TO COLLECT

For the average American, authentic Arts & Crafts furniture has become all but unaffordable. Furniture that is signed by its maker and has its original finish and upholstery now sells for thousands of dollars. Cabinetmakers sell authentic reproductions, but the good ones are, again, thousands of dollars.

And the stuff available in furniture stores varies somewhere between not entirely bad and unspeakably awful. So it's official. The only way you are going to be able to afford authentic Arts & Crafts furniture is to build it yourself. That's where this book comes in.

During the last decade, many of the *Popular Woodworking* staff members have been building Arts & Crafts furniture for our homes and for publication in *Popular Woodworking* magazine. Some of these designs have been adaptations. For example, the Arts & Crafts sideboard on page 188 owes a huge debt to four or five sideboards produced by one or another of the Stickley brothers. But instead of creating a museum copy, David scaled the proportions down a bit to fit into a modern home. Other projects in this book have been taken from photos of original pieces, examples we found in museums or, in the case of the Shop of the Crafters Morris chair on page 100, an exact replica was made from the original.

Arts & Crafts furniture is remarkably simple to make. In fact, it's no coincidence that just as the Arts & Crafts movement was coming into its own in 1900, the manual training movement became an important force in schools. It was the first time American schools had sought to teach handicrafts, including woodworking and sewing. In fact, Gustav Stickley (1858-1942), one of the spiritual fathers of the movement, urged students in his shop class to build Arts & Crafts-style furniture because of its simple joinery and honest construction.

So as you embark on building your own American classics, you can rest assured it has been part of the learning experience for woodworkers for more than a century.

THE MYTHICAL MOVEMENT

The Arts & Crafts movement itself was founded on good intentions, cloaked in philosophy and popularized through advertising and marketing. The now-popular legend is that the Arts & Crafts movement came about because people at the turn of the centu-

Leopold Stickley

ry rejected the mass-produced and ornate furnishings of the Victorian "Golden Oak" period and longed for furniture that was honest, simple and made by hand. And while it's true that the founders of the movement had pure intentions, the reality is that most of the people involved in producing Arts & Crafts goods during this period were more concerned with exploiting a furniture fad.

Most historians trace the origin of the American Arts & Crafts movement to Englishmen John Ruskin (1819-1900) and William Morris (1834-1896), whose name has been given to the Morris chair, though no one has ever been able to convince me he ever even sat in one. According to David M. Cathers' seminal work on the movement, *Furniture of the American Arts & Crafts Movement*, Ruskin believed that the industrial age had dehumanized workers who were slaving in England's early industrial factories. To break the bonds of the machine and create an improved social order, workers needed to return to creating handmade objects. In essence, Ruskin wanted a return to the old medieval guild system.

William Morris agreed and came up with an idea to actually do something about the situation. He founded a company in 1861 that put these principles into practice. The idea was that people would make beautiful objects by hand that the middle class could afford. In this way, the workers' lives would be improved, and the level of taste and quality of goods in the marketplace would also improve. Unfortunately, as you probably well know, making things by hand is slow and very expensive. As it turned out, the only people who could afford Morris' beautiful wares were the very wealthy. So in 1881, Morris allowed machines into his workshop to remove the drudgery of routine tasks for his workers; it also made the furniture more affordable.

Morris' and Ruskin's ideas, however, were flourishing in the minds of the right people in America. Elbert Hubbard (1856-1915), the founder of the Roycrofters, and Gustav Stickley traveled to Europe and were exposed to these ideas. They came back to the United States and, within a year or two, a movement was born. Stickley spent some time experimenting with different designs and was producing his first line of Craftsman furniture by 1900. Hubbard founded a printing company. After he expanded his building, he needed to give the carpenters something to do. Legend has it that they built a few tables for the new buildings. When visitors toured his place, they wanted to buy the tables, and so a new furniture company was born. Both companies were more like craftsmen's guilds than traditional cabinet shops of that time period. Both began producing furniture mostly by hand. And both would eventually reject this idea in order to stay in business.

As soon as other furniture makers saw the popularity of this new style, they began to copy it. They developed their own lines of furniture made from white oak, and they used the same marketing tactics employed by Stickley and Hubbard, who preached about the virtues of handmade furniture.

Charles P. Limbert's catalog No. 112 is a good example of some of the puffery that the public was eager to swallow. "Our heavy tops are solid planks," Limbert wrote. "We use no strips on the edges to make them appear heavier." Well, I can tell you with certainty: That declaration is a load of bunk. I've inspected half of a dozen examples of his furniture that use buildup strips on the edges; as a matter of fact, one of them is in my living room. At the Roycroft Shop in East Aurora, New York, visitors were shown the work area, which featured some massive woodworking benches, a lot of hand tools and not a machine in sight. Visitors were never shown the mechanical tenon cutters, saws or sanders. Handmade objects were all the rage. But only the machine could deliver these products at a price the public could afford.

Most woodworkers, like myself, are quick to forgive the furniture makers of that time because we struggle

A Welsh cupboard similar to this drawing was noticed by Leopold Stickley during an exploratory visit to Chester, England.

with this same dilemma every day we're in the shop. I enjoy cutting dovetails by hand, but you'd have to pry my ³/₄-hp jointer out of my cold, dead hands before I'd give it up. So is my work a product of handwork or is it merely machining the wood to an exact tolerance? Modern woodworking machines have reduced the tedium of many time-consuming tasks. Would you enjoy woodworking if you had to spend three solid days surfacing all your stock with a scrub plane? Probably not. So, if you feel a tinge of guilt as you fire up your hollow chisel mortiser, wondering if you're being true to the movement, you can rest assured that Stickley, Hubbard and others felt exactly the same way. And, in the end, they chose the path that took the drudgery out of construction and allowed the woodworker to enjoy the simple act of creation.

ABOUT THE MANUFACTURERS

Probably hundreds of companies were producing Arts & Crafts furniture around the turn of the century, and probably even more are producing it today. To give you a feel for the history behind the pieces in this book, we've included short profiles of the major manufacturers we've highlighted, including the major stylistic elements you'd find on original pieces.

WHO WERE THE BROTHERS STICKLEY?

When most people see a piece of Arts & Crafts furniture, they inevitably ask if it's a Stickley. It's a horrible question to try to answer. That's because several Stickleys were building furniture at the time. Gustav Stickley had his own firm, Craftsman Workshop. His brothers, Leopold and

Popular Woodworking's reproduction of item #255, the Limbert Waste-paper Box. Plans for this project are included on the accompanying CD-Rom.

John George, founded L. & J.G. Stickley. Brother Charles had his own firm called Stickley and Brandt. And all of the brothers were involved, at one time or another, with the Stickley Brothers company. It's interesting to note that before the Arts & Crafts movement began about 1899, all five of the Stickley brothers were involved in building period reproduction chairs, exactly the kind of stuff that they would later rail against. The first brother to make this switch was, of course, Gustav. Between 1900 and 1916, Gustav's Craftsman Workshops in Eastwood, New York, produced what is now considered the best work of the day. His furniture is characterized by through-tenons that have been reinforced by dowels, bold but pleasing proportions and an absolutely first-class finish. Though most people think of Arts & Crafts furniture as universally dark brown, Gustav offered a finish that was brownish-green and another that had a tinge of gray. I've seen both of these finishes on original and reproduction furniture, and I'm surprised more woodworkers haven't given them a try.

His case pieces are marked by heavy, copper hardware (though he is said to have preferred square oak knobs) and shiplapped backs that have a small chamfer on the seam between the boards. Later examples of his work show that he used a plywood back. All of his furniture was signed, usually with an imprint of a joiner's compass and the Flemish expression, *Als ik kan*. This translates to As I can, or As best I can.

Gustav also published *The Craftsman* magazine — a publication devoted to all things Arts & Crafts. While it was a vehicle for selling his goods, *The Craftsman* also offered complete plans for furniture, a heavy dose of philosophy, as well as floor plans and decorating tips for the ideal home. By 1912, his business was in decline. The world went to war, and when that was over, there was little interest in the Arts & Crafts movement. The style had been supplanted by an interest in Art Deco styles originating in Europe, colonial pieces from America's past and, eventually, modernism that was inspired by machines. Gustav died in 1942 while living with his daughter. Apparently he was still experimenting with finishes to the very end; his descendants found small patches on the underside of the furniture in his room that had been used as sample boards.

L. & J.G. STICKLEY: THE OTHER BROTHERS

Leopold and John George's company in Fayetteville, New York, is worthy of note because it survives to this day. The work that came from L. & J.G. Stickley looked a lot like the furniture from the Craftsman Workshop, with only minor alterations. According to Bruce Johnson's account of the company, L. & J.G. Stickley's copies were of the highest quality. Other imitators of Gustav's furniture would use dowels to assemble the furniture and simply nail a fake tenon end onto a leg to suggest a through-tenon. L. & J.G. Stickley's shop appeared dedicated to quality workmanship.

Above is item #340 from an early-1900's Limbert catalog, and at right is the Popular Woodworking reproduction of the same two-door bookcase. Plans for the project are found on page 40.

In fact, in a couple of instances, items produced by L. & J.G. Stickley exceeded the workmanship at Craftsman Workshop. For example, in order to get quartersawn ray flake on all four sides of a table leg, Gustav would glue quartersawn veneer onto the two sides that showed the plain-sawn grain. L. & J.G. Stickley used quadrilinear post construction. This involves taking four pieces of wood and essentially cutting a lock miter on all of the edges to make a table leg. It creates a superior leg.

Unlike their brother Gustav, Leopold and John George were willing to change their furniture line to match their customers' tastes. The company issued its last Arts & Crafts catalog in 1922 (six years after Gustav went out of business) and began producing a line of colonial reproduction furniture in cherry. The company's 1950 catalog is interesting because it reads exactly like the company's 1914 catalog. You only need to replace the word *oak* with the word *cherry*:

"It was furniture that took full advantage of the durability and workability of the wild cherry wood ... furniture with broad flat surfaces that revealed the beautiful figure of the wood to advantage and that melted into pools of liquid fire when candlelight gleamed onto its carefully rubbed and polished finish."

After Leopold's death in 1957, his descendants sold the business to Alfred and Aminy Audi, who began producing Arts & Crafts furniture again in 1989.

OTHER STICKLEYS
Furniture collectors generally consider the other companies bearing the Stickley name to have been manufacturers of lesser furniture, though occasionally one piece will surprise you. One of my favorite pieces of furniture is a Stickley and Brandt side chair with a spring seat. The workmanship and finish rivals that of pieces from the Craftsman Workshop.

CHARLES P. LIMBERT COMPANY:
CURVES AND CUTOUTS
Three of the projects in this book are reproductions from the Charles P. Limbert Company's catalog. Unlike many of the imitators of the day, Limbert's factory in Grand Rap-

ids, Michigan, turned out an extensive line of Arts & Crafts furniture that was much less massive and rectilinear than the Stickley lines. Many of Limbert's pieces had a decidedly European influence. Curves and cutouts were common on some pieces. On other pieces, he clearly was trying to take customers away by imitating the Stickleys.

As customers' tastes changed, Limbert was ready. Late in the period he introduced a popular line of "Ebon-oak" furniture, which was made from oak inlaid with ebony. The rocking chair featured on page 108 is from this collection. It is considered one of the finest rockers of the era and co-mands a high price tag at auction.

GREENE & GREENE:ARCHITECTS WITH A FLAIR FOR FURNITURE

It's not really fair to lump Charles and Henry Greene's architectural firm with furniture manufacturers, but it's necessary. The Greene brothers, like Frank Lloyd Wright, were not in the business of producing furniture. However, they wanted to design the furniture that went into the homes they built for wealthy clients. (And when the clients couldn't afford their fur-niture, they insisted the client purchase furniture from Gustav Stickley.)

Greene & Greene furniture is noteworthy because of its unabashed Asian influence. Instead of oak, Greene and Greene used mahogany as their primary wood. Instead of using straight stretchers on chairs or tables, the Greene brothers' furniture incorporated a "cloud lift," a gentle bump, into the designs. And their signature design ele-ment included placing inlaid ebony pegs into the major joints. Sometimes these pegs were structural; sometimes they concealed screws.

Like furniture designed by Wright, Greene & Greene designs are rare and highly sought after. Some pieces fetch hundreds of thousands of dollars. In fact, some pieces, such as the Greene & Greene entry bench featured on page 116 have disappeared altogether into the black market.

SHOP OF THE CRAFTERS: EUROPEAN DESIGNS FOR THE MIDWEST MAN

We've always had a soft spot in our hearts for furniture from the Shop of the Crafters because the company is lo-cated in the same town as our editorial offices: Cincinnati, Ohio. Oscar Onken (1858-1948) began as a picture framer and then in 1904 founded his own furniture company that produced a full line of Arts & Crafts furniture. The furni-

Limbert's Arts and Crafts workshop attached this leather tag trademark to each piece of cabinetwork they created.

ture was more European in flavor than most, and many pieces relied heavily on inlay or veneer. Unfortunately, the construction techniques Onken used were not always up to par with those used by the Stickleys. His Morris chairs, for example, used dow-els at the major joints instead of mor-tise-and-tenon joints.

The Shop of the Crafters cata-log was geared mostly toward men. The furniture itself was massive and overbuilt, sometimes to the point of looking clunky. And Onken's catalog was filled with cellarettes and smoking stands, two of the pieces of furniture reserved for a man's den of the period.

ROYCROFT SHOP: PRINTING, METAL-WORKING AND WOODWORKING

Elbert Hubbard was a successful soap salesman who turned philosopher after an 1894 encounter with Wil-liam Morris in England. Hubbard was impressed by Morris' press and his guild of workers who were making furniture, wallpaper, textiles and books. So Hubbard returned to the States and set up a company that imitated Morris' Kelmscott Press. From his shop in East Aurora, New York, Hubbard produced his magazine, *The Philistine*, and a series of books called Little Journeys, which contained biographies of influential reformers (including Morris), philosophers, musicians and scientists.

His campus and his flamboyant personality attracted the attention of the public, which flocked to his shop. They wanted to buy the furniture they saw there, and he let them. According to Bruce Johnson, it's unlikely that Hubbard designed the furniture made by the Roycroft Shop; that task was handled by others. But the furniture is some of the most massive and well built on the antique market today. And it was considerably more expensive than furniture sold by Gustav Stickley. Even as the demand for the heavy furniture waned and other manufacturers began to shift gears, the Roycrofters stuck to their guns, even after Hubbard himself was drowned in the sinking of the *Lusitania* in 1915. Furniture making continued until the 1930s, but by 1938 the shop was bankrupt.

BYRDCLIFFE ARTS COLONY: PERHAPS THE EARLIEST HIPPIES IN WOODSTOCK

The Byrdcliffe Arts Colony was an experimental utopian community founded by Ralph Radcliffe Whitehead (1854-1929) in 1902 in Woodstock, New York. It was to be a

ISN'T ARTS & CRAFTS JUST ANOTHER FURNITURE FAD?

In 1990, a friend of mine who had been collecting Arts & Crafts furniture for five years told me that I should wait to purchase a few antique pieces because the bottom of the market was about to fall out. According to him, the Arts & Crafts revival, which had begun in the 1970s, was going to take a serious nosedive, and soon the furniture would be affordable for everyone. At the time, I was eyeing a Shop of the Crafters Morris chair that had been languishing in an Anderson, South Carolina, antiques market for months with a $360 price tag.

"Just wait," he said. "And the price will come down."

I couldn't wait. I bought the chair. And it's lucky I did. The bottom has yet to fall out of the market. The American public has a seemingly inexhaustible hunger for all things Arts & Crafts — from Morris chairs to the plates that cover your light switches. The current revival, according to some estimates, has now lasted longer than the original movement. But, every year, I hear the same refrain from people inside and out of the movement: It's going to end some day, so watch out. Perhaps they're afraid they'll end up like Gustav Stickley did, forgotten and living with his daughter, experimenting with finishes on tiny patches of wood on the underside of his bedroom furniture.

Now, I'm sure that the craze surrounding Arts & Crafts will die down a bit. And maybe some of the people who are producing junk won't be able to sell it anymore. But the important thing to remember here is that the Arts & Crafts style has now been recognized as an important period in furniture history, like the heyday of 18th-century American cabinetmaking. And while colonial reproductions are hard to come by in the superstores, the market for authentic antiques and quality handmade reproductions in this style is as strong as ever. This is likely the future of Arts & Crafts.

So if you enjoy the clean lines and honest workmanship of Arts & Crafts furniture, I think you are going to enjoy this book and relish the furniture you build using it. And if you take extra special care to peg all of your tenons with dowels, if you account for wood movement as best you can, and if you cut each joint as tight as possible, I'm sure your great-grandchildren are going to feel the same way about your furniture, too.

place where artists and craftsmen could work together to produce beautiful objects for sale much like a modern-day commune.

It never quite worked out that way. Wendy Kaplan estimates the colony turned out fewer than 50 pieces of furniture. Apparently some of the pieces were so heavy and massive that shipping them was difficult. And because they were made by hand — frequently with carvings — they were unaffordable for most people. By 1905, the founder — Ralph Radcliffe Whitehead — had closed the doors to the woodshop.

CONSTRUCTION AND FINISHING TECHNIQUES

ach of the project chapters in this book includes step-by-step construction directions that should provide adequate information, for all but the very new woodworker, to successfully build each project. We've also included the specific finishing processes used for each individual project. We'll talk more about finishing later. Where possible we have endeavored to teach new methods and simplify complicated processes.

In addition to these fairly thorough directions, we felt it appropriate to include this section on construction and finishing techniques specific to Arts & Crafts furniture designs. While none of these joints or finishing techniques is unique to Arts & Crafts furniture (except for ammonia fuming for finishing), when a number of them occur in a single piece there's a good chance that it fits in the Arts & Crafts category.

CONSTRUCTION

On the following, pages we will discuss construction techniques for a number of types of mortise-and-tenon joints — including blind, through, pegged, wedged and keyed tenons. We will also take a look at the use of quadrilinear construction for legs and posts, corbels for esthetics and support, shiplapped construction for use with solid wood backs, and the use of pattern routing to make identical esthetic shapes. With basic woodworking knowledge and the detailed instruction of these techniques, you will be able to build almost any Arts & Crafts furniture piece.

MORTISE AND TENON

It's not really going too far to say that you can't build a piece of Arts & Crafts furniture without using a mortise-and-tenon joint somewhere. The type and complexity of mortise-and-tenon joints varies from project to project, but this was a popular joint with the Arts & Crafts craftsman. Happily, they weren't nearly as fond of dovetails, which take a bit more skill.

The basic mortise-and-tenon joint, or blind tenon, consists of a square hole cut into one piece of wood, with a correspondingly sized nub cut on the end of the mating piece of wood. Square peg A in square hole B. Simple. This joint gets used in chair construction to join legs and stretchers, to attach back splats to back rails and then the back rails to the back legs. Simple mortise-and-tenon joinery also sees frequent use in stile-and-rail door construction and in stile-and-rail panel construction in case pieces. This makes lots of sense because the strength offered from this joint is amazing. When you add the option of wedged or pegged tenons the joint is nearly indestructible. Make it a through-tenon with a key, and this remarkably strong joint can be taken apart to collapse the piece of furniture and easily move it. The mortise and tenon are handy and versatile joints, so let's talk about how to make them.

There are two basic schools of thought on all mortise-and-tenon construction. In one, you cut the mortise, or hole, first, then fit the tenon to the mortise. In the other, you make the tenon first and then fit the mortise. Neither

Mortises (made using a moritser at left) and tenons (as shown being made on the table saw above), create the mortise and tenon joint that is a staple in Arts & Crafts furniture.

is wrong, but the mortise-first method has benefits that most of us at *Popular Woodworking* agree with. So, let's start with making the mortise, and hopefully you'll see why it's the better method.

MORTISES

There are a few ways to make a mortise. The traditional method is with a chisel and mallet, defining the shape of the mortise and slowly paring away the wood with the chisel. If you count the number of mortises in either the box spindle chair project or the sideboard project, you may decide hand cutting is a labor-intensive method. The tool of choice is a dedicated square-chisel mortiser. Designed to cut $\frac{1}{4}$", $\frac{3}{8}$" or $\frac{1}{2}$" mortises, these clever tools not only drill out the hole, but with the use of an attached four-sided chisel, they square the corners. The mortiser allows you to set the depth of the mortise, and make accurate, square mortises, quickly and with relatively little difficulty. While you may not be looking for more machinery for your shop, if you plan on building any amount of Arts & Crafts furniture, you may want to seriously consider a mortiser.

Another option is to use an existing drill press. While the drill press won't square out the corners of the mortise for you, it certainly will speed up the operation. Then you head back to basics and simply square out the corners with your hand chisel. Another option with a drill press is a mortising attachment. This attachment turns your drill press into a mortiser. The one difference is the distance the drill press lever must travel to create the same depth hole as the mortiser. Because of the way the machines are geared, the mortiser can create the same hole with a third of the travel necessary on a drill press.

No matter which method you choose, the mortising process is the same. Start by carefully marking the location of the mortise. The usual procedure is to cut the mortise in the center of the face of the piece. The mortise width should be one-third the thickness of the piece, and the depth should be approximately two-thirds the width. So if your door stile is $\frac{3}{4}$" × $1\frac{1}{2}$", the mortise should be $\frac{3}{8}$"-wide, centered on the $\frac{3}{4}$" face, and be approximately 1" deep. The mortise formed by this method is referred to as a blind mortise and tenon because the joinery will not be visible on the finished piece.

The only other option is a through mortise, which is cut all the way through the piece of wood. In any through-cutting situation, take care to avoid tear-out on the exit side of the mortise. The easiest way to do this is by using a backing piece. While this piece will help a lot, there will probably be some tear-out. Make sure that the tearout side is on the face that the tenon's shoulder will seat against, helping to hide the imperfect mortise.

TENONS

Now that we've talked about mortises, let's look at the tenons. A tenon can be cut a few different ways. Either two or four sides can be pared away (basically performing a rabbet cut), to leave less than the thickness or width of the piece. The sides of the tenons are referred to as the cheeks, and the top of the notch left after the cut is referred to as the shoulder. If a tenon is cut with four cheeks, the shoulders will hide imperfections caused by cutting the mortise. Since the usual shoulder is only about $\frac{3}{16}$"-wide, it won't hide everything, but if your mortise is that sloppy, it won't make a very good joint either.

To cut a tenon, the usual method is to use a table saw. A router table can also be used, and there's still the old faithful handsaw if you've got the extra time and energy. To make tenons on the table saw, the first step is to define the shoulder, thereby determining the length of the tenon. Set your rip fence for the length of the tenon, including the blade thickness in the dimension (you'll be cutting

Quadralinear Post

Through-mortise and wedged tenon.

the shoulder height to the left of the blade, or, said another way, the cut will include the thickness of the blade). You should cut the tenon $\frac{1}{16}$" shorter than the depth of your mortise to leave a place for the glue to pool. Square the miter gauge to the blade, and with the blade set at a height to cut a little less than the shoulder width, lay the tenon piece flat on the saw; with the end against the rip fence, push the miter gauge and piece through the blade, cutting on two or four sides as required. For example, if you are cutting a tenon for the above-mentioned $\frac{3}{8}$"-wide, by 1"- deep mortise on $\frac{3}{4}$" material, the rip fence is likely set for $\frac{13}{16}$" (including the $\frac{1}{8}$" blade thickness), and the blade height would be set for a little less than $\frac{3}{16}$" high. All four sides can be cut with this setting.

Next, reset the fence for the width of the tenon, plus the width of the shoulder, and change the height of the blade to the actual length of the tenon. In our example this would be $\frac{1}{16}$" between the fence and blade, and the height would be $\frac{15}{16}$". By running the piece on end with the wider side against the fence, the two wider cheeks are formed. The fence is then reset to trim the two other cheeks to size. Some woodworkers choose to cut the cheeks first, then define the shoulders, but, by following that order, you will end up with the waste piece trapped between the blade and fence, causing a kickback.

Unless you have a certain amount of comfort and experience on the table saw, running the cheek cuts with the piece upright is best performed with a support jig behind the piece to keep the piece square to the table and to help control the cut. Another option is a tenoning fixture designed for the table saw to cut tenons. While a useful, accurate and efficient device, it costs a little more, and I actually find it a little time-consuming. Still another option, and also time-consuming, is to leave the piece lying flat after the initial shoulder defining cut and use repeat passes to nibble away the rest of the tenon waste.

Although following these steps to cut the tenon should give you an accurate fit to your mortise, you should cut test pieces to check the size as you go. A mortise-and-tenon joint should be a snug fit, but you shouldn't have to use too much force to put it together. Also, too loose and your joint will have less strength. It's best to have the tenons a little thicker than necessary, then carefully fit them to the mortise with a shoulder plane, chisel or a little sanding.

THROUGH-TENONS

Beyond the basic blind mortise and tenon is the through-tenon. With the mortise cut all the way through the piece, either the tenon can be cut flush, then wedged into the end of the tenon, or it can be left long to extend beyond the outer face of the piece. If left long, the end of the tenon can be chamfered on four edges to leave a decorative edge, then pegged (we'll talk more about this). Or the tenon can be left very long and a key added to secure the joint (more about this, as well).

PEGGED TENONS

Pegging a tenon is a great way to make an already strong joint even stronger. To peg a tenon, after it has been glued and seated in place in the mortise, drill a hole through the side of the leg or other mortised piece, going through the center of the tenon and on through into the opposite side of the mortise. Insert a dowel of corresponding diameter into the hole and glue it in place in the hole, then cut the dowel flush to the surface. The extra strength provided by this "wooden nail" should be obvious at this point, but over time it will be even more useful. As wood ages, it has a tendency to shrink a little, which can allow a tight mortise-and-tenon joint to loosen up. The peg can hold the joint tight, even if the tenon shrinks in the mortise. Pegging is a fine idea for blind or through-tenon construction.

KEYED TENONS

In a keyed tenon, another through-mortise is drilled in the extended length of the tenon (partially hidden by the mortised leg or piece), and another piece of wood (the key), cut in the shape of a wedge, is tapped into the hole to pull the joint tight. The keys can be plain or decora-

Corbels offer support, as well as a decorative embelishment.

Shiplapped backs allow for solid wood movement.

tive depending on the designer or your choice. Specific directions for through-tenon, pegged and keyed joints are included with the individual projects.

QUADRILINEAR POSTS

One of the most appealing features in the somewhat understated Arts & Crafts furniture is the beauty of the wood figure. Using traditional quartersawn white oak in a piece and two faces of each piece will show the attractive medullary rays, which appear as flakes or bands of lighter translucent material. To use this figure to its best design capability, it's best to have the rays show on every face. This isn't really possible on all pieces, but it can, and has been, achieved on legs and posts. While Gustav Stickley opted to add quarter-sawn veneer to the non-quartersawn faces, his brother Leopold came up with a mechanical (and more durable) method he dubbed the quadrilinear post. If you take thinner (³⁄₄") material and miter the long edges, the glued-up post will have four quarter-sawn faces. Add a strip in the center of the hollow

piece to form a solid post. Not only is this attractive, but this is also a more economical use of materials. Leopold went even further than just mitering the edge and formed an interlocking miter. A variation on that locking miter is now available as a router bit used in box building to form a lock-miter joint. While it works great for boxes, Leopold would recognize its benefit on the quadrilinear post. Setup for using the lock-miter bit takes some precision, but once the bit is set up in a router table, the final visual effect is dramatic.

CORBELS

A fairly distinctive feature in Arts & Crafts furniture is the use of sweeping bracket-like supports to stabilize tops, arms and seats. These supports, or corbels, offer a delicate style element as well as strengthening the piece. Though the corbel is not peculiar to Arts & Crafts furniture (the shape and use is found in a number of architectural designs), it is common to the style. Corbels are seen in a number of shapes and sizes, and while we've provided some instruction on how they should look in the specific projects, we recommend a certain amount of personal choice to help make the piece your own. Corbels are simple to make once the shape is determined. After rough-cutting the pieces to shape on the band saw, clamp the pieces together (corbels hardly ever travel alone), and sand them smooth and to match. Attaching

Pattern-routing a cloud lift for a Greene & Greene project.

corbels is simple. Because of the grain orientation, corbels can be glued to a leg or cabinet side with simple clamping pressure, forming a strong long-grain glue joint.

SHIPLAPPED BOARDS

An lot of today's cabinetry uses ¼"-thick plywood for backs. Our ancestors didn't have that commercial luxury and instead used solid wood backs. But one-piece solid wood backs are an unstable construction detail and definitely not economical. So they borrowed a joint from their shipbuilding brethren and used an overlapping edge joint, allowing them to use solid boards of random and thinner width to form the back. Frequently they added a slight chamfer to the joined edges of the boards to further separate the pieces. This design appears in many Arts & Crafts pieces, and while some of the projects in this book substitute plywood backs to save money, the shiplap design is an authentic and attractive design element.

PATTERN ROUTING

Another frequent design element is the use of arches on stretchers and aprons. Even more prevalent in the work of the Greene & Greene brothers is the use of stepped designs on the stretchers and aprons with rounded corners. The Greene brothers referred to this design element as a cloud lift, and the design has decidedly Asian influences. In most cases these design elements repeat identically on pieces. To get them to match, pattern routing is a handy technique. Make a plywood template in the shape of the required piece, then use a router bit with a ball-bearing guide to make any number of pieces in the same shape.

FINISHING ARTS & CRAFTS FURNITURE

Achieving the perfect finish on a piece of Arts & Crafts furniture is perhaps the biggest challenge faced when building in this style. After all, the designs are generally straightforward and the construction techniques are not difficult to master with a little practice. We've tried dozens of different ways to color the wood to achieve that perfect, mellow tone so indicative of Arts & Crafts. And while we haven't found the perfect one-step solution, we're a lot closer than we were a few years ago.

SANDING

Before you color your wood, pay attention to the sanding process. White oak is a tough wood that requires more sanding than other cabinet woods such as cherry or maple. For sanding white oak, we recommend using a random orbit sander. Begin at 100-grit, then go to 120 and, finally, 150. Now, stop. Here's the thing: random orbit sanders minimize the scratches left on the wood, but with white oak, you need to go one step further. If you want to eliminate the tiny "pig tails" or swirls that soak up stain, you have to hand sand your project.

Use a sanding block loaded with 150-grit paper, turn on the radio and turn off your brain. This is the only road we know to a swirl-free finish. As you sand, examine the surface with a low, raking light source. It will clarify any swirls left on the surface.

Arts and Crafts finishes can be tough to get "just right." After years of practice, we've come up with a couple of methods that please us. This Stickley side table was finished with a water-based dye, followed by a coat of boiled linseed oil, a coat of glaze, then three coats of a clear finish.

Always make a sample board of your work before you color your project. That way you won't have to learn about "refinishing" just yet.

AMMONIA FUMING

Gustav Stickley and his imitators fumed their oak furniture with ammonia. Stickley recommended in an issue of *The Craftsman* magazine that the home woodworker fume furniture in this manner: The furniture must be fumed in an airtight room. One solution is to build a fuming tent from sheets of plastic and 2×4s. Robert Lang gave this a try for the Harvey Ellis bookcase on page 30. Or if you have to fume an entire roomful of furniture at once, there's the story about a guy who rented a truck and fumed all the pieces in there.

Once the furniture is in an airtight room, place shallow dishes of high-strength ammonia in the room, seal it up and wait. Ammonia purchased at the neighborhood grocery store isn't strong enough; find someone who sells aqua ammonia (a mixture containing twenty-six percent ammonia). Stickley said 48 hours should be a long enough time period to produce the desired color. The longer you wait, the darker the color. After 48 hours, lightly sandpaper the surfaces, then fume the piece again. Then add a top coat of wax, shellac or another clear finish.

Is ammonia the best way to finish Arts & Crafts furniture? Our experience on the Ellis bookcase showed us that fuming white oak with ammonia is an exercise in faith. The color doesn't look right until the piece is finished with shellac and dark wax. There is also a distinct risk that some parts won't come out the same color as others, or, perhaps worse, that there will be some sapwood present that won't take on any color at all.

Add to this the reality that working with the higher strength ammonia can cause health risks, and the return on the effort begins to become minimal. Especially when

we've been able to create some beautiful finishes on many of the pieces in this book, with more consistent results and much more safely.

Stickley himself said the process can be troublesome. Unless you know what you're doing or are working with someone who does, we recommend you stick to traditional stains, dyes and glazes.

DYE AND GLAZE

Some of the nicest finishes we've achieved incorporated a reddish water-based dye, followed by a coat of shellac, then a coat of warm brown glaze, followed by three coats of a clear finish. If using a water-based dye, rag a thin coat of clear water over the entire project before you apply the dye. Water raises the grain of the wood. Allow the water to dry, then sand off the raised grain by hand with 150-grit sandpaper. Now, when the dye is applied, it won't raise the grain nearly as much.

Our reddish dye of choice is Moser's Light Sheraton Mahogany. It comes in a powder that is mixed with hot water. Follow the directions on the package, then dilute it by half. Rag it on your project using a lint-free cloth. Be careful not to overlap the edges too much; the color can build up quickly. Allow the dye to dry overnight.

Moser also makes an alcohol-based version of this dye, but it is more susceptible to fading then the water-based. However, it does dry faster.

Next, seal the wood to prepare for glazing. This can be done any number of ways: Add a coat of boiled linseed oil and let it dry overnight; or brush/wipe on a thin coat of orange shellac or wiping varnish (varnish that has been thinned with mineral spirits). Shellac gives a warmer tone than a clear finish does and dries much faster than a wiping varnish. Once this sealing coat is dry, don't worry that it looks so red. Adding the warm brown glaze will "kill" some of the red color.

Most woodworkers are mystified by glaze. Essentially, it's a thin paint or a thick stain professional painters use for faux effects. It always goes on between coats of a film finish. If applied directly to the wood, it's not glazing, it's staining. Sometimes that works fine, too, though you should try a sample board using only glaze and a top coat.

Applying glaze is easy. Use a cheesecloth to apply a thin coat to one surface of your project. Let the glaze set up for a few minutes and allow it to "flash." This means that the surface of the finish goes from shiny to dull. Then, take a second cheesecloth and begin wiping away the excess glaze with even and gentle strokes. Wipe the surface until you achieve the tone you want and then stop. Now, move on to the next surface.

When your entire project is glazed, allow it to sit overnight. Cover it with three coats of a clear finish, sanding between coats with a sanding sponge (fine grit) or 360-grit lubed sandpaper.

ARTS & CRAFTS BOOKCASE

A simple, knockdown, turn-of-the-century classic provides lots of storage for your favorite books.

By Kara Gebhart-Uhl

My mom has a bookcase in every room of my parent's house. Most of them are stuffed two-rows deep with paperbacks, hardbacks, picture books and travel books and still, whenever I visit, I find even more novels and novellas piled on top of end tables, underneath coffee tables, by the sides of chairs and on the backs of toilets. But I'm like her — I love collecting books.

Tired of moving my own piles of books every time I needed a place to set a drink down, I decided to build a bookcase of my own. This project serves as a nice challenge for the beginning woodworker and as a great weekend project for those more skilled. Its Arts & Crafts style is emphasized by mortise-and-tenon joinery, wedges and Stickley-style (sans ammonia) finish. While the ends remain forever assembled, a few good whacks to the wedges and the whole project comes apart, stacks together and can be transported easily in the trunk of a car.

GETTING STARTED

In keeping with the Arts & Crafts tradition, I bought rough quartersawn white oak for this project, which I jointed and planed. Don't have a jointer or planer? No problem. Head out to your local home center and purchase some dimensional lumber, in a species to suit your taste. The shelves can be cut from 1×8s, as can the rails and stiles, with some waste.

When purchasing your lumber, be picky. Choose knotfree heartwood (you don't want pieces with a lot of sap) that has lots of figure. Determine which pieces are the most attractive and mark those for the most visible parts of the project. Now cut all your pieces to size according to the cutting list.

TEST MORTISE

The first step to building this bookcase is tackling the joinery and assembling the sides. It's important that the project's tenons fit snugly into the mortises, which means first making a test mortise. This will allow you to check the size of your tenons throughout the tenon-cutting process, ensuring accuracy. There are twenty-four mortises in this project. Do yourself a favor and, if you don't already have one, buy a hollow chisel mortising machine (about $250). A mortising attachment for your drill press or a $\frac{3}{8}$" Forstner bit are also acceptable options.

To make your test mortise, first select a piece of scrap from this project. Some sappy waste will do just fine. As a rule of thumb, mortises should be half the thickness of your tenon's stock. Because this project's tenon stock is $\frac{3}{4}$" thick, the mortises need to be $\frac{3}{8}$" thick. It's also a good idea to make your mortises about $\frac{1}{16}$" deeper than the tenons are long. This will keep the tenons from bottoming out in the mortises. The depth isn't as important as the width in a test mortise, so simply make your test mortise as deep as the longest tenon is long. Because the rails have $\frac{3}{4}$"-long tenons and the stiles have 1"-long tenons, the test mortise for this project needs to be $1\frac{1}{16}$" deep.

If you've never used a hollow chisel mortiser before, check out *A New Manual for Mortisers* (August 2001 issue #123, available for sale at www.popwood.com). Cut your test mortise.

TABLE-SAW TENONS

Now it's time to cut the twenty-four tenons. Sure this sounds like a lot, but with a dado stack and a miter gauge,

A few quick passes is all it takes to cut both sides of the rails' tenons (above left), using a dado stack and a miter gauge. The same table saw setup will take care of the edges of the tenons (above right).

Use a test mortise to check the fit of your tenons throughout the tenon-cutting process. This ensures accuracy.

Use the edges of the rails' tenons like rulers to mark the beginning and end of each mortise in the stiles.

you'll breeze through this step in no time.

First, install a ⅝" dado stack in your table saw. Set the fence for the finished length of your tenon and set the height of the dado stack to about ³⁄₁₆", which is the depth of your shoulders on your tenon. I cut the rails' tenons first, so the finished length was ¾". Hold the piece about ¹⁄₁₆" from the fence and push it through the blade, using your miter gauge. Now hold the piece directly against the fence and, using your miter gauge, push it through the blade again. Repeat this same procedure for the edges of the tenon.

After you've cut your first tenon, make sure that it fits snugly into your test mortise. If satisfied, keep cutting. Remember to set the fence for 1" once you're ready to cut the tenons on the end of the stiles.

BACK TO THE MORTISER

To cut the mortises, first use the diagrams to measure where the rails start and stop along the stiles. Now use your rails to lay out the locations of your mortises, as shown above. Cut each mortise a little over each measured line so that you're able to maneuver the rails for perfect positioning during glue up. Cut all the stiles' mortises. You'll cut the mortises in the feet after the sides of the bookcase are assembled.

Before assembling the sides, use your table saw, plane or chisel to cut a ³⁄₁₆" × ³⁄₁₆" chamfer on the stiles' top four edges, which is a traditional Arts & Crafts look.

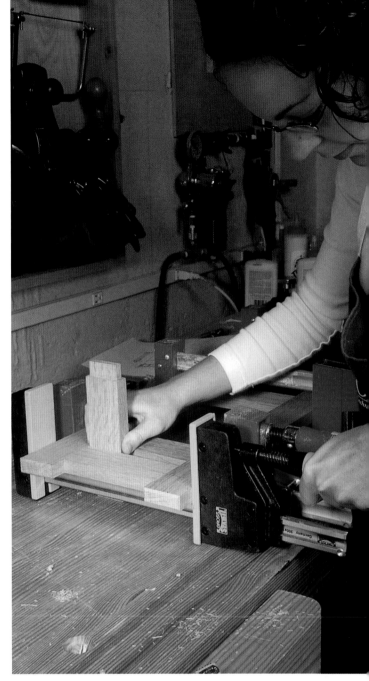

Slide an extra rail (which is ¾" thick) into the space between the top two rails to ensure a perfect slot for the top shelf.

ASSEMBLING THE SIDES

Now that the rails and stiles are complete, it's time to assemble the sides. First, dry fit everything together. Choose the face sides of your pieces carefully. Remember: Your most visible pieces should be your most attractive. Clamp the assembly together.

Check for gaps, squareness, mistakes or anything else that might cause panic during glue up. Use the extra space you cut (when you mortised slightly over the measured lines) to maneuver the rails until they're in their appropriate places. If it's tight, try hitting them with a mallet. Once you're positive that everything is perfectly positioned, use a ruler to draw lines across the joints. These lines will be

Use the diagrams to measure where the stiles start and stop on the feet. Like the rails, use the edge of the stiles' tenons like rulers to mark the beginning and end of each mortise.

STURDY SHELVES

With the sides assembled, it's time to cut the shelves. First you need to cut notches in the shelves' corners. The top and bottom shelves' notches are 2¼" long by ¾" wide, allowing enough overhang for the wedges. The notches in the two middles shelves are ¾" long by ¾" wide.

Once you've measured and drawn where the notches start and stop, head to the table saw to cut the notches on the top and bottom shelves. Because the table saw's blade is curved and because you won't be running the entire length of the board through the blade, you must be a little creative in your cutting. First, correctly position your fence and raise your blade to its appropriate height. Then, with a grease pencil, draw a line on the fence where the blade enters the table. Now, draw a line on your work where the cut should stop. Run the piece through until the two lines meet, stop and pull the piece back. Carry the line on the piece over to the other side, flip the shelf over and again run it through until the two lines meet, as shown in the photograph on page 28.

Head to your band saw and cut the remaining part of the top and bottom shelves' notches away. Now cut the

your guides during glue up. Now take everything apart, put glue in the mortises, clamp and let dry.

BAND SAWN FEET

Once the glue has cured, it's time to cut the feet. Each foot has two mortises and a detail cut using the band saw. Use the diagram to lay out the shape of the feet on each piece. Lay out and cut your mortises, again going a little over each line for maneuverability during assembly.

Now head to the band saw. Cut the feet to shape as close to your lines as possible. The closer you get, the less cleanup you'll have to do. Remove the saw marks with a chisel. Dry fit the sides and feet, draw your guide lines, take the sides and feet apart and then glue them together.

arts & crafts bookcase
INCHES (MILLIMETERS)

REFERENCE	QUANTITY	PART	STOCK	THICKNESS	(mm)	WIDTH	(mm)	LENGTH	(mm)	COMMENTS
A	4	stiles	white oak	¾	(19)	2	(51)	38	(965)	1" TOE
B	10	rails	white oak	¾	(19)	2	(51)	7	(178)	¾" TBE
C	2	feet	white oak	¾	(19)	2	(51)	12	(305)	
D	2	top & bottom shelves	white oak	¾	(19)	7	(178)	39	(991)	
E	2	middle shelves	white oak	¾	(19)	7	(178)	36	(914)	
F	8	wedges	white oak	½	(13)	½	(13)	2⅛	(54)	

TBE = tenon, both ends; TOE = tenon, one end

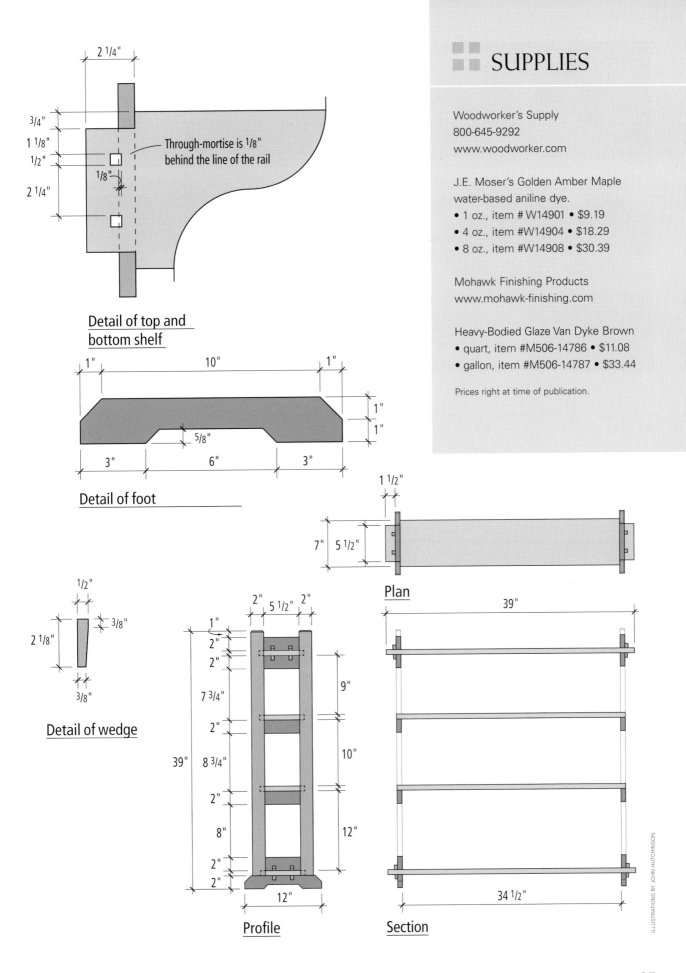

2 1/4"

3/4"
1 1/8"
1/2"
1/8"
2 1/4"

Through-mortise is 1/8"
behind the line of the rail

Detail of top and bottom shelf

1"   10"   1"

1"
1"

5/8"

3"   6"   3"

Detail of foot

SUPPLIES

Woodworker's Supply
800-645-9292
www.woodworker.com

J.E. Moser's Golden Amber Maple
water-based aniline dye.
• 1 oz., item # W14901 • $9.19
• 4 oz., item #W14904 • $18.29
• 8 oz., item #W14908 • $30.39

Mohawk Finishing Products
www.mohawk-finishing.com

Heavy-Bodied Glaze Van Dyke Brown
• quart, item #M506-14786 • $11.08
• gallon, item #M506-14787 • $33.44

Prices right at time of publication.

1 1/2"

7"   5 1/2"

1/2"

2 1/8"   3/8"

3/8"

Detail of wedge

2" 5 1/2" 2"
1"
2"
2"
7 3/4"
2"
8 3/4"
2"
8"
2"
2"
39"
12"

9"

10"

12"

Profile

Plan

39"

34 1/2"

Section

ILLUSTRATIONS BY JOHN HUTCHINSON.

When cutting the shelves' notches, draw a line on your table saw's fence to determine when to stop cutting. Because of the table saw's curved blade, more material will be cut away on the underside of the piece than on the top.

notches on the middle shelves, using only the band saw.

The whole bookcase is held tightly together by tapered wedges that snug into through-mortises in the top and bottom shelves. Cut the mortises in the top and bottom shelves, as shown at left.

TAPERED WEDGES

If you haven't done so already, plane the stock for your wedges down to ½" thick. Measure and make a mark ⅜" from the top of each wedge, and another mark ⅜" wide from the bottom of each wedge. Draw a line, connecting your marks. Cut the taper, using either your band saw or a sander. Clean up the wedges with your chisel. Test fit the wedges, as shown at far right.

FINISHING TOUCHES

After all of your hard work, the last thing you want to do is slack off when it comes to sanding. First, clean up all your edges with a sanding block and a chisel. Next, sand everything, starting with 100 grit and then moving on to 150. Hold each piece up to the light, making sure you have all the scratch marks removed. Break the edges.

Because this is an Arts & Crafts piece, I decided on a Stickley-style finish, without ammonia's danger. First apply J.E. Moser's

3/4"-long tenons on rails

1"-long tenons on stiles

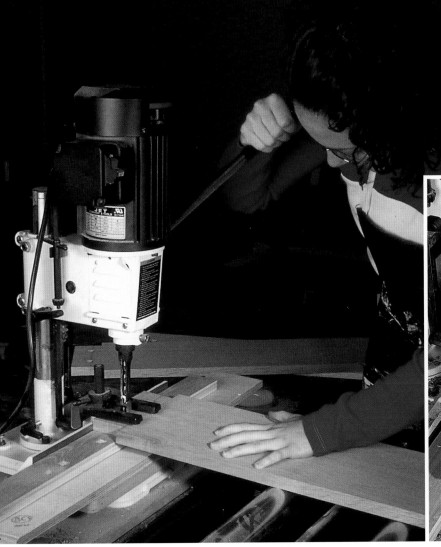

Wedges slide through mortised holes in both the top and bottom shelves. Use the diagrams to lay out the locations of the $1/2$" x $1/2$" mortises. Note on the diagram how the mortises are located $1/8$" behind the line of the rails.

Golden Amber Maple water-based aniline dye. Let it dry overnight. Next, apply Mohawk Van Dyke Brown glaze. Let it, too, dry overnight. Finally, apply your favorite topcoat. Check out the Supplies box on page 27 for ordering information.

Most of the tapered part of the wedges should slide through each mortise. As the wedge gets wider, you will need a mallet and a block of wood to finish pounding them down to a uniform height.

HARVEY ELLIS BOOKCASE

A faithful reproduction of the epitome of Arts & Crafts design.

by Robert W. Lang

Gustav Stickley once wrote that the best way to learn furniture design was to build a proven design. He wrote that the student "learns from the start the fundamental principles of design and proportion and so comes naturally to understand what is meant by thorough workmanship." This bookcase is one of the finest examples of proportion and detail that make the Craftsman style more than just a simple piece of furniture.

In 1903 Harvey Ellis designed this glass-door bookcase while working as a designer for Stickley. The first time I saw an original example of this piece of furniture I was struck by how perfectly proportioned it was and how well all of the details combine.

These details also present some challenges in building. While this is a relatively simple piece, the joinery must be precisely executed. Before I began, I spent some time tuning up our table saw and jointer, made sure my squares and measuring tools were in order, and sharpened my chisels and planes.

TRUE TO THE ORIGINAL

Original Craftsman furniture was occasionally made in mahogany or figured maple, but the vast majority was made from quartersawn white oak. This method of sawing yields more stable material than plain sawn oak, and the distinctive rays can be absolutely stunning. White oak is much more of a furniture wood than red oak, giving a smoother and more refined appearance.

In addition to using this wood, I also decided to use the same method of finishing that was originally used, fuming the finished piece with ammonia, and using shellac followed by wax.

Tannic acid in the wood reacts with the fumes from the ammonia, yielding a distinctive coloration in the rays and flecks, as well as in the rest of the wood. Staining, glazing and dyeing can come close to the color of an original Stickley piece, but fuming can match it exactly.

I had to glue stock together to obtain the widths required. Because the final color was dependant on a chemical reaction, and the tannic acid content of white oak will vary from tree to tree and board to board, I was careful to match boards for color as well as for figure. I also cut most of the parts for the door from the same piece of wood so that the color would be as close as possible.

MORTISING WITH A TEMPLATE

I began the joinery work with the through mortise-and-tenon joints at the bottom of the case sides. I made a template from ½"-thick plywood, which helped me locate the mortises and the arched cut-outs. I cut the mortises in the template with a ½"-diameter bit in my plunge router, guided by the router's fence, and squared the ends with a chisel and a rasp.

I could have used this same method on the actual cabinet sides, but by using the template I only had to do the layout work once, and if I slipped with the plunge router, the damage would be to a piece of plywood, not my finished end panel.

With the template clamped to the bottom of the end panel, I drilled most of the mortise with a ⅜" Forstner bit, and then used a router with a flush trim bit to trim the sides of the mortises flush to the template. I used the smallest diameter flush trim bit I had to minimize the amount of material left in the corners. With the template still clamped to the panel, I used the edges of the mortise in the template to guide the chisel in the corners. A riffler and a flat rasp completed the work on the mortises.

DADOS AND RABBETS

On the inside of the end panels there is a dado to hold the bottom and a rabbet from the top down to the dado to house the back. I made both of these cuts with a router and a ¾"-diameter straight bit. I used a shop-made T-square jig for the dado, and used the router's edge guide to make the rabbet, stopping at the dado for the bottom. I also ran a ¾"-wide by ¼"-deep rabbet along the back edge of the cabinet bottom.

The template locates the through mortises precisely, as well as the arched cut-out and the location of the dado for the bottom of the case.

harvey ellis bookcase
INCHES (MILLIMETERS)

REFERENCE	QUANTITY	PART	STOCK	THICKNESS	(mm)	WIDTH	(mm)	LENGTH	(mm)	COMMENTS
CARCASE										
A	1	top	oak	¾	(19)	14	(356)	36	(914)	
B	2	sides	oak	¾	(19)	13	(330)	57¼	(1454)	
C	1	bottom	oak	¾	(19)	13	(330)	31½	(800)	
D	1	bottom edge trim	oak	½	(13)	¾	(19)	32	(813)	
E	2	arched rails	oak	¾	(19)	5	(127)	33¼	(844)	31" between tenons-tenons extend ⅜" past sides
F	2	face frame stiles	oak	⅞	(22)	1½	(38)	50½	(1283)	
G	1	face frame rail	oak	⅞	(22)	1⅛	(29)	29	(37)	28" between tenons
H	2	applied pilasters	oak	¼	(6)	1	(25)	50½	(1283)	
I	2	capitals	oak	⅞	(22)	2⅛	(54)	1⅛	(29)	
J	2	shelves	oak	¾	(19)	11⅛	(282)	30⅞	(784)	
DOORS										
K	2	stiles	oak	¾	(19)	2½	(64)	49⅜	(1255)	Door opening is 28" × 49⅜"
L	1	top rail	oak	¾	(19)	2½	(64))	24½	(623)	23" between tenons
M	1	bottom rail	oak	¾	(19)	3½	(89)	24½	(623)	23" between tenons
N	2	intermediate stiles	oak	¾	(19)	1¼	(32)	44⅜	(1128)	43⅜" between tenons
O	1	intermediate rail	oak	¾	(19)	1¼	(32)	24	(610)	23" between tenons
P	3	top lights	glass	⅛	(3)	7⁵⁄₁₆	(186)	7⁵⁄₁₆	(186)	
Q	3	lower lights	glass	¾	(19)	7⁵⁄₁₆	(186)	35¹³⁄₁₆	(910)	
R	18	glass stops	oak	¼	(6)	¼	(6)	7⁵⁄₁₆	(186)	
S	6	glass stops	oak	¼	(6)	¼	(6)	35¹³⁄₁₆	(910)	
X	1	door stop	oak	¼	(6)	2	(51)	49⅜	(1255)	
BACK										
T	2	stiles	oak	¾	(19)	1½	(38)	37³⁄₁₆	(945)	
U	2	rails	oak	¾	(19)	1½	(38)	37³⁄₁₆	(945)	28½" between tenons
V	1	mid rail	oak	¾	(19)	2	(51)	37³⁄₁₆	(945)	28½" between tenons
W	12	back panel slats	oak	¼	(6)	4⅞	(124)	37³⁄₁₆	(945)	Shiplapped

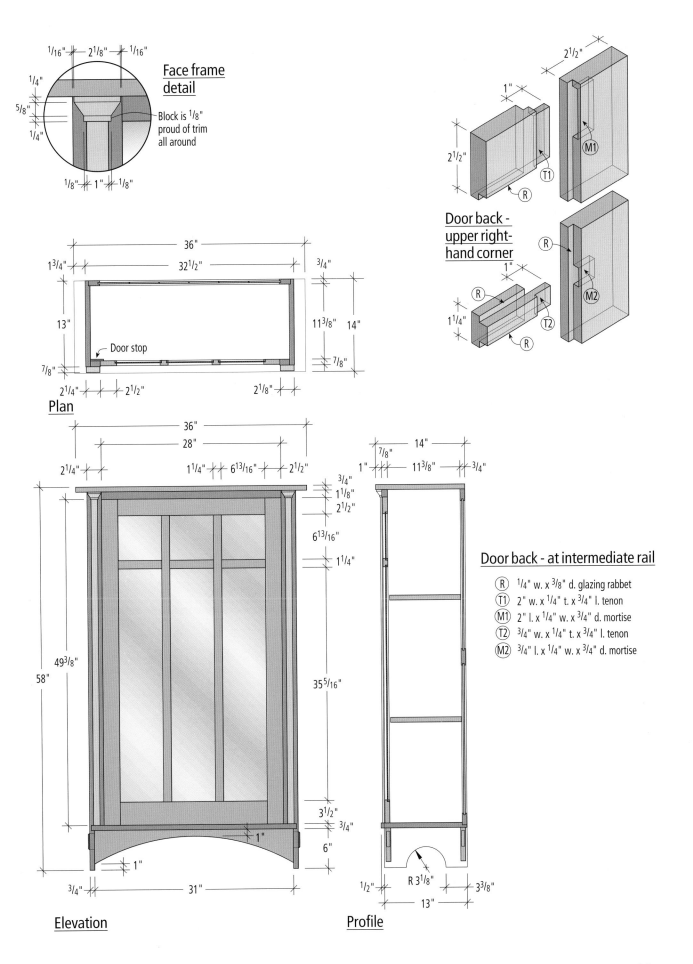

Face frame detail

1/16" 2 1/8" 1/16"

1/4"

5/8"

1/4"

Block is 1/8" proud of trim all around

1/8" 1" 1/8"

Door back - upper right-hand corner

2 1/2"

1"

2 1/2"

M1

T1

R

R

1"

R

1 1/4"

T2

R

M2

Plan

36"

32 1/2"

3/4"

1 3/4"

13"

11 3/8" 14"

Door stop

7/8"

7/8"

2 1/4" 2 1/2" 2 1/8"

Door back - at intermediate rail

R 1/4" w. x 3/8" d. glazing rabbet
T1 2" w. x 1/4" t. x 3/4" l. tenon
M1 2" l. x 1/4" w. x 3/4" d. mortise
T2 3/4" w. x 1/4" t. x 3/4" l. tenon
M2 3/4" l. x 1/4" w. x 3/4" d. mortise

Elevation

36"

28"

2 1/4" 1 1/4" 6 13/16" 2 1/2"

3/4"
1 1/8"
2 1/2"

6 13/16"

1 1/4"

49 3/8"

58"

35 5/16"

3 1/2"
3/4"

1"

6"

1"

3/4" 31"

Profile

14"

7/8"
1" 11 3/8" 3/4"

1/2" R 3 1/8" 3 3/8"

13"

The long mortises on the ends of the rails are cut with this tenoning jig that rides along the table saw fence.

After the tenons are trimmed to fit with a shoulder plane and scraper, the exposed ends are rounded with a block plane.

With the work on the side panels complete, I turned to the tenons on the ends of the two arched rails that sit below the bottom and penetrate the sides.

I always like to "sneak up" on the fit of tenons, especially when they are exposed. The tricky part with through tenons is that the final cut that yields a good fit must also be smooth enough to give a good finish. I made the initial cuts on the table saw, using a jig that rides on the fence as shown.

With the bottom in place in its dado, I held the rails in place, and marked the locations of the top and bottom of the tenons directly from the mortises in the end panels. I made these cuts on the band saw, then I cleaned up all the saw marks with a shoulder plane. As I got close to a good fit, I switched to a card scraper. Once I had the tenons fitting nicely, I took a piece of $3/32$"-thick scrap, and placed it on the outside of the cabinet with its edge against the tenon. I then marked a pencil line around the tenons. This established a starting point for the rounded ends of the exposed tenons. I used my block plane and a rasp to bevel and round over the ends of the tenons, shown above.

After the tenons were complete, I marked the midpoint of the arch, and drove a finishing nail $1/8$" below that point. I also made a mark $3/8$" in from each end at the bottom edge of the rail. I then bent

a $1/8$"-thick strip of wood across these three points, and marked the curve with a pencil. The curves in the end panels had been marked from the template, and all of these cuts were made with my jigsaw.

The next task was to join the two stiles and top rail that make up the face frame of the carcase. I cut tenons on the end of the rail with a stack dado set in the table saw, and made the mortises at the top of the two stiles with a hollow

With the rails already glued to one stile, the shiplapped boards for the back panel are slipped into the groove in the rail. When they were all in place, I glued on the remaining stile.

chisel mortiser. I glued the rail between the stiles, and set this subassembly aside while I worked on the back panel.

PANELLED BACK

Backs in original Craftsman pieces varied depending on when they were made, and could be V-grooved or shiplapped planks, or frame-and-panel assemblies. I chose to make a back panel, as this would help keep the cabinet from racking.

The stiles and rails for the back are all ¾"-thick material, with a ¼"-wide by ⅜"-deep groove centered in one edge. Mortise-and-tenon joints hold the panel together, and the ¼"-thick shiplapped panels float in the grooves in the stiles and rails. You also could use ¼"-thick plywood for the back panels, or make the entire back from one piece of ¾"- thick plywood.

To assemble the back, I first glued one end of each of the three rails into one of the stiles. After letting the glue dry overnight, I slipped the shiplapped panels into place, then applied glue to the tenons on the rails, and clamped on the remaining stile.

ASSEMBLING THE CASE

With one of the end panels flat on the end of my assembly table, I inserted the tenons for the bottom rails part way in their mortises, and then applied glue to the tenons. This keeps the glue from squeezing out on the outside of the joint. I tapped the rails home with a dead-blow mallet,

and then eased the bottom in to its dado, as shown below. With these parts together, I put glue on the tenons of the rails, and edge of the bottom before clamping down the remaining side panel.

I then laid the cabinet on its back, and glued and clamped the face frame in place. After letting the glue dry for an hour, I glued the trim piece on the front edge of the bottom. The seam between the face frame and the end panel is covered by a ¼"-thick strip that runs from the top edge of the bottom to the bottom of the top face-frame rail.

These small additional pieces add interest to the design by creating steps in an otherwise flat surface. They also hide the joints and display quartersawn figure on the front of the cabinet.

I made a template out of ½"-thick baltic birch plywood that located the holes for the pegs that support the two adjustable shelves. After drilling the holes, the carcase was complete, except for the two blocks that cap the trim on the top front of the cabinet. I laid out the

To control glue squeeze-out on the exposed tenons, I get the tenon started in the mortise, then apply glue directly to the tenon.

With the two bottom rails in place, I spread glue on the top edges of the rails and in the dado before tipping the bottom in to place.

After spreading glue on the end of the bottom, and the cheeks of the tenons, the remaining cabinet side is carefully put in place.

Because of the mechanical fit of the rails and bottom, it only take a couple clamps to secure the bottom of the case assembly.

The trapezoid shaped block is laid out on each end of a long piece of wood to make cutting and handling easier.

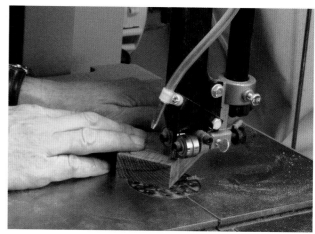

All of the cuts to form the capital block were made on the band saw, as shown here. The final cut will be made after the block is smooth.

Leaving the block attached gives me plenty of material to clamp in the vise while I smooth out the saw marks with a rasp, followed by a file, and then 150-grit sandpaper.

Standing the cabinet upright, I glued the trim piece to the front edge of the cabinet bottom. A 1/4" thick piece of trim will be added to cover the joint between the cabinet side and the face frame.

blocks on each end of a piece of wood about a foot long to give me room to hold them while cutting them on the band saw (shown top right).

This extra material also provided a way to hold the blocks in my bench vise while cleaning them up with a rasp. After all the surfaces were smooth, I glued them in place.

DOOR

With the back panel completed, and the case parts assembled, It was time to work on the door. The glass sits in a 1/4"-wide by 3/8"-deep rabbet and is held in place with 1/4"-square strips of wood. The outer stiles and rails are held together with mortise-and-tenon joints. The intermediate stiles and rail also have tenons on their ends. The door

tenons all have a step in them to accommodate the rabbet for the door's glass. The 1/4"-wide mortises are in line with the inside of the rabbet.

At the upper portion of the bookcase door, the intermediate rail joins the two narrow stiles with a half-lap joint as shown on the next page. I made the joints for the outer stiles and rails, and then clamped the door together to lay out the joints for the intermediate stiles and rails. I cut these joints, as well as the all tenons for all the door parts, with a stack dado set in the table saw.

I assembled the door in stages, to avoid putting together a lot of parts at once. I assembled the half-lap joints first. The top and bottom rails were then put on the ends of the smaller stiles and clamped. While this assembly was

Half-lap joints hold the intermediate stiles and rails of the doors together.

The half-lap joints, as well as all of the tenons for the door were cut with the dado head on the table saw as you can see here. The block clamped to the saw's fence locates the cuts without trapping the parts between the dado cutter and the fence.

drying, I cut the mortise for the lock, and carved the recess to inlay the brass escutcheon for the keyhole.

I secured one of the long stiles in my bench vise (as shown at right), and put glue in the mortises before placing the tenons of the rail assembly. Next I put some glue on the top edges of the tenons on the rails. Then I tapped the second rail in place before I began clamping.

FUMED FINISH

Fuming white oak with ammonia is an exercise in faith; the color doesn't look right until the piece is finished with shellac and dark wax. There is also a distinct risk that some parts won't come out the same color as others, or, perhaps worse, that there will be some sapwood present that won't take on any color at all.

Twenty-six percent ammonia is used in blue print machines, and is a much stronger solution than household ammonia, which is about five percent. Such a strong chemical requires great care in handling, as the fumes can quickly damage eyes, skin and lungs. Make sure to where gloves, goggles and a respirator when handling it. I also took steps to minimize the time that the ammonia was exposed to the environment in our shop.

Before fuming the entire piece, I did some tests on scraps. As I worked on this project, I saved the cutoff pieces from the end panels and top. I put these, along with other scraps in a plastic container with an airtight lid. I put some ammonia in a small plastic bowl in the larger container, sealed the lid, and let this sit for twenty-four hours. Satisfied that the final result would be close to matching, I built a frame from inexpensive one-by-three pine and covered it with 4-mil-thick plastic sheet, as shown on page 38.

I tucked the plastic under the wood frame at the floor, and secured it to the frame with spring clamps to get an airtight seal. I left one end open so that I could place the assembled cabinet and all of the parts inside. Once ev-

I assemble the door in stages. Here I'm placing a subassembly of the intermediate stiles and rail to one of the door stiles. The remaining stile will be placed on top and clamped.

After sanding all of the parts, I placed them in an airtight fuming tent, located by the back door of the shop.

After "fuming" for 24 hours the tent was aired out and the plastic removed. Here you can see the construction of the tent frame, and the change in color.

erything to be fumed was inside, I clamped most of the opening closed, leaving just enough room at the bottom to reach in and pour the ammonia in to a plastic container. After this, I sealed the rest of the end and waited a day.

When it came time to remove the cabinet from the tent, I put on my goggles, gloves and respirator, opened the bottom of the end, and put a lid on the plastic container inside. I then put a fan in the opening, and exhausted the fumes outside. After letting the fan run for an hour, I opened the tent completely.

Most of the pieces came out close in color, but there were a few parts that were a bit lighter, and a couple edges that didn't take at all. Overall though, I was happy with the results, and prepared to deal with the inconsistencies.

The first step after fuming was to smooth all of the surfaces with a nylon abrasive (Scotchbrite) pad, and give

everything two coats of garnet shellac, in a two-pound cut. I then mixed some aniline dye (Liberon Fumed Oak light) with some alcohol. With a 1"-wide sash brush, I applied the dye to the lighter areas, brushing on slight amounts until the color was close. I followed this with two more coats of shellac.

The shellac changes the dirty-looking brownish gray of the fumed oak to warm brown. The photos at right show the progression of the color from raw wood, fuming and shellac. The color from the shellac, however, was just a bit too orange, and needed to be waxed to achieve the desired rich brown I was looking for. I smoothed all the surfaces with 320-grit sandpaper, followed by a Scotchbrite pad.

The final step in finishing was to apply dark paste wax, which fills the open pores of the oak, and tones down the color from the garnet shellac, leaving the piece a rich warm brown.

With the finish complete, I installed the glass in the door, holding it in place with $1/4" \times 1/4"$ glass stop. I mitered the corners, and attached the stop to the inside of the openings with small gauge pins.

All that remained was to install the lock and escutcheon in the door, hang the door and attach the top with figure-

The quartersawn white oak in its natural color.

After exposure to ammonia fumes for 24 hours, the oak has turned a grayish brown color.

Garnet shellac adds some color, and highlights the distinctive grain. Dark wax will complete the finish.

8 fasteners. I placed three fasteners in the front and back rails, and one in the center of each of the end panels.

Harvey Ellis's association with Gustav Stickley lasted only a few months before Ellis died in January 1904. However, Ellis's influence on Arts & Crafts design was tremendous. The details he produced for Stickley have served as hallmarks of the period.

Ellis related the arrangement of spaces in good design to the notes in a musical chord. This bookcase combines the practical and architectural elements that he is known for in perfect harmony, and serves as a fitting tribute to his genius.

SUPPLIES

Lee Valley Tools
800-871-8158 or leevalley.com
1 • 1³/₈" mortise cabinet lock
    #00N25.35, $11.20
1 • ¹/₂" extruded brass escutcheon
    #00A03.01, $2.70

Rockler
800-279-4441 or rockler.com
2 • Antique brass ball tip hinges 3" long × 2" wide
    #56962, $29.99 pair
8 • Desktop fasteners
    #21650, $2.39/package of 8

Craftsman Plans
craftsmanplans.com
1 • Large format shop drawings, includes full size details
    and cut list, #GST700, $16.95

Prices as of publication date.

LIMBERT BOOKCASE

Show off your pottery, books and good taste by building an authentic reproduction of a turn-of-the-century classic.

By Christopher Schwarz

In 1996 I stopped purchasing Arts & Crafts furniture, and this bookcase is the reason why. After collecting Arts & Crafts furniture since 1990, I had amassed a small but nice collection on my salary as a newspaper reporter. However the piece I wanted but never could find is a glass-front bookcase. So I patiently saved my money and went to an auction in Chicago, ready to buy this very bookcase, which had been featured prominently in the auction's catalog.

I was outbid. Well, completely blown out of the water is more like it. I went home that day with two smaller pieces that, while nice, were not exactly what I wanted. So like any scorned woodworker, I plotted and planned. I sought out dimensions from auction catalogs and reprints of historical materials. And when I was ready, I built the bookcase I'd always wanted. Limbert pieces were almost always made from quartersawn oak or ash, but I decided that cherry with a deep mahogany finish was what I wanted.

Everything about this piece is as authentic as I could get, from the knob to the shiplapped beadboard back. My only compromises were some non-mortise hinges (I'm convinced Limbert would have used these if Amerock had been making them in 1904), and a thin bead of silicone to help hold the glass in place. Construction is simple — well within the reach of most beginning and intermediate woodworkers. The top, bottom and gallery back rest in dados and rabbets in the sides. The beadboard back is screwed into rabbets on the case members. And the doors are simple mortise-and-tenon construction. In fact, the only tricky part is the mullions on the doors. But if you take some care when building them, you should have no problem at all.

You need about 50 board feet of 4/4 cherry (that's 1" thick) to build Limbert's #340 bookcase, and not a scrap of plywood. Begin by surfacing all your material and gluing up the panels you'll need for the sides, top, bottom and shelves.

START WITH THE SIDES

Begin working on the case by cutting the $\frac{3}{8}$" × $\frac{5}{8}$"-deep rabbets on the back edges of the top, bottom and side pieces for the back. The rabbeting bit I own for my router table wasn't large enough to make this cut easily, so I made the rabbet in two passes on the table saw. While you're at the saw, cut the $\frac{5}{8}$" × $\frac{3}{8}$"-long tongues on the ends of the gallery back. These tongues allow the gallery back to lock into the rabbet on the side pieces.

Now it's time to mill the $\frac{3}{8}$"-deep dados in the sides that will hold the top and bottom in place. Make a simple plywood jig (it takes about five minutes) to cut these dados. Here's how to do it: first study the photo at left to see generally what the jig looks like. Basically it's two pieces of plywood with two pieces of scrap nailed to them. You'll notice that the two pieces of plywood that the router rides on are different widths. This is no accident. One of them is 4" wide and the other is 2½" wide. The dado that holds the top needs to go 4" from the top edge. The dado that holds the bottom needs to go 2½" from the bottom edge. With this little jig, all you need to do to make a perfectly placed dado is put the 4" wide part flush against the top edge of the side. Clamp the jig in place, and make the dado cut using a pattern bit (with a top-mounted bearing) that's chucked into your plunge router. Turn the jig

This plywood jig cuts the dados in the sides that hold the top and bottom pieces. Here I'm cutting the dado for the bottom. Note how the edge of the jig is flush to the bottom of the case.

around and put the 2½"-wide edge against the bottom edge and cut the dado for the bottom.

Here's the easy way to make the jig. Rip the two pieces of plywood to size and place them on top of one of the side pieces. Now put pieces of ¾"-thick scrap under the plywood that's the same thickness as the sides. Now take another piece of scrap that's exactly as thick as your top

and bottom pieces and place it between the two pieces of plywood.

Press the pieces of plywood together against the piece of scrap between them and nail the plywood to the wood below. Your jig is done.

Place the jig on top of the sides, clamp it down and rout the ¾"-wide × ⅜"-deep dados for the top and sides. You'll need to make these dados in at least two passes to be safe.

Before you can assemble the case, you need to cut the ½" radius on the front corner of the side pieces and the front corners of the top piece, which extends beyond the front of the case by ¼". Make the pattern using a piece of plywood. Cut the radius on the plywood using a band saw and then sand it smooth. Use this pattern with a pattern-cutting bit in your router to shape the corners.

Now sand all the case parts up to 150 grit and get ready to assemble them.

ASSEMBLY

To assemble the case, I recommend you use polyurethane glue. First, it is superior to yellow glue when joining long grain to end grain. Second, it has a long open time so you have about 20 to 40 minutes to make sure your cabinet is square.

If you've never used polyurethane glue, let me tell you that you should use as little as possible because the foamy squeeze-out is no fun to clean up. I like to coat one part that's being glued with a very thin (but consistent) film of the glue.

Then I wipe a little water on the part it's being joined

limbert bookcase
INCHES (MILLIMETERS)

REFERENCE	QUANTITY	PART	STOCK	THICKNESS	(mm)	WIDTH	(mm)	LENGTH	(mm)	COMMENTS
A	2	sides	oak	¾	(19)	12	(305)	46	(1168)	
B	1	top	oak	¾	(19)	12¼	(311)	31¼	(793)	
C	1	bottom	oak	¾	(19)	12	(305)	31¼	(793)	in ⅜" dado
D	1	gallery back	oak	¾	(19)	4	(102)	31¼	(793)	in ⅜" dado
E	1	kick	oak	¾	(19)	2	(51)	30½	(775)	in ⅜" × ⅝" rabbet
F	2	adjustable shelves	oak	¾	(19)	10½	(267)	30⅜	(772)	
G	1	back	oak	⅝	(16)	31¼	(793)	38¾	(984)	in ⅜" × ⅝" rabbet
H	4	stiles	oak	¾	(19)	1¾	(45)	38	(965)	
I	2	top rails	oak	¾	(19)	1¾	(45)	13¾	(349)	1" TBE
J	2	mid rails	oak	¾	(19)	1	(25)	13¾	(349)	1" TBE
K	2	bottom rails	oak	¾	(19)	2	(51)	13¾	(349)	1" TBE
L	2	mid stiles	oak	¾	(19)	1	(25)	13	(330)	½" TBE
M		retaining strips	oak	¼	(6)	¼	(6)			

TBE = Tenon Both Ends

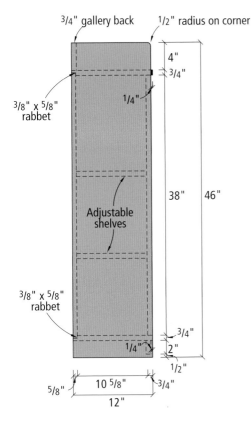

3/4" gallery back 1/2" radius on corner

4"
3/4"
1/4"

3/8" x 5/8" rabbet

38" 46"

Adjustable shelves

3/8" x 5/8" rabbet

3/4"
1/4" 2"
1/2"

5/8" 10 5/8" 3/4"
12"

Profile

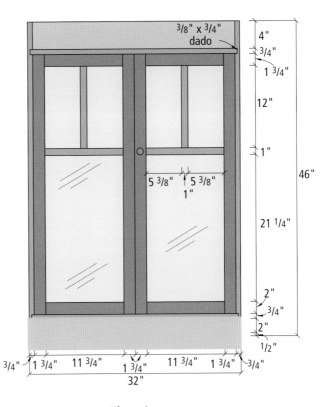

3/8" x 3/4" dado

4"
3/4"
1 3/4"

12"

1"

5 3/8" 5 3/8"
1"

46"

21 1/4"

2"
3/4"
2"
1/2"

3/4" 1 3/4" 11 3/4" 1 3/4" 11 3/4" 1 3/4" 3/4"
32"

Elevation

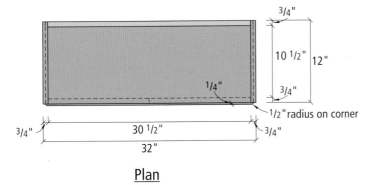

3/4"

10 1/2" 12"

1/4"
3/4"

1/2" radius on corner

3/4" 30 1/2" 3/4"
32"

Plan

to. Moisture activates the glue and speeds curing. Glue the top, bottom and gallery back between the sides. Clamp up your case and let it sit overnight.

When the glue has cured, take the case out of the clamps and drill the holes for your adjustable shelf pins. I made a plywood jig using my drill press and a 5 mm bit. I drilled holes every 3" and placed each row 2" from the front and back of the cabinet. Finally, glue the kick to the bottom of the case. I cut biscuit slots in the bottom and in the kick to keep the piece aligned as I clamped it to the bottom piece.

THE BACK

If you've never built a solid wood shiplapped back, I think you're going to find the reward is well worth the effort.

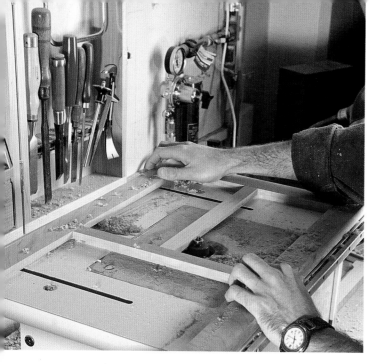

Cut the rabbet for the glass using a rabbeting bit in your router table. After the rabbet is cut, you'll need to square the edges with a chisel. Because this work is delicate, make sure your chisel is super sharp.

Build the back before you build the doors because the back, when screwed in place, holds your case square. A square case is critical when hanging your doors.

Make your back pieces out of any scrap pieces of cherry you have lying around. Narrow pieces are OK. You just want to make sure that the width of the pieces will add up to 31¼" when in place in the rabbet in the case sides.

Begin by cutting ⁵⁄₁₆"-deep × ¼"-wide rabbets on the edges. I like to use a rabbeting bit in a router table. Cut the rabbet on both long edges of the boards (one on the front face of the board and the other on the back) for the back boards — except the boards that will go on the outside. Those need the rabbet on only one edge. Now cut the bead on one edge of the tongue pieces using a beading bit in your router table. Beading bits look confusing at first. Just remember to run the boards on edge through your router table.

Now fit your back pieces in place in the rabbet in the case. Put quarters between your back boards to space out the boards. This allows the back to expand and contract with the seasons. When everything

Get a pocketful of quarters when putting the back in place. You want the back to expand and contract with the seasons, and the thickness of a quarter is just about right.

fits, screw the back boards in place. Use only two screws to attach each back board: one centered at the top and one at the bottom. (This will prevent your back from self-destructing later.) On the boards on the ends you can also screw the back boards into the side rabbets.

DOORS

I like to build my doors to the exact size of the opening and then fit them to size on the jointer. These doors are built using mortise-and-tenon joinery. I cut my tenons on a table saw using a dado stack and then used them to lay out my mortises.

All the tenons for the doors are ⅜" thick. The tenons on the rails are all 1" long. The tenons on the middle stiles are ½" long. I cut ³⁄₁₆" shoulders on all the tenons. When cutting your mortises, make them ¹⁄₁₆" deeper than the tenon is long. This prevents your tenon from "bottoming out" in your mortise.

Check the fit of everything and then glue up the doors. When the glue is dry, you need to cut ⅜" × ⅜" rabbets on the back side of the door to hold the glass. The best way to do this is to use a bearing-guided rabbeting bit in your router table as shown in the photo above.

Take it slow in the corners so you don't blow out the wood around the middle stile and middle rail. Sand your doors and get ready to hang them.

GET A PERFECT GAP

The goal when hanging an inset door like this is to get a ¹⁄₁₆" gap all around. If your case is square and your doors are square, it's going to be a simple task.

DEALING WITH WARPED DOORS

Once you hang your doors, you might find that the stiles don't line up just right. No matter how flat you plane your stock, there's still a chance that your stiles won't be perfect and one will bend out in front of the other. Sometimes this is caused by clamping too tightly. Sometimes it's squirrely wood.

There are two ways of dealing with this. First, you can make your door parts out of two thin pieces of cherry laminated together. I made these stiles from two pieces of ½" cherry that I glued together at the face and then planed the lamination down to ¾".

This process produces a primitive form of two-ply plywood that will resist warping.

Second, after you hang your doors, you can cheat by removing the warp with a handplane. With the doors hung in the case, mark the one that sticks out. Use a pencil to draw a line on the edge of this proud door all along the place where it juts forth.

Take the door off its hinges and plane the stile down to that line using a handplane. Rehang the door and check your work.

Start by putting one of the doors in place and holding the stile against the side. This is where you're going to find out if everything is square. If things are square, you can just start shaving off a little bit from the stiles and rails until you have the gap you want.

If things aren't square, you need to make some tapered cuts on your doors. You can do this on your jointer, but I prefer to use a handplane to shave off the excess. This allows you to stop your cut exactly where you want it. Keep working at it until the gap looks reasonably uniform.

Now hang the doors. I used Amerock non-mortise hinges. These hinges are adjustable so you can get your inset doors lined up just right. And installing them is a snap.

First screw the hinges to the case. Then attach the doors to the hinges using spring clamps. Drill pilot holes for your screws and screw the doors to the hinges. Remove the spring clamps. While you're at it, add the knob and the catches you've chosen to hold the doors shut.

Remove all the hardware and then cut some ¼" × ¼" retaining strips to hold the glass in place. Sand everything to 150 grit and prepare for finishing.

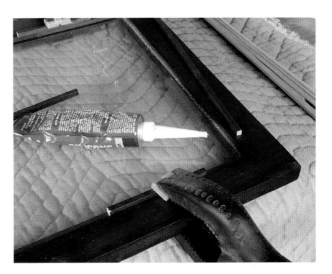

Put down a thin bead of silicone in the rabbet, then put the glass on that. Then lay down another bead of silicone and press the wooden retaining strip into place to cover the goop. Now your doors look good when both open and shut.

FINISHING

Begin the finishing with a water-based dye. I use Moser's Light Sheraton Mahogany dye (from Woodworker's Supply, 800-645-9292, item #844414). Then I covered the entire project with one coat of Behlen's Van Dyke Shading and Glazing Stain (from Woodworker's Supply, item # 916-759). Wipe the glaze on with a cheesecloth. Allow it to flash after a couple minutes, and then wipe off the excess until you achieve an even tone. Allow the glaze to dry overnight. Finally, apply three top coats of a clear finish, such as lacquer.

GLASS

Normally I would pin the strips to the doors to hold the glass in place. But because the mullions are so small this was out of the question. Silicone to the rescue. Put a small bead of 100-percent clear silicone (available at any home center) in the rabbet, and place the ⅛"-thick glass in place. Then run another small bead of silicone in the gap between the wood and the glass and press the wooden retaining strips in place. Use spring clamps to hold them in place while the silicone sets up.

Now that the bookcase is done, I plan to set it up in my study, right where I always envisioned it. And the first thing I'm going to put in there is all those auction catalogs I don't have any more use for.

LIMBERT TABOURETTE

This historical reproduction is easier than it looks, thanks to a tricky rabbet.

by Christopher Schwarz

The curves, cutouts and captured shelf of this small table make it look like a daunting project for the beginning woodworker. But thanks to some sharp design work from our project illustrator, this tabourette actually is duck soup.

Or, should I say, "rabbet" soup.

At the core of this table is an unusual rabbet joint that joins the four legs of the table. The rabbets nest inside one another and, when assembled, look like a pinwheel when viewed from above. As a bonus, this joint allows you to make all four legs from one simple template.

But how do you clamp such a curvy form with this unusual joint? If you own a nail gun, then you already have the answer.

This noteworthy joint might be the only thing that separates my reproduction from a museum original. Using historical photographs, we went to great pains to ensure this tabourette looks exactly like the table that appeared in Charles P. Limbert Co.'s 1905 furniture catalog. If you are unfamiliar with Limbert furniture, you should know that this Grand Rapids, Mich., company produced Arts & Crafts furniture with a European flair. Instead of straight lines and massive proportions, Limbert preferred curves. The furniture remains popular to this day. The #238 sold for $7 in 1905;

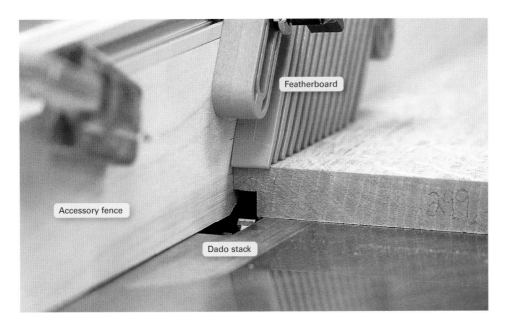
Accessory fence
Featherboard
Dado stack

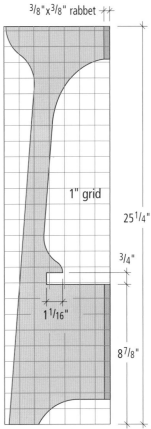
3/8"x3/8" rabbet
1" grid
25 1/4"
3/4"
1 1/16"
8 7/8"

Leg pattern

a recent example fetched $1,600 at auction. Constructing this replica, as you'll see, is easier than affording an original.

START WITH THE LEGS

You can build this project with just two 8'-long 1×8s, making it affordable and easy to build — even if you don't have a jointer or a planer in your shop. Limbert's company built this table in quartersawn white oak, though we've also built it in walnut and cherry for a more contemporary look.

The first order of business is, as always, to get your stock flat and true. Cut all your pieces to length and true one long edge of each board. Set aside the four boards for the legs and glue the remaining boards edge-to-edge to create the panels you will need for the top and shelf.

You're going to make the legs using a plywood template, a router and a pattern-cutting bit. But before you start cutting curves, you should first cut the 3/8" × 3/8" rabbet on your four legs that will join the four pieces together.

This rabbet is the most critical part of the project. It needs to be precise to ensure the legs nest together seamlessly, so check your work carefully as you go. An inexpensive dial caliper will make the work easier.

I like to cut my rabbets on the table saw using a dado stack that's buried in an accessory fence. This allows me to cut my rabbets in one pass and has given me consistent results — especially when I add a

featherboard to the setup, as shown in the photograph.

With your rabbets cut, fit the four pieces together to check your work. Tweak your saw's settings until everything fits. You'll be able to tune up your joints by hand later by using a traditional shoulder plane.

With the patterns taped together, attach it to a piece of plywood using a spray adhesive. This 3M product is available in the glue section of most home-center stores.

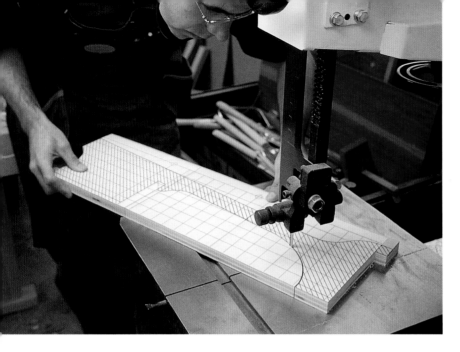

When trimming your pattern to rough size, cut as close to the line as you dare. The closer you are now, the less you'll labor your router later. But if you go over the line, you'll be in trouble.

ONE TEMPLATE, FOUR LEGS

With the rabbets cut, it's time to make the plywood template that will shape the legs. You can use the scaled diagrams we've provided, or you can download a full-size drawing of one from our web site at popwood.com. Click on "Magazine Extras" for details. The file will allow you to print out the legs on three sheets of letter-sized paper and stick them directly to your plywood with a spray adhesive. (There also is a full-size pattern of this table's shelf on our web site.) To make the template, you can use thin ¼" plywood if you like, though thicker plywood, such as ½" or ¾", will make your routing easier, as you'll see later on.

Using your band saw or jigsaw, cut slightly wide of the line. Leave a small nib of waste at the foot and the top of the leg that will allow you to screw this template directly to your lumber.

Clean up the curves on your template using sandpaper or files. Make the curves as smooth as possible. To ensure your curves are fair, I recommend you shape a piece of scrap with your template before you move on to the real thing. A trial run will point out rough spots or bumps that need more attention with the file.

To rout the shape of the legs, first lay the pattern on your work and line up the long, straight edge of the pattern with the rabbeted edge of the piece. Trace this shape onto your wood.

Remove the pattern and trim your leg close to this line using a jigsaw or band saw – get within ¹⁄₁₆" to make it easier on your router and pattern-cutting bit. Save your fall-off pieces because they can help you clamp the legs together later in the game.

There are a couple of ways to rout the legs. You can do the operation on a router table, if your table is big enough. Or you can clamp the work to your bench and use a hand-held router.

The real trick is the router bit itself. There are two kinds of pattern-cutting bits: One has the bearing at the end of the bit; the other has the bearing above the cutting flutes. I generally prefer bits with the bearing on the end, especially when working with a hand-held router. That's because you can work with the pattern clamped to your workbench (if your pattern is thick enough). If this is the route you choose, clamp the pattern to your bench using a vise and bench dogs – make sure your bench dogs don't interfere with the bearing on the end of the bit. Affix the work to the pattern with screws and double-sided tape and rout it to shape.

With the shape routed, you'll immediately see that the notch that holds the shelf will need some additional work. The round router bit won't cut that area square, so square out this section with a jig saw, band saw or even a handsaw and chisels – whatever works for you. This also is the

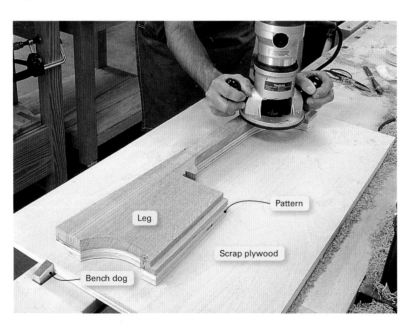

I nailed my pattern to a piece of scrap plywood and clamped that to my bench. This made routing the leg a simple operation that could be done in one pass.

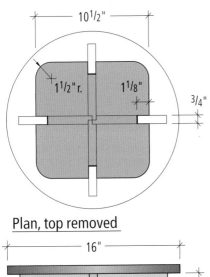

Plan, top removed

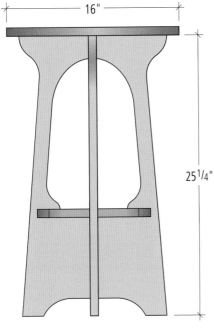

Elevation

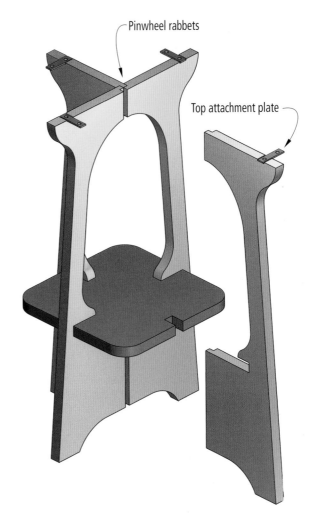

Pinwheel rabbets

Top attachment plate

Exploded view

limbert tabourette
INCHES (MILLIMETERS)

REFERENCE	QUANTITY	PART	STOCK	THICKNESS	(mm)	WIDTH	(mm)	LENGTH	(mm)
A	4	legs	white oak	3/4	(19)	8	(203)	26*	(660)
B	1	top	white oak	3/4	(19)	16	(406)	16	(406)
C	1	shelf	white oak	3/4	(19)	10 1/2	(267)	10 1/2	(267)

* Item is slightly oversized for pattern-routing

time to remove the small pieces of waste that you used to screw the work to your template.

Shape the other three legs in the same manner. Remove all the machining marks with sandpaper or hand tools (a spokeshave and smoothing plane would be appropriate). Then move on to the shelf, top and assembly.

THE OTHER CURVES

After shaping the legs, the top and shelf are pretty simple. The lower shelf requires notches on the four sides and round corners, as shown below. You can make a template for this operation, too. Cut the

A template for the shelf can simplify things if you're making several tables. I cut the notches on each edge of the pattern with a table saw and cleaned out the interior waste with a chisel. Double-sided tape held the shelf on the pattern during routing.

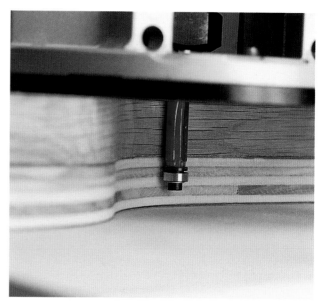

Move the router around the piece in a counterclockwise pattern. As the grain changes direction in the piece, you might want to climb-cut a bit in places (cutting clockwise) for a cleaner cut. Just keep a firm grip on the router when you do this.

notches with the same tools you used to clean up the notches in the legs.

You can round the top in a variety of ways depending on what sort of tools you have. A circle-routing jig like the one featured in our October 2003 issue ("The Magic Trammel Jig") is ideal. You also could cut it close on a band saw or jigsaw and sand it round on a disc sander.

This is the best time to finish the table's parts. Begin by sanding all the surfaces. Start with #100 grit, then move up to #180 or #220. I'm a hard-core hand-tool enthusiast so I skip the sandpaper and use a smoothing plane and a card scraper to prepare my wood for finishing. Either way is fine. Once your wood is perfect, tape off all your glue joints with blue painter's tape.

I use a tried-and-true finishing process we've developed in our shop that emulates the deep reds and browns of a fumed ammonia finish without the downsides of that dangerous chemical. We explained the entire process in detail in our June 2002 issue ("Arts & Crafts Finish," available for sale at our web site).

Essentially, you dye the project with a reddish half-strength water-base aniline dye. After that's dry, wipe on a coat of Valspar warm brown glaze. Then add a topcoat finish – we spray lacquer. The finish takes some time, but it's worth the effort. See the "Supplies" box for ordering what you'll need for this finish.

ASSEMBLY

Putting the base together is easier than it looks; the trick is to do it in stages. First study the pinwheel rabbet in the diagram. Then take two of the legs and join them at a 90°

angle as shown in the illustration. Here's how: Put glue in the rabbet, put the lower shelf in place and nail the two pieces together. You read that right, nail it. I've used a 23-gauge pinner and an 18-gauge nailer for this operation. Both fasteners work, but the smaller pins are less likely to split the wood.

Place the fasteners so that when you assemble the entire table the nail holes will be covered by the other rabbets.

Now add a third leg to your first assembly in the same way.

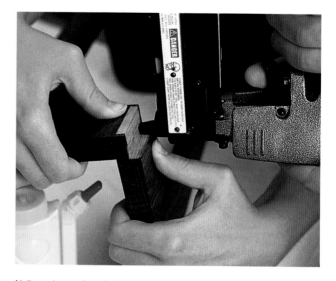

Nail one leg to the other so that the nail holes will not show when the piece is together. It's easy to do, but it's also easy to make a mistake. Use the diagram as a guide and an extra set of hands helps immensely.

What you have left is what you see in the construction drawing: A three-legged table with a groove running down the assembly. And you have a fourth leg with its mating rabbet. Attaching this leg is a bit of a trick. I recommend either band clamps or making clamping cauls.

If you want to make clamping cauls (as shown above) you can use the fall-off pieces from band-sawing the legs to shape. These work, but they won't mate perfectly. The better way is to print out another copy of the leg pattern and use that to saw and sand a set of cauls. To make the cauls easier to clamp to your project, tape the cauls to your clamps' heads. This allows you to assemble the project by yourself.

Using your cauls, clamp the fourth leg in place until the glue is dry, then attach the top. I used brass mending plates that have two screw holes bored in them. These simple bits of hardware allow the top to move with the seasons. To install them on the table's base, use a chisel to make a notch that's just a little bigger than the mending plate. The plate needs to pivot a bit when the top expands and contracts. (If you don't want to use mending plates, the "Supplies" box tells you where to get desktop fasteners, which function similarly.)

The notches shown in the photo are $3/32$" deep × $5/8$" wide and are $1\frac{1}{8}$" in from the outside edge of each leg. Screw each plate to the base. Once you install all four, screw the base to the top.

Now that you're done, be sure to save your templates and clamping cauls. Because you're ready to go into production.

I made clamping cauls using the patterns for the legs. Sand the edges of the cauls to avoid marring your finished edges. I also taped the cauls to my clamps, which made them easy to get in position without help.

The shallow notch at the top of each leg holds the mending plates ($1.50 for a set of four from my local home-center store). Make the notch a bit wider than the plate to allow it to pivot. This allows the top to expand and contract with the seasons.

GREENE & GREENE PLANTER TABLE

An indoor/outdoor plant stand that lets you water without worrying about spills on the furniture or floor below.

By Steve Shanesy

This table made a humble first appearance in *Popular Woodworking* as a prop in a photo of a featured project, the Blacker House's Greene and Greene Bench. Well, not only was the bench a hit with readers, but we had lots of calls about the table as well.

As a table/plant stand/dry sink, the project is a real hybrid. And like many projects produced in home workshops, this one was an answer to a particular problem. You see, my wife presented me with the bonsai tree shown in the photo. All of the sudden I was responsible for an 18-year-old miniature "tree."

Bonsai require frequent watering. Their sandy soils need a thorough drenching every day. The inevitable run-off begged for a solution easier than a daily trip to the kitchen sink. So I devised a plan for a table with a dry-sink top lined with a copper pan to catch the water.

It works well and looks good. The Japanese design influence provides just the right setting for a Japanese bonsai tree.

Construction follows the same principles and techniques as are typical for small tables: an arrangement of aprons at the top and stretchers set about mid-leg. In lieu of a top, the copper pan slips in from below and is supported by a plywood bottom that is held in place with cleats screwed to the aprons. The principal materials are redwood (although red cedar would be a less expensive alternative) and outdoor-grade plywood. The copper pan is sheet metal and is simple to fabricate.

Cut out the legs, aprons and stretchers following the cutting list. You can cut the stretchers about $\frac{1}{8}$" wider than given so there's a little left to trim when routing them with a template to finished shape. The legs are cut from redwood 2x material and the rest is $\frac{3}{4}$" stock.

Now use Baltic birch, medium density fiberboard (MDF) or some other material without voids to make templates for routing the patterns on the aprons and stretchers. It's best if the template thickness is at least $\frac{1}{4}$" and not more than $\frac{1}{2}$". Make the templates to the shapes indicated by the diagrams. Be sure the edges are smooth after cutting them.

When the templates are done, position the one for the side stretchers or aprons. Make it easy to find the right position by penciling a center line across the width of the template and the width of the parts. Then it's just a simple matter of matching up the center lines and leaving a fraction of overhang along the width. Now trace the template shape on the parts and cut out the shape, leaving $\frac{1}{8}$" or less waste to be trimmed with the router.

When done, position the template on the part again and tack it in place with wire brads. Two should be sufficient. Now use a "pattern" router bit (a straight bit with a bearing of equal size as the diameter of the bit) in a router and secure the router in a router table. Elevate the bit to a height where the bearing rides against the template and the cutting edge of the bit will trim the overhanging waste from the part. Use this procedure for all the parts that are shaped from the two templates.

Now position the parts in their correct locations relative to the legs. Follow the diagram for these locations. Mark the aprons and legs for two #10 biscuits each and the stretchers for a $\frac{3}{8}$" dowel. The biscuit slots will overlap, so cut one end off one of the biscuits about $\frac{1}{2}$" back. Cut the slots and drill the holes. Dry assemble the parts.

The finished shape of the stretchers and aprons is made using a template that guides the bearing on top of the router bit.

Before assembly, rout a ¼" radius detail on the stretchers, legs and aprons.

After taking the table apart, change the router to a ¼" radius bit with a bearing. Run all the edges of all the parts with the following exceptions: Leave the ends of the aprons and stretchers square and the inside top edge of the aprons; the bottom end of the legs remain square and the inside corner of the legs where the aprons start and stop are also square.

Now, before assembling with glue, presand the parts where it's easier now than later. When done, glue the two ends with stretchers first and let them dry, then glue up the long sides and center stretcher to complete the assembly.

Finish the woodworking portion of the project by cutting the plywood bottom and the redwood strips that will be tacked to the inside top of the aprons. With the bottom, notch the corners so it can slip in place without interfering with the legs. For the redwood strips, rout the ¼" radius detail on one edge of a ¾"-thick piece, then rip

the piece off to ¼" thickness, and repeat until you have the four pieces required. You can glue and clamp these in place or simply glue and nail them.

These strips provide a lip for the copper pan to seat to when installed from the bottom and give a clean, finished look to the "dry sink" top.

When the pan is complete, set the table upside down, position the pan, set the plywood bottom on top of it then screw cleats to the apron sides to hold the pan and bottom snugly in place.

Because of the anticipated water abuse — including an occasional rain soaking while outdoors during the summer months — I left the table unfinished and will let time provide a very pleasing patina. Best of all, and assuming I can provide the proper care for the bonsai tree for the next 18 years, the table will still be just the right size.

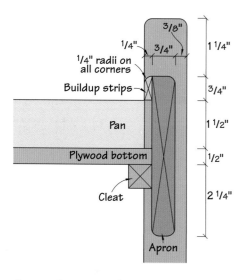

Cross Section of Pan and Apron

After the parts are shaped, cut slots for biscuits into the legs for joining the aprons. Center the slots in the apron ends, then elevate the biscuit joiner with a ¼" piece of plywood to provide the correct offset for the inside of the apron when cutting the leg slots.

greene & greene planter table
INCHES (MILLIMETERS)

REFERENCE	QUANTITY	PART	STOCK	THICKNESS	(mm)	WIDTH	(mm)	LENGTH	(mm)	COMMENTS
A	4	legs	redwood	$1^3/_8$	(35)	$1^3/_8$	(35)	$29^1/_4$	(743)	
B	2	aprons	redwood	$^3/_4$	(19)	5	(127)	18	(457)	
C	2	aprons	redwood	$^3/_4$	(19)	5	(127)	14	(356)	
D	2	stretchers	redwood	$^3/_4$	(19)	2	(51)	14	(356)	
E	1	stretcher	redwood	$^3/_4$	(19)	$2^1/_2$	(64)	$18^1/_2$	(470)	
F	2	build-up strips	redwood	$^1/_4$	(6)	$^3/_4$	(19)	18	(457)	
G	2	build-up strips	redwood	$^1/_4$	(6)	$^3/_4$	(19)	14	(356)	
H	1	bottom	plywood	$^1/_2$	(13)	$14^3/_8$	(366)	$18^3/_8$	(467)	
I	2	cleats	poplar	$^3/_4$	(19)	$^3/_4$	(19)	8	(203)	

One piece of copper sheet metal, 17" × 21"

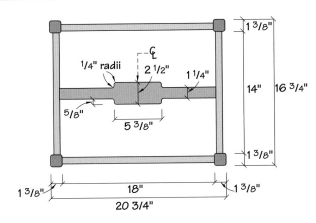

Plan

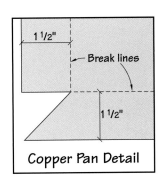

Copper Pan Detail

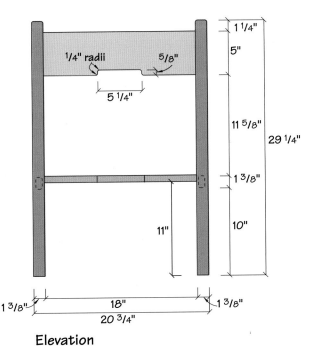

Elevation

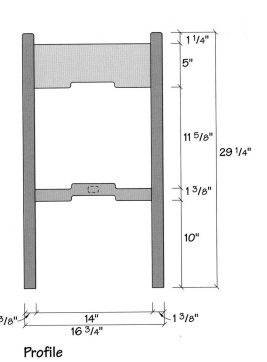

Profile

MAKE A WATERTIGHT PAN

Cutting, bending and soldering the copper for the pan is nothing to be intimidated by. You can cut the copper sheet metal on your table saw using a carbide crosscut blade, trim the corners with an ordinary pair of snips, bend the stock with a simple plywood jig and solder it to make it waterproof just as you would when joining copper plumbing. I picked up the copper from a roofing company that uses this material for flashings. I paid a few bucks for the piece I needed. To fabricate the pan, just follow these simple steps.

1. Carefully measure the inside dimension of the table from the inside corners of the legs, not the inside of the aprons.

2. Cut your copper to this size on the table saw (make sure you are wearing safety glasses and that the thin metal stock cannot slip under the fence).

3. If it matters on the copper you are using, turn the piece so that the good side is face down on your bench. Then measure from each edge and mark the height of the pan side, 1½". Score the material to make a crisp, square edge when bent. Score all four edges similarly.

4. Use your combination square and mark a 45° angle from each corner to the intersection of the score lines at each corner. Now cut away one of the triangles made in each corner.

A simple method for bending using plywood cut with a 45° angle and clamps. This ensures a bend in a straight line and a point to bend to. Clamp the metal to a table with the area to be bent overhanging the edge of the bench.

After drawing a line from a corner to the intersection of two score lines, cut out one of the triangular shapes from each corner using snips.

Heat the copper at the point where you want the solder to flow.

After clamping the overhanging piece, bend upward until the mitered edges close. Then remove the clamps. Repeat for each side

5 Cut a piece of ¾" plywood that's at least as long as the longest side of the copper so that you end up with two pieces with a 45° angle on a long edge. Make one piece the height of the pan side and the other at least 6" wide. Finally, cut one more piece with square edges only that is as wide as the pan side.

6 With the scored side down, place one edge of the copper so that the score line and the edge of the bench are the same. Clamp the wider plywood piece over the copper so that the point of the plywood angle is also at the edge of the bench. With the overhanging copper, make a sandwich of the copper, the square-edged plywood below and angle-edged plywood above. Be sure the points of the plywood angles touch and securely clamp the sandwich together.

7 Bend the edge of the copper up until the plywood angles close. Repeat the process until all four edges are bent. If the sides are not quite square, tap them with a hammer along the length of the bend.

8 Solder the corners together. First coat the surfaces with flux. Position the corner so it's square and lightly clamp with a steel clamp. Thoroughly heat the parts, especially close to the corner until the solder flows and is drawn in between the surfaces. Allow to cool and repeat for the other corners. When done, add water to the pan and check for leaks. Clean any flux residue with soap and water.

LIMBERT FURNITURE   TURN of the Century Editions

GUSTAV STICKLEY'S CRAFTSMAN FARMS
The Quest for an Arts and Crafts Utopia

Alden A. Watson → HAND TOOLS

GREENE & GREENE SIDE TABLE

Simple joinery makes a table in the classic style
of the Greene brothers a rewarding and easy
project for woodworkers of any skill.

by Steve Shanesy

If you don't mind a little cheating, you can make this table quite simply. You see, the "pegged" mortise-and-tenon joints aren't really pegged at all. They are simple dowel joints, and the "pegs" are merely inlaid and applied pieces of ebony. But even if you feel the slightest twinge of guilt about taking such short cuts — please don't. The brothers Greene and Greene, renowned architects and designers of the late Arts & Crafts period, didn't hesitate a moment to use screws in their classic furniture. So a little liberty on this project follows right along in the tradition.

I built this table from cherry. The legs require 2"-thick material and the top requires 1½"-thick stock. The aprons and stretchers finish out at ⅞" thick. If you use thinner material, you could reduce both the top and legs by ½", and the aprons and stretchers could go to ¾" stock. That will keep the proportions just about right.

Prepare all your stock to the final sizes as given in the cutting list. Next prepare the template for routing the so-called "cloud lift" patterns on the aprons and stretchers. These are a Greene and Greene signature design and were borrowed from the Japanese.

CLOUD LIFT TEMPLATE

The two-sided template is made from ¼" Baltic birch plywood with the two patterns (one is slightly longer than the other) cut on the long edges of the same piece. Plan on using the template along with a straight router bit with a bearing of the same dimension as the bit diameter. Draw the design on the plywood following the dimensions in the diagram. The "lift" is ¾". Before band sawing to the line, drill ½" holes in the inside corners of the pattern.

When routing the cloud lifts, the top-mounted bearing on the straight router bit follows and duplicates the pattern shape onto the table apron. Before routing, most of the waste material is removed with a band saw. Note the aprons ends are aligned with pencil marks on the template and the part is held to the template with brad nails.

Here I'm rounding over the edges with a ¼"-radius router bit. Almost every edge on the project gets this treatment. The exception is where parts join together, such as the apron and stretcher ends, and apron top edge.

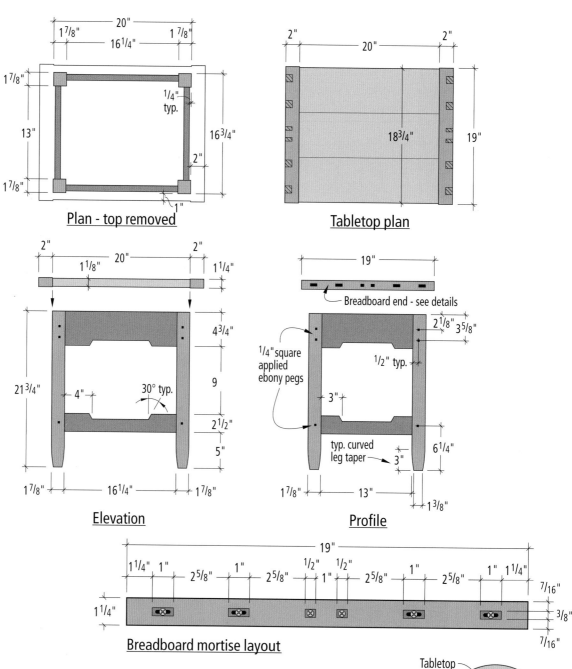

Plan - top removed

Tabletop plan

Elevation

$1/4$" square applied ebony pegs

typ. curved leg taper

Breadboard end - see details

$1/2$" typ.

Profile

Breadboard mortise layout

greene & greene side table
INCHES (MILLIMETERS)

REFERENCE	QUANTITY	PART	STOCK	THICKNESS	(mm)	WIDTH	(mm)	LENGTH	(mm)
A	4	legs	cherry	$1^7/8$	(47)	$1^7/8$	(47)	$21^3/4$	(552)
B	2	aprons	cherry	$7/8$	(22)	$4^3/4$	(121)	$16^1/4$	(412)
C	2	aprons	cherry	$7/8$	(22)	$4^3/4$	(121)	13	(330)
D	2	stretchers	cherry	$7/8$	(22)	$2^1/2$	(64)	$16^1/4$	(412)
E	2	stretchers	cherry	$7/8$	(22)	$2^1/2$	(64)	13	(330)
F	1	top	cherry	$1^1/8$	(28)	$18^3/4$	(476)	20	(508)
G	2	breadboards	cherry	$1^1/8$	(28)	2	(51)	19	(483)

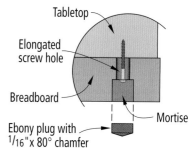

Tabletop

Elongated screw hole

Breadboard

Mortise

Ebony plug with $1/16$" x 80° chamfer

Breadboard plan detail

RIGHT-SIZING DOWELS

A dowel that's even slightly oversized in diameter can cause all sorts of problems – the worst of which is actually splitting the part to be doweled. This not only happens because the dowel is a snug fit, but also because the glue in the hole has nowhere to go once you insert the dowel. If the glue can't escape, it can prevent the dowel from inserting completely and can actually prevent the parts to be joined from closing completely.

If your dowels are too snug, there's an easy fix called a dowel skinner. In this project, I found my $^3/_8$" dowels were too tight for my $^3/_8$" hole. The solution was to drill a hole in $^1/_8$" or thicker mild steel, that's $^1/_{64}$" smaller than the dowel. Then just drive your dowels through the hole with a hammer and you'll get a perfect fit.

Drilling these holes is much easier than band sawing such a tight radius. After carefully band sawing to the line, sand the band-sawn edges so that they are smooth and straight. Next, on the template, mark each pattern edge with a line that represents the ends of the two different lengths of aprons and stretchers used in the project.

Before using the templates to rout the design, first band saw away most of the waste on the parts. Using the template, draw a pencil line of the design on each apron or stretcher, then band saw to about $^1/_{16}$" from the line. The router will clean up the rest.

To prepare for routing, set up a router table with a router and the $^1/_2$" straight bit as mentioned earlier. No fence is required for this type of pattern cutting. To begin routing, align the part so that the ends match up with the lines previously drawn and so that the leading edge of the pattern aligns with the edge of the part. Attach the part to the template using two small brad nails. You can putty the nail holes later, but even so, select the "b" side of the part that will go to the inside of the table base as the side to nail to. Run each part this way. If you use cherry, do your best not to hesitate in the corners of the cut to minimize burning.

Simple joinery makes this project quite easy. A pair of dowels join each apron and stretcher end to the leg. This vintage Stanley #59 doweling jig makes this process especially easy due to its adjustability (see the story on page 63), particularly when drilling the holes in the legs to provide the $^1/_4$" setback of the aprons.

No mortising machine? You can still speed along the process of cutting the plug holes in the breadboard ends. After marking out the locations, drill out most of the waste, then square up the ends and side walls with a chisel.

DOWEL JOINTS FOR BASE

To assemble the legs, aprons and stretchers, drill the holes for the $\frac{3}{8}$" dowels and sand the parts to 150 grit. Use two, 2"-long dowels for each joint and position them so that when assembled, the apron sets back $\frac{1}{4}$" from the outside face of the leg.

When all the dowel holes are drilled, dry-fit the assembly before actually gluing it together. When I assembled my base, I glued and clamped it in two stages. First assemble one set of legs, aprons and stretchers. Then complete the assembly after the first assembly is dry. Take care not to apply too much glue because squeeze-out in the joint is difficult to clean up and can lead to finishing problems later.

MAKE THE TOP

Now turn your attention to the tabletop. The breadboard ends with ebony plugs are another Greene and Greene signature detail. I made the breadboard ends $\frac{1}{8}$" thicker than the top, leaving them $\frac{1}{16}$" proud of the thickness of the rest of the top. They also are slightly longer. This additional length anticipates eventual expansion of the top.

Prepare your top's main boards and glue them up. When dry, square up the top and cut it to its final size. The breadboards are attached easily with a $2\frac{1}{2}$"-long screw in each of the plugged holes. Be sure and make elongated screw slots in the breadboard to anticipate wood movement in the top. To make the square grooves in the breadboard ends, use a mortising machine or chain drill the holes and then square them up with a chisel. The depth of the hole is 1". The size of the small holes is $\frac{3}{8}$" wide by $\frac{1}{2}$" long. The longer holes are 1" long.

Before attaching the breadboards to the top, go back to the router table and round over the long edges of the top and the outside edges of the breadboards. The edges of the top and breadboards that join together remain square. As with the table base, pre-sand the top before assembling the top and breadboard ends. When done, clamp the ends to the top so they remain in perfect position while screwing the ends in place.

SHAPE THE LEGS

Next, turn to the legs. First shape the bottom to the gradual tapering curve as seen in the diagram. Start the detail 3" up from the bottom. The slight curved taper removes only $\frac{1}{4}$" per side at the end of the leg. Now make a template of the pattern so you can draw a pencil line for each side of the leg. Then band saw and sand to the line.

With the parts of the table base shaped, go back to the router table and insert a $\frac{1}{4}$" roundover bit in the router. Run the profile on all the long edges of the legs, stretchers and aprons, except for the top edge of the apron, which remains square.

EBONY PLUGS AND PEGS

The ebony plugs used on the table all stand about ⅛" proud of the surface. The top of each plug is shaped so that it looks faceted, or slightly beveled on the top. The ebony plugs for the breadboards are first made as a ⅜" x ½" long stick. Carefully make two 10° cuts on one of the long ⅜"-dimension edges to create two of the facets. Next cut them to length, but a little long. Fit each one as they are installed. I fit mine by sanding. Also sand the other two facets on the top surface. When ready to install, add a slight amount of glue and carefully tap them into place. The process is a bit tedious, but it takes just about an hour to complete.

The smaller pegs for the mortise-and-tenon joints are ¼" square. To make these, cut an ebony stick ¼" square and about 12" long. Facet the top to make a shallow pyramid shape by sanding, then hand-saw off the shaped end about ⅛" long. Repeat the process until you have at least 24 "plugs." To apply the "plugs" use cyanoacrylate (what most people call Super Glue). Carefully mark the location of each plug, add a tiny drop of glue and set it in place. The glue cures quickly and no clamping is required.

Finish sand the top and base with 220 grit sandpaper. This last sanding must be done by hand due to the plugs projecting off the surface. I finished the project using two coats of a clear satin finish spray lacquer that comes in an aerosol can. A wiping varnish or polyurethane also would be appropriate. Whichever finish you use, sand lightly between coats for the smoothest results.

You're almost done. Attach the top to the base using whatever method you prefer. I used 1"-square wooden cleats and screws. Again, be sure your method of attachment accommodates wood movement in the top.

OLD STANLEY DOWELING JIG THE BEST

There was a time when I used a lot of dowels in furniture building. Back then, the jig I used was the self-centering kind. A few years ago a woodworker friend showed me a vintage Stanley doweling jig he picked up at a flea market. Its design is quite similar to the current Stanley offering, but the quality of the materials are far superior to today's models.

The great feature of this design is the variability of spacing the dowel hole locations and the ease of aligning the hole center to your predetermined location. Since purchasing my own vintage Stanley, my self-centering jig hasn't come out of the drawer. Chances are you can buy your own vintage Stanley #59 or #60 at auction on eBay (ebay.com). Just make sure the one you bid on is complete. The bushings for guiding your drill are interchangeable depending on which size hole you want. A complete jig would include bushings for ¼", 5⁄16", ⅜", 9⁄16" and ½" drill bits. These rigs can generally be bought on eBay for about $25.

If you do buy one of these tools without bushings (or if you need odd-size bushings), Stanley still sells them as replacement parts. Call 800-262-2161 during business hours and select the option "replacement parts."

GREENE & GREENE SIDEBOARD

by Robert W. Lang

In 1907, the architectural practice of brothers Charles and Henry Greene was at its peak of popularity in southern California, with several houses under construction. Equally busy was the workshop of Peter and John Hall, another pair of brothers who were responsible for the actual construction of the ultimate bungalows designed by Greene and Greene.

In addition to acting as general contractors, the Halls were also responsible for all of the interior woodwork and the furniture for these magnificent homes. In researching this piece, I tried to discover what the original details were, and also tried to place myself in the setting in which the original work was done. Given the volume of work performed in the Halls' millwork shop, this furniture must have been made as efficiently as possible.

The original version of this serving table was made from mahogany with ebony accents for the Freeman Ford home in Pasadena, Calif. My version is about 12" shorter than the original and about 6" narrower. In planning this project, I wanted to come as close as I could to the details of the original piece. I found an amazing online resource for original Greene and Greene drawings and photographs. See the article, "The Greene & Greene Virtual Archives" on page 68 for more information.

Ebonized plugs and cloud lifts are two Greene & Greene original details.

DIGGING FOR THE DETAILS

In many Greene and Greene reproductions, the finished project doesn't look quite right, or the methods used are terribly inefficient. In highly detailed projects like this, half the battle is making nice details quickly. The other half is the sequence in which the work is performed.

Many times people follow someone else's reproduction, rather than referring to an original example. The problem with this is that details get changed or exaggerated, and then are taken as good examples. The style gets watered down and the methods become too complicated. I wanted to make this piece as it would have been made by the Hall brothers; excellent workmanship done efficiently, faithful to the design.

I also wanted the color and character of the mahogany to look the way original pieces do. It took some detective work and head scratching to work out the methods and

greene & greene sideboard
INCHES (MILLIMETERS)

REFERENCE	QUANTITY	PART	STOCK	THICKNESS	(mm)	WIDTH	(mm)	LENGTH	(mm)	COMMENTS
A	1	top	mahogany	$7/8$	(22)	18	(457)	$69^3/4$	(1772)	$1/4$" × $3/8$" tongue each end
B	2	breadboard ends	mahogany	1	(25)	3	(76)	$18^1/4$	(463)	$1/4$" × $3/8$" groove one edge, $1/4$" × $5/8$" × 2" groove both ends
C	8	legs	mahogany	$2^3/4$	(70)	$2^3/4$	(70)	$29^1/8$	(740)	
D	2	top end rails	mahogany	$7/8$	(22)	$5^5/8$	(143)	13	(330)	$1/2$" × $1^1/4$" × $4^5/8$" tenon each end
E	2	lower end rails	mahogany	$7/8$	(22)	6	(152)	13	(330)	$1/2$" × $1^1/4$" × 5" tenon each end
F	4	front/back top rails	mahogany	$7/8$	(22)	$5^5/8$	(143)	$8^1/4$	(209)	$1/2$" × $1^1/4$" × $4^5/8$" tenon each end
G	2	front/back cloud lift rails	mahogany	$7/8$	(22)	$6^3/8$	(162)	$21^1/2$	(546)	$1/2$" × $1^1/4$" × $4^5/8$" tenon each end
H	4	front/back bottom rails	mahogany	$7/8$	(22)	6	(152)	$8^1/4$	(209)	$1/2$" × $1^1/4$" × 5" tenon each end
I	2	front/back bottom mid rails	mahogany	$7/8$	(22)	6	(152)	$21^1/2$	(546)	$1/2$" × $1^1/4$" × 5" tenon each end
J	72	plugs	walnut	$3/8$	(10)	$3/8$	(10)	$5/16$	(8)	ebonized
K	2	splines	walnut	$1/4$	(6)	$7/8$	(22)	6	(152)	ebonized
L	2	cleats	mahogany	$7/8$	(22)	$7/8$	(22)	$10^3/8$	(264)	
M	2	cleats	mahogany	$7/8$	(22)	$7/8$	(22)	$18^7/8$	(479)	

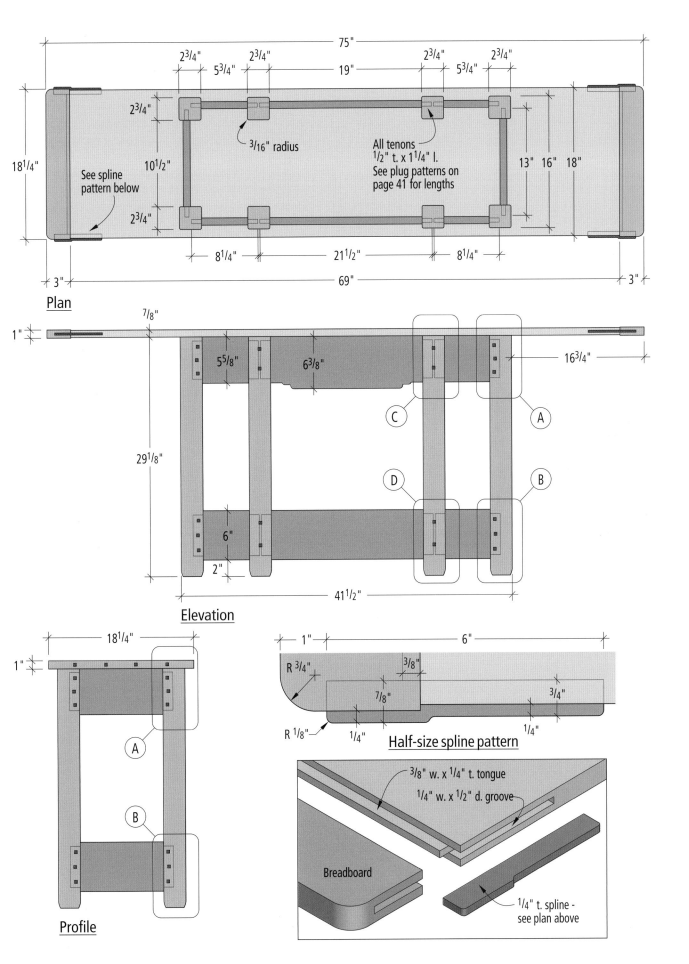

75"

2³/₄" 2³/₄" 2³/₄" 2³/₄"

5³/₄" 19" 5³/₄"

2³/₄"

3/16" radius

All tenons
1/2" t. x 1¹/₄" l.
See plug patterns on
page 41 for lengths

18¹/₄"

10¹/₂"

2³/₄"

See spline
pattern below

2³/₄"

13" 16" 18"

8¹/₄" 21¹/₂" 8¹/₄"

3" 69" 3"

Plan

7/8"

1"

5⁵/₈" 6³/₈"

16³/₄"

C A

29¹/₈"

D B

6"

2"

41¹/₂"

Elevation

18¹/₄"

1"

A

B

Profile

1" 6"

R ³/₄" 3/8"

7/8" 3/4"

R ¹/₈" 1/4" 1/4"

Half-size spline pattern

3/8" w. x 1/4" t. tongue

1/4" w. x 1/2" d. groove

Breadboard

1/4" t. spline -
see plan above

THE GREENE & GREENE VIRTUAL ARCHIVES

The University of Southern California hosts an amazing online collection of original drawings, photographs, correspondence and other documents from the work of Charles Sumner Greene and Henry Mather Greene. You can find it online at: usc.edu/dept/architecture/greeneandgreene/index.html

The database of digital images can be searched by project name or by type of object. Once a document has been found, you can zoom in and pan around on individual drawings and photographs. Background information and other reference material is also available.

I was able to find an original black and white photograph of the table featured in this article, and while drawings for this table don't exist, I looked at working drawings for other furniture from the same house, as well as a finish formula from the William Thorsen house.

This material served as the basis for how I made the details of this table. The shape and projection of the square plugs and splines on the breadboard ends, the treatment of the edges of the legs and top, and the finish color were all completed by following the details shown in these original documents.

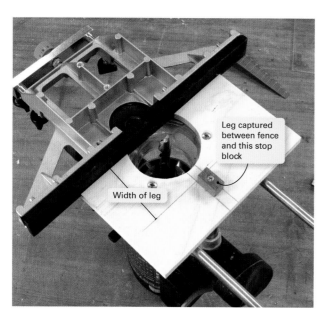

The small block on the sub-base is the same size as the bit, placed farther away than the width of the leg from the fence.

The block is lined up with the bit so that the template can be made to the exact size and location of the mortises.

materials. In the end, this table looks more like the original than most reproductions.

My plans called for 32 mortise-and-tenon joints and 72 square plugs. The plugs on the legs appear to be going through the mortise-and-tenon joints that connect the rails to the legs. If you look closely at the inner set of legs on the previous page, you will notice that the plugs are centered in the width of the legs.

The only way these plugs could be functional would be if the tenons were long enough to cross the midpoint of the leg. If that were true, then the tenons would need to be reduced in thickness, so that they could cross each other. This would complicate these joints as well as weaken them. This set of plugs is just for show.

I also questioned the need for pinning all three of the plugs at each of the corner joints. One would be sufficient to reinforce the joint. Pinning all of them could weaken the tenons, and introduce problems when the rails expand and contract seasonally. I decided to pin only the middle of each tenon and make most of the plugs only decorative.

The original drawings detailed the breadboard ends, the splines and the way they are attached with screws behind the plugs.

Our local wood supplier had 3"-square by 30"-long leg blanks in stock, so I decided to purchase eight of them instead of milling my own out of 12/4 material. You might need to glue up the leg blanks from two or more pieces to get the thickness of 2¾".

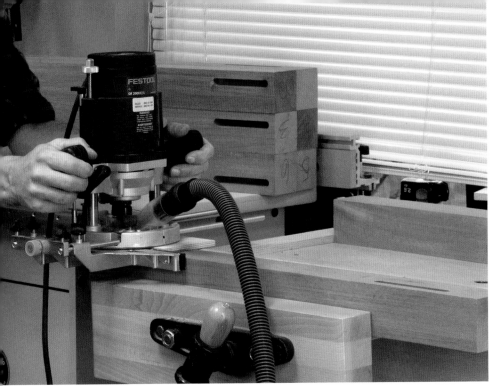

With the template and the leg held in the vise, the fence on the router places the cut laterally, and the block hits the template to locate the ends of the mortises. Using this method allowed me to mill all 32 mortises quickly and precisely, without doing any layout work on the legs.

The rest of the material all has a finished thickness of ⅞" except for the breadboard ends, which are a full 1" thick. I had wood that was long enough to make all of the top rails out of one piece and all of the bottom rails out of the other. I kept them in order to match grain and color around the entire table, which adds a nice touch.

WHICH LEG IS WHICH?

After laying out all of the legs and rails for grain direction and orientation, I numbered each leg on the plan view of my drawing, and wrote the number on the top of each leg to keep them in order as the work progressed. I also marked each end of the rails with the number of the leg it joined to.

My first task was to find an efficient way to cut all the mortises. Instead of using a hollow chisel mortiser, I decided to use a plunge router along with a template to quickly locate all of the cuts.

MORE MORTISES PER HOUR

The fence for the plunge router was used to locate the distance in from the edge of the leg to the mortises. In order to set the beginning and end of each mortise, I added a sub-base to the router as shown below, and attached a ½"-square block of wood to the sub-base. This size block matched the diameter of the bit I was using. I placed it in line with the router bit and square to the fence. The template was made to the exact length of the leg, with the notches cut at the end points of each mortise. After the notches were cut, I added a stop to locate the template at the top of each leg.

I took the four outer legs, and with a lumber crayon, marked the general location of the mortises on adjacent corners. I marked the four inner legs on opposite sides. These marks were to keep straight which surfaces were to be mortised. The exact locations of the mortises would come from the template without my needing to locate and mark each one.

I put each leg, along with the template in my bench vise, with the surface to be mortised facing up. I then rout-

A small-diameter flush-cutting bit follows the template and shapes all of the cloud lifts accurately and identically leaving only minimal sanding to be done.

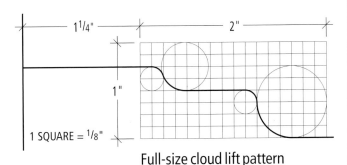

1¼"   2"

1"

1 SQUARE = ⅛"

Full-size cloud lift pattern

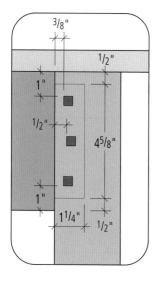

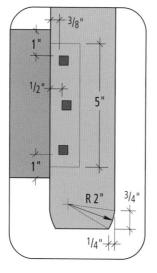

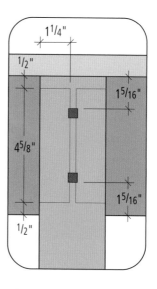

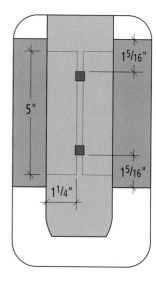

Plug pattern A

Plug pattern B and bottom of leg detail

Plug pattern C

Plug pattern D

ed the mortises, plunging back and forth until I reached the final depth of 1¼".

I cut all of the tenons on the rails with a jig on the table saw, coming in ³⁄₁₆" from each face and ½" from each edge to form the tenons. I used a rasp to round off each of the tenon shoulders to match the rounded ends of the mortises I routed earlier.

To make the cloud lift patterns on the center rails, I made a template out of ½"-thick plywood, carefully filing the inside and outside curves at the corners. I then rough cut each of the cloud lifts with the band saw, and used the template and a ¼"-diameter flush trimming bit in the router to cut each rail to the pattern.

I fit each of the tenons, trimming with my shoulder

plane, and then made a dry run assembly of the entire base of the table.

PRODUCTIVE METHOD FOR PLUGS

With 64 square plugs to make for the table base, I didn't want to lay out the location of every hole. So I made a template the width and height of the legs and marked out the center points of each of the plugs, drilling a ⅛"-diameter hole at each of these points. I marked all of the legs by sticking my awl through each hole and into the face of the leg.

With a ⅜"-diameter Forstner bit in my drill press, set to bore ¼" deep, I drilled a hole for each of the square plugs. I could have made these holes with the mortiser, but with

The tenons are adjusted to fit with my shoulder plane. A piece of scrap plywood attached to the bench acts as a bench stop to hold the work .

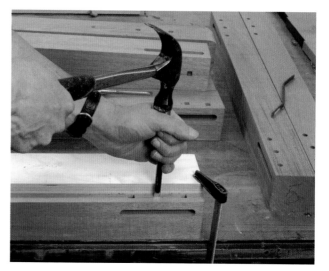

A modified chisel from a hollow chisel mortiser turns round holes square with just a few hammer taps. Plywood clamped to the leg keeps the chisel straight.

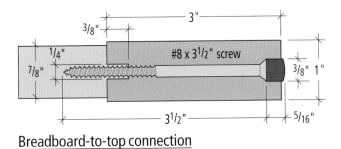

Breadboard-to-top connection

◫ SUPPLIES

amazon.com
Photographer's Formulary Potassium
Dichromate 100 grams, $7.49

some of the squares offset ⅛" from the others, I didn't want to set up the mortiser fence three times. With the center points marked from the template, I saved time.

To make the holes square, I took a worn out ⅜" chisel from the mortiser, ground the points off the end, and with a conical bit in a Dremel tool, sharpened the back of each corner of the chisel. I clamped a scrap of plywood to the face of each leg with its edge tangent to each row of holes as shown below right. This kept the chisel square to the edge of the legs, and with a few smacks of the hammer the round holes were now square. I could have used a standard chisel and made four cuts on each hole, but this would have taken four times as long.

The bottoms of the legs were radiused with a 2"-radius round-over bit. I set up the bit in the router table, so that the radius ended ¾" up from the bottom of each leg and ¼" in. Using a thick block of wood to back up the legs, I moved each edge of the leg bottoms across the bit as seen in the photo below.

Before finish sanding all the parts to #220 grit, I used a roundover bit in my router to ease all of the edges to a ³⁄₁₆" radius on the legs, and a ⅛" radius on the rails and edges of the tabletop.

Just a portion of a 2"-radius roundover bit shapes the bottoms of the legs.

NOT EBONY, BUT EBONIZED

In original Greene and Greene furniture the square plugs were made of ebony, but I decided to use walnut, ebonizing them with a solution made from vinegar and steel wool. I took a pint of white vinegar and dropped in a shredded pad of steel wool. After letting this soak for several days, I strained the liquid through a coffee filter to remove any metal.

Because I would be coloring the legs and the plugs separately, I wanted to shape the plugs and cut them to finished length before putting them in place.

To make the plugs, I ripped strips about ¹⁄₆₄" over the size of the ⅜" square holes. Using the miter gauge on the band saw I cut 1" long blocks. These were long enough to round over and bevel the ends before cutting them to final length. I put a slight dome and bevel on each end of the 1"-long blocks with a quarter-sheet pad sander, and set up a stop block on the miter gauge for the band saw ⁵⁄₁₆" away from the blade. Carefully holding the blocks against the miter gauge with the point of an awl, I cut them to length.

The last step was to put a small chamfer on each of the back edges with a chisel. The chamfer let me get the plugs started in the holes before driving them in with a dead-blow mallet.

The top was glued up from three 1"-thick boards, and after surfacing it to ⅞", I trimmed it to length. Each end of the top has a ¼"-wide by ⅜"-long tongue to hold the breadboard ends. I clamped a piece of plywood across the top to serve as a straightedge for the router to mill the tongues, as shown above right.

I used a ¼" straight bit in the router table to cut the groove in the center of one edge of the 1"-thick end pieces. I then raised the bit to 2" above the table to cut the ⅝"-deep slot in the end of the breadboard to receive the splines. The last slot to cut was in the top for the other end of the splines. This was made with a slot-cutting bit in my hand-held router.

I made the first spline, and I used it as a pattern for the remaining three. I cut the splines a little oversized on the band saw and then fixed them to the pattern with double-sided tape. I used the flush-trim bit in the router to make exact copies of the splines. With a little sanding on the

The breadboard end is attached to the tabletop with screws and the ebonized walnut spline is glued in the slot in the table only.

A piece of plywood clamped across the top guides the router to cut the tongue for the breadboard ends.

edges, and a few strokes of my block plane to adjust the thickness, the splines were ready to be ebonized.

The breadboard ends are held to the ends of the tabletop with #8 × 3½" screws. I drilled oversized holes through the ends, and moved the bit side to side in the two outer holes to elongate them. With glue applied only to the middle 6" of the tongue, I put the ends in place, temporarily inserted the splines to align the breadboard ends and tightened the screws.

AUTHENTIC COLOR UNCOVERED

One of the most interesting discoveries I made on the Greene and Greene Virtual Archives was a recipe for the finish for the furniture from another house. I have always admired the rich, vibrant color of the mahogany in original Greene and Greene furniture, something rarely seen in most reproductions of their work.

The formula called for a treatment of potassium dichromate applied "as work proceeds" followed by a "filler" composed of four colors mixed in linseed oil. Potassium dichromate is a powerful oxidizer and must be handled carefully. I wore a respirator while mixing it and gloves while applying it. After experimenting, I used a solution of ⅜ ounce of powder to a quart of distilled water.

For the colors, I used artist's oil colors. Chrome Yellow (3½ parts of the formula) and Raw Umber (3 parts) were easy selections. White Lead (2⅝ parts) is no longer made, so I used Titanium White. The last color listed was Sylvan Green (⅛ part), and I couldn't find an oil color with this

The solution of potassium dichromate oxides the mahogany, turns it a rusty orange color and gives it an aged patina. After this treatment, a green stain made of artist's oils and Danish oil is applied.

After wiping off the excess, the mahogany is left a rich, reddish brown color. This is the same technique used in original Greene and Greene furniture. After the stain dries, three additional coats of oil are applied.

name. Because it was a small part of the original mixture, I took a guess and used Hooker's Green.

I squeezed out the colors in the proportions given on a scrap of plywood and mixed them together with a pint of Danish oil. Following a recipe, I hadn't thought about what color would be the result. I was expecting a rich, reddish brown and was surprised to see a shade of green I haven't seen since my son has been out of diapers.

I was ready to abandon the experiment because of the horrendous color I had mixed, but curiosity won and I tried it on my sample board. After wiping off the excess, I was pleased to find a truly wonderful color and sheen on the mahogany. What first appeared as a mistake makes sense technically. On a color wheel, the red from the chemical treatment and the green from the stain are opposite each other, producing a perfect color.

FINISH NOW, ASSEMBLE LATER

Before I did any assembly work, I brushed on the potassium dichromate solution and wiped each part dry. Letting the parts dry overnight, I applied the stain I had mixed, waited about five minutes and wiped off the excess. Doing all of the color work before assembly let me get an even coat on all the surfaces of all the parts. This saved me from reaching in and around the legs and rails on the assembled table base.

After letting the color coat of oil dry overnight, I assembled the table base in stages. I first glued and clamped the four pairs of outer and inner legs. After these had been in the clamps for an hour, I glued the longer center rails in between each subassembly. Finally I glued the four end rails between the front and back assemblies to complete the base of the table.

With the table base together, I drilled $1/4$"-diameter holes through the mortise-and-tenon joints in the central plugs of the outside legs. I inserted $1\frac{1}{4}$"-long dowels in each of these holes, driving the ends flush with the bottom of the square holes.

I dipped the plugs in my ebonizing solution and applied it to the visible parts of the splines with a brush. After these small parts were dry, I put a small amount of glue on the end of each plug and drove them into place, as shown at right. The splines were driven into their slots after I applied glue to the slots in the top only.

Once the coloring of the wood is complete, the table base is assembled in stages. Here I'm gluing the center rails between each subassembly.

A small, flat riffler is used to clean up the edges of the square holes. A slight chamfer on the back of the oversized square plugs gets them started in the holes before they are driven home with a dead-blow mallet.

I screwed $7/8$"-square cleats to the inside of the two end rails, and to the two long front and back rails so that I could attach the top to the base with screws. With 107 parts now in their proper places, I gave the entire table three additional coats of Danish oil.

Greene and Greene hold an important place in the history of American design, melding the influences of the Arts & Crafts movement with Japanese design elements in a unique way. Making this piece provided an opportunity to practice authentic detailed work. Had I been working for the Hall brothers in 1907, with a houseful of trim and many more furniture pieces to go, I would have been just warming up.

THE LOST STICKLEY TABLE

A one-of-a-kind table reappears after 100 years.

by Robert W. Lang

Most original Gustav Stickley furniture can be easily identified by model number. This was, after all, factory-made furniture and pieces were designed to be made in multiples. When you come across an antique, you can look it up in an old catalog to identify it. However, the only known example of this small table appeared at a Sotheby's auction in late 2004.

This uncataloged piece was likely a prototype, never put into factory production. What makes it unique is the front and back splay of the legs. It's this slight angle that gives this table more character than straight-legged versions that were mass produced. It's also the likely reason this piece never got beyond the prototype stage.

This table features many of the Stickley design elements that appear in other pieces. There isn't much material in it, but there is a good deal of labor-intensive, head-scratching joinery involved. This probably made it too expensive to be marketed at a reasonable price, but that does make it a great project on which to practice and develop joinery skills.

The anonymous cabinetmaker who built this prototype lived when it was a great time to be a woodworker. Hand-tool skills had not yet been forgotten, and machinery was in use to make life in the shop easier.

Using a full-size section drawing is essential; it lets me set angles and shows the exact sizes of parts without any of the risks of measuring.

As I planned how I would make this piece, I realized it made sense to do some of the work with machine methods, while on other parts it would be quicker and easier to make some joints by hand.

FIRST THINGS FIRST

Before cutting any lumber, I made a full-size section drawing on a piece of plywood. This helped me plan the sequence of building, and the sizes of the joints. It also established a reference to the exact size and shape of the parts.

While I was building this table, I referred to this drawing rather than relying on calculations, numbers and measuring. My CAD program tells me that the angle of the legs is 3.56° and that the length of the bottom edge of the rail between the legs is 15¹⁷⁄₃₂". Neither of those pieces of information is needed, and trying to build to the numbers instead of referring to the full-size drawing only slows things down and invites mistakes.

I made the legs by laminating two ¹³⁄₁₆"-thick pieces together, then covering the edge seams with ⅛"-thick veneer that I resawed from the same boards I used for the other parts of the legs. This is the method originally used by Gustav Stickley to show quartersawn figure on all four

Thin veneers tend to buckle when clamped. Gluing them in a stack applies even pressure to keep them flat.

An angled block of scrap wood tilts the leg to cut an angled mortise parallel to the top of the leg.

The angled mortises on the lower rails were roughed out with a Forstner bit on the drill press. A tapered block under the workpiece makes the holes at the correct angle.

edges of a leg. To keep the thin pieces flat, I glued and clamped all of the legs together at one time.

After trimming the edges of the veneer flush with my smoothing plane, I cut the angles at the top and bottom of each leg. I then returned to the full-size layout to locate the mortises. The mortises in each leg are in different locations, so I marked each leg's position in the table on its top. As I made other pieces, I marked which leg they joined to with a red lumber crayon.

The mortises on the back of the front legs, and the front of the back legs are parallel to the top and bottom of

After squaring the corners of the mortise with a chisel, I use a rasp to finish smoothing the inside of the angled joint.

the legs. I put an angled block of scrap on the bed of the hollow-chisel mortiser to make these mortises.

THE BEST MADE PLANS

I planned on making the remaining mortises in the legs with the mortiser, but on the second mortise, the machine broke down. Faced with a deadline, I switched to plan B and made these mortises with my plunge router.

The through mortises that pierce the lower front and back rails are at an angle to the face, and I'd planned to use an angled block on the bed of the mortiser to make them. Instead, I used a similar setup on the drill press. I removed most of the waste with a Forstner bit, then cleaned up the openings with chisels and rasps.

I made the straight and standard tenons on the ends of the lower rails on the table saw. I used a miter gauge to cut the tenon shoulders, and a jig that rides on the fence to cut the cheeks.

I considered making the angled cuts on the remaining tenons on the table saw, but realized each angled setup would need to be done twice: One to the right and one to the left. I decided to make a guide block that could be reversed for my handsaw, as seen in the photos at the top of the next page.

This was a quick and accurate method, and I was able to make all four saw cuts for each joint in sequence. This helped to keep the parts in order, and prevented making any miscuts by machine.

I dry-fitted the front and back legs with the top rails, and checked this assembly against my full-size layout. The angles matched, so I knew I could determine the length and angle of the lower stretcher directly from the full-size

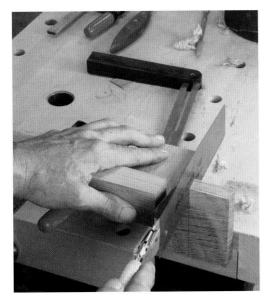

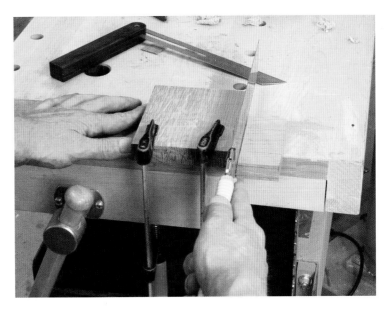

The quick and easy way to make the angled cuts for the through tenons is with a handsaw, guided by an angled block of wood.

These angled shoulder cuts would be tricky to make with power tools.

drawing. The critical length on this part is the distance between the shoulders of the through tenons. The angled parts of these tenons are short, but they need to be exact. I didn't want to risk a miscut on the table saw, so I used another angled block to guide my handsaw.

THE KEY TO A GOOD FIT

I did use the table saw tenoning jig to cut the wide cheeks of the through tenons on the lower stretcher, and the band saw to cut the edge cheeks. I made all of these cuts a hair big. Through tenons always demand some hand fitting. I used chisels, rasps and a shoulder plane to fit the tenons, checking the fit frequently as I came close to the finished size.

With the through tenons fit, there were only two mortises remaining: Those for the keys that hold the lower stretcher to the lower rails. These look difficult, but are actually the easiest joints to make in the piece. With the tenon fit in its mortise, I made a pencil mark at the intersection.

Taking the pieces back apart, I made another line slightly behind the first one. This puts the mortise just behind the intersection, and ensures that the key pulls the two lower rails tightly together. Luckily a repair part for the mortiser arrived, and I could cut these mortises with one stroke of the ½" chisel. I used a piece of scrap under the tenon to support it while the cut was made.

In most pieces with a keyed tenon, the mortise is angled slightly to allow the key to wedge in place. Because the rails are tilted back and the stretcher is horizontal, the angle of the rail allows the key to wedge in a straight mortise. To make the keys, I cut a few long pieces of scrap

to slightly more than the ½" width of the mortise by ⅝". I cut pieces about 6" long, and cut the taper on the band saw. I used my block plane to remove the saw marks, and bring the keys down to a snug fit.

This method let me get a good fit without worrying about the length of the keys. When I was happy with the fit, I marked ¾" above and below the protruding tenon to get the finished length of the keys.

The last parts to be made were the narrow rail below the drawer and the web frame. The rail is thin so that it can be turned 90° to show quartersawn figure on its face. It is also beveled to be parallel with the front faces of the legs. The web frame is made from poplar, and is mortise

After fitting the through tenon, the location of the second mortise is laid out, keeping the back of the hole just behind the face of the rail.

REFERENCE	QUANTITY	PART	STOCK	THICKNESS	(mm)	WIDTH	(mm)	LENGTH	(mm)	COMMENTS
A	1	top	white oak	$^{13}/_{16}$	(21)	$15^3/_8$	(391)	21	(533)	
B	2	top aprons	white oak	$^{13}/_{16}$	(21)	$4^1/_4$	(108)	$17^7/_8$	(454)	$1^1/_4$" ATBE
C	2	lower rails	white oak	$^7/_8$	(22)	$5^1/_4$	(133)	$13^5/_8$	(346)	$1^1/_4$" ATBE
D	1	lower stretcher	white oak	$^3/_4$	(19)	$3^7/_8$	(98)	$22^1/_4$	(565)	$1^{13}/_{16}$" BSTBE
E	4	legs	white oak	$1^5/_8$	(41)	$1^7/_8$	(47)	27	(686)	angle both ends
F	1	back apron	white oak	$^{13}/_{16}$	(21)	$4^1/_4$	(108)	$13^5/_8$	(346)	$1^1/_4$" TBE
G	1	rail below drawer	white oak	$^{13}/_{16}$	(21)	$^{13}/_{16}$	(21)	$12^5/_8$	(321)	$^3/_4$" TBE
H	1	drawer front	white oak	$^{13}/_{16}$	(21)	$3^1/_2$	(89)	$11^1/_8$	(282)	bevel both edges to fit
I	2	tenon keys	white oak	$^1/_2$	(13)	$^5/_8$	(16)	2	(51)	taper to fit through tenons
J	2	drawer sides	maple	$^5/_8$	(16)	$3^1/_4$	(82)	$15^7/_8$	(403)	
K	1	drawer back	maple	$^5/_8$	(16)	$3^1/_4$	(82)	$11^1/_8$	(282)	
L	1	drawer bottom	maple	$^1/_4$	(6)	$10^1/_2$	(267)	$15^1/_4$	(387)	
M	2	web frame stiles	poplar	$^3/_4$	(19)	2	(51)	$17^1/_4$	(438)	notch around legs
N	2	web frame rails	poplar	$^3/_4$	(19)	2	(51)	$9^3/_4$	(248)	$^3/_4$" TBE
O	2	drawer runners	maple	$^{11}/_{16}$	(17)	$^9/_{16}$	(14)	$15^3/_4$	(400)	fit between legs & beside drawer
P	2	drawer stops	maple	$^{11}/_{16}$	(17)	$^9/_{16}$	(14)	6	(152)	fit behind drawer

TBE=tenon both ends; BSTBE=beveled shoulder tenon both ends; ATBE=angled tenon both ends

The mortise is cut with one plunge of the hollow-chisel mortiser. A piece of scrap below the cut supports the tenon, keeping the wood from breaking on the back side.

As the tenon key is fit, the length above and below the through tenon changes. I leave the key long and mark the length once I have a good fit.

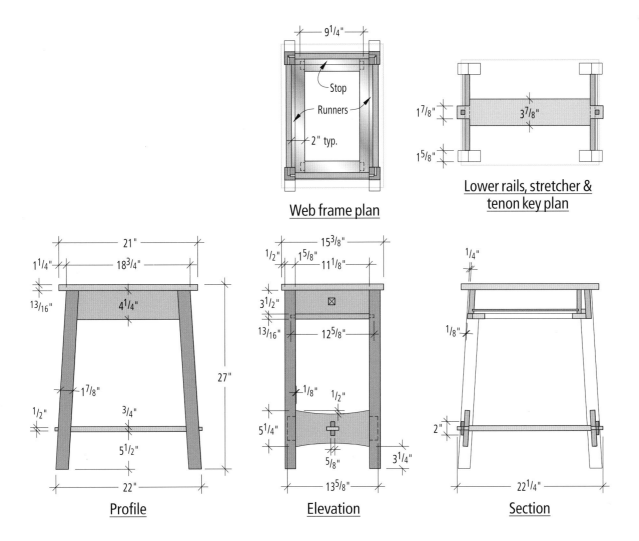

Web frame plan

9¼"

Stop

Runners

2" typ.

Lower rails, stretcher & tenon key plan

1⅞"

3⅞"

1⅝"

Profile

21"

18¾"

1¼"

13/16"

4¼"

27"

1⅞"

½"

¾"

5½"

22"

Elevation

15⅜"

½"

1⅝"

11⅛"

3½"

13/16"

12⅝"

1/8"

½"

5¼"

5/8"

3¼"

13⅝"

Section

¼"

1/8"

2"

22¼"

and tenoned together. When I had all the joints fit, I made a dry assembly of the table. Then I took the pieces back apart so I could plane, scrape and sand all of them before gluing the entire table together.

I glued in stages, making subassemblies of front and back legs, and the top aprons. I cut some angled blocks and attached them to the top of the legs with masking tape so that the clamps would pull straight on the angled legs.

After letting the glue dry on these, I put one of the leg assemblies flat on my bench. I put glue in the mortises, and put in the upper-back rail, the small rail below the drawer, and the lower rails, with the stretcher in place between them. I then brushed glue on the tenons, and placed the second leg assembly on top. Turning the table upright on my bench, I clamped the joints and began to worry about the drawer.

Half-blind dovetailed drawers don't bother me, but I'd never made one with the face tilted back at an angle. I decided to lay out the tails with the same angles they would have if the drawer front were vertical. This makes the top and bottom angles of the tails different in relation to the

After cutting the key to length, I round the edges above and below the completed joint.

The assembled web frame is notched around the legs. After fitting the drawer runners between the legs, they are screwed in place, and the drawer stop is also attached with screws to the frame.

slanted drawer front which made the layout tricky, but it looked right when the joints were completed.

After cutting the tails by hand, I laid out the pins on the ends of the drawer front, and removed most of the waste with an upcut spiral bit in my trim router. This speeds things up, and gives a perfectly flat surface where the back of the tail rests on the bottom of the pin. I then used a chisel to pare down to the layout lines.

The pull was made from a cutoff piece from one of the legs. I trimmed it down to 1¼" × 1¼" by about 3" long. The pull finishes at 1⅛" but the extra length gave me something to hold on to while cutting it to shape. I laid out the shape of the pull on two adjacent faces, and cut it out on the band saw. I didn't worry about the exact size of the radius below the pyramid shaped top; that would come from the shape of my rasp.

After cutting one face, I taped the scraps back on the block with clear packing tape and cut the adjacent side. With the rough cutting complete, I clamped the extra

length in my vise, and finished shaping the pull with a rasp. The finished pull is held to the drawer front with a #8 × 1¼" screw from inside the drawer.

I wanted an authentic looking finish, but didn't want to go to the trouble of fuming it with ammonia. I used W.D. Lockwood Dark Fumed Oak aniline dye (wdlockwood. com or 866-293-8913) diluted with alcohol. I brushed on the dye, and wiped it with a rag. I then brushed on two coats of amber shellac. After letting the shellac dry, I attached the top with figure-eight fasteners. I took off the gloss of the shellac with a Scotch-Brite pad and applied a coat of paste wax.

After routing most of the waste, I use a chisel to pare the pins down the rest of the way. The router quickly establishes a consistent depth.

I laid out the tails with the same angles from horizontal that I would have if the drawer front were vertical. The knob is cut with the band saw, and shaped with a rasp.

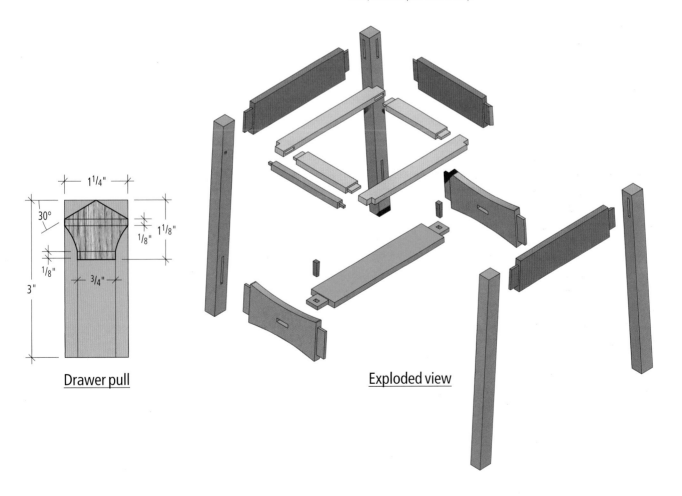

Drawer pull

1¼"

30°

1⅛"

⅛"

⅛"

¾"

3"

Exploded view

PRAIRIE-STYLE COFFEE TABLE

An anachronism in its time, this table now fits perfectly in our homes.

By David Thiel

Frank Lloyd Wright would probably be dismayed to see a coffee table built in his Prairie furniture style. In fact he and his fellow early 20th-century designers all would have been disturbed by the concept of a coffee table. Eating or drinking in the living room? Unheard of! That type of informality in furniture is a product of the latter half of the 20th century.

But, there is a fine, old Russian proverb that says necessity is the mother of invention. And so I offer you the Prairie-style coffee table. At least it'll keep my kids from leaving plates, glasses and remote controls on the floor.

This project is an adaptation of a number of Wright's pieces, utilizing applied moulding to a generally simple design. The shelf is placed high on the legs and extends beyond the base to match the wide and low look of Wright's Prairie-style buildings and furniture.

The construction is simple, with the most complicated joint being a mortise-and-tenon attachment on the legs, which I've simplified even further for you.

GROUND-UP CONSTRUCTION

I started building the table at the base with the four legs. For a larger table I would have used a mitered or lock-mitered leg to make sure the dramatic grain commonly found in quartersawn white oak was visible on all four sides of the legs. But for a table

this small, the work really didn't justify the benefit, so I started with 2" × 2" white oak turning blanks, choosing the straightest grain possible.

With the legs cut to length, the first step is to mark the mortise locations and then make the mortise holes. Traditionally it makes sense to make the mortises and then fit the tenon to the mortise. Because I'm short-circuiting the tenon process by using part of the stretcher as the tenon,

The lower stretchers tie into mortises cut in each of the four legs. I made the mortises 1/2" wide so I wouldn't have to cut tenon cheeks on the stretchers. Unfortunately I only had a 3/8"-wide mortising chisel, so I overlapped the mortise cuts to achieve a snug 1/2"-wide mortise.

With the mortises cut, it was time to assemble the three-piece stretchers. To ensure a square fit, I first squared the center stretcher piece while it was fit into the mortise. Remember, no glue at this point!

I needed to make the mortise match the tenon this time. The photo on page 83 shows the details.

The next step is assembling the stretchers. This is where the fun starts. The two stretchers are of an I-beam design, with a top and bottom that are horizontal, and a middle piece that is oriented vertically. The top and bottom stretcher pieces are 9½" long, which is the actual size of the space between the legs. The middle stretcher is 11" long. When the three pieces are assembled, the middle piece extends ¾" on either side, creating the tenons.

It's important that the stretchers fit tightly against the legs, so I assembled the stretchers while they were in place

in the legs. Before you do that, though, sand all the pieces, because it's next to impossible to sand inside the channel once the stretcher is assembled. By squaring the stretchers to the legs while assembling, everything fits tight without a lot of extra fitting.

The other part of the support structure on the table is the shelf. Traditionally this would be positioned much lower, but the Wright design dictates a higher shelf. Useless you say? Posh! It's the perfect height for hiding the remotes and the TV Guide. Maybe they won't all end up stuck in the couch cushions if they have a proper home.

The shelf is attached to the legs using dowels. I used

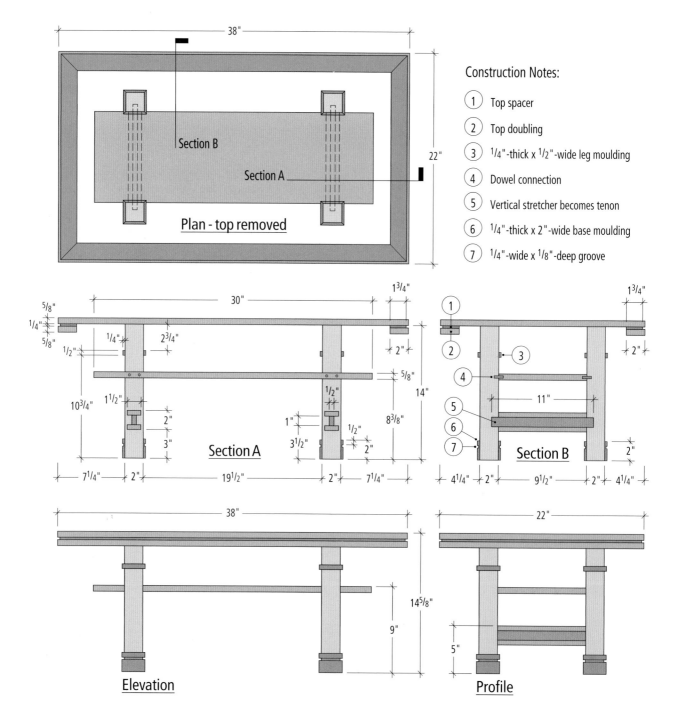

Construction Notes:

1. Top spacer
2. Top doubling
3. ¼"-thick x ½"-wide leg moulding
4. Dowel connection
5. Vertical stretcher becomes tenon
6. ¼"-thick x 2"-wide base moulding
7. ¼"-wide x ⅛"-deep groove

Plan - top removed

Section A

Section B

Elevation

Profile

REFERENCE	QUANTITY	PART	STOCK	THICKNESS	(mm)	WIDTH	(mm)	LENGTH	(mm)	COMMENTS
A	1	top	white oak	5/8	(16)	22	(559)	38	(965)	
B	2	top spacers	white oak	1/4	(6)	1 3/4	(45)	21 1/2	(546)	MBE
C	2	top spacers	white oak	1/4	(6)	1 3/4	(45)	37 1/2	(953)	MBE
D	2	top doublings	white oak	5/8	(16)	2	(51)	38	(965)	MBE
E	2	top doublings	white oak	5/8	(16)	2	(51)	22	(559)	MBE
F	1	shelf	white oak	5/8	(16)	9 1/2	(241)	30	(762)	
G	4	legs	white oak	2	(51)	2	(51)	14	(356)	
H	4	stretchers	white oak	1/2	(13)	1 1/2	(38)	9 1/2	(241)	
J	2	stretchers	white oak	1/2	(13)	1	(25)	11	(279)	3/4 TBE
K	32	leg mouldings	white oak	1/4	(6)	1/2	(13)	2 1/2	(64)	MBE
L	32	leg mouldings	white oak	1/4	(6)	2	(51)	2 1/2	(64)	MBE

*MBE=miter both ends; TBE=tenons both ends

With the center stretcher square, it's simple to pin the upper and lower stretchers in place, maintaining the square relationship and forming the tenons on the stretchers simultaneously.

The shelf is dowelled into the legs to make assembly simple. A dowelling jig makes this even easier. Locate the dowel holes on the legs 4³/₄" down from the top of the legs and centered. The locations on the shelves are 4¹/₄" in from the ends and centered on the thickness of the shelf.

only one dowel per leg as shown in the photos. Because it's such a small table and the top is attached to the legs as well, one dowel is adequate.

However, if you look at the drawing, we've shown two dowels at each location. One thing that's nice about this design is if you cared to scale this up to dining table size, all the proportions would still work and it would be an attractive larger table. In that case, two dowels per leg would be recommended.

At this point, leave the stretchers and shelf separate from the legs. We still have some detailing to do on the legs themselves before assembling the base.

MITERING SMALL MOULDINGS
There are two moulding details on the leg — a lower "foot" and a small upper strip. The upper piece is simply ¹/₄" × ¹/₂" material mitered around the perimeter of the leg. The lower moulding is ¹/₄" × 2" material that has a ¹/₈" ×

¼"-wide groove cut into the length, ½" down from the top. I cut the groove in two passes on the table saw on a long strip before mitering the pieces to length.

The first time I ever saw one of Wright's Prairie designs, I looked at the mouldings and thought, "Wow, that's simple! All you do is miter the pieces and nail them on!" Well, that is the process, but it's not as simple as it seems. While fitting a single miter isn't too awkward, getting four miters to align perfectly around a leg is darn tricky. In fact, this step turned out to be the most difficult part of the project.

I started out assuming that I could simply use my miter saw and a stop block to cut the pieces. But working with such small pieces is actually a little scary. Your fingers are too close to the blade. A table saw could work as well, if you have a sled that works with the blade either tilted or beveled to 45°. But, again, the small pieces and the concern of tear-out make it a task not for the faint of heart.

Instead, I relied on a slower method, but one that proved more reliable. After rough-cutting the moulding pieces to length (using a clamping jig on the miter saw). I hand-fitted each piece using a small disk sander with the table set to a 45° angle.

TINY NAILS

After fitting the pieces to the legs, it's a good time to sand all the pieces before attaching the mouldings. It's just easier to get in the corners this way. Then it really is as simple as adding a little glue and nailing them in place. Actually, I pinned the pieces in place using a 23-gauge pneumatic pinner. I love this tool. The pins are so small that the hole looks like a freckle on the wood. The holes are easily filled, or you can actually be a little lazy and let the stain cover up the hole.

One tip when using a pinner (or nailer) like this: Rather than drive all the pins straight into the piece, angle the pins toward one another. While it's unlikely the pins will fail, this will add extra strength to help keep the moulding from ever pulling loose.

Start with the lower moulding, setting the leg upright on your work surface as you attach the pieces. This helps to make sure you have a flat bottom to the leg and helps align the pieces at the miters.

The next step is the upper mouldings. You'll need to add some location lines to the legs to orient these mouldings. Measure down 2¾" from the top of the leg to the top of the mouldings.

BASE ASSEMBLY

At this point you're ready to assemble the base. Work two of the legs flat on your work platform, with the mortises facing up. Add glue to the one set of dowels and tenons, and attach the shelf and two stretchers to the legs. Then add glue to the remaining dowels and mortises, and attach the other two legs.

After running the ⅛"-deep x ¼" groove in the lower mouldings using the table saw, they were ready to miter and hand-fit on a sanding disk. This is the tricky part, so take your time. Then glue and pin the pieces in place.

The same mitering technique is used to fit and then attach the upper mouldings on the legs. Remember that part of the leg is hidden behind the top's built-up edge, so locate the moulding 2¾" down from the top of the legs.

At this point, stand the base up and allow the legs to sit flat on the work platform. Then clamp across the legs to hold everything together while the glue dries. Use a square to double check the angle of the legs to the shelf while clamping the base. Set this aside to dry and turn to the top.

DOUBLING THE TOP

Part of the look of the top is achieved by recessing a piece of ¼"-thick material between two thicker pieces, leaving a ¼" x ¼" channel that creates a delicate shadow line on the top's edge.

One of the other benefits of this process is making the top look more substantial without adding too much weight.

Start with the main top glued-up and trimmed to finished size. The spacer and doubling material also are solid white oak, cut to width and thickness as given.

The spacers required to create the ¼" × ¼" shadow line are mitered and held ¼" in from the edges, then pinned in place (no glue). The pieces don't need to be 1¾" wide. My scrap was narrow, but no one will know.

The doubling pieces work the same as the spacers, but they're held flush to the top piece. A square works well to orient the pieces before pinning through the spacers into the top.

Now flip the top upside down and mark the corners ¼" in from each edge. By holding the spacer pieces at this off-set you will create the recess for the shadow line.

A note here on wood movement: Because the top is solid wood, it will move across the width with seasonal changes in humidity. If you attach the spacers and dou-bling across the ends of the top with glue, they will likely break or shift with this movement. Because of this, I didn't use glue and simply pinned the pieces in place. I used a few extra pins, but because of how thin the pins are, they're more likely to bend slightly with the wood move-ment, rather than tear the top apart.

Attach the spacers, mitering the corners. I used ½" pins at this point, holding the pieces ¼" in all the way around the top.

The doubling is next and it's important to align the doubling flush to the top piece for a good look. I used a square against the table to align the doubling, then used 1⅛" pins to nail through the doubling and the spacer into the top.

ATTACHING THE TOP

I attached the top to the legs using figure-eight-shaped fasteners that are recessed into the tops of the legs — not just recessed, but also given a little extra space so the fasteners can swivel on the screws in the legs. This solves the wood-movement problem at this joint, allowing the top to expand with changes in humidity without affecting the base.

Drill a hole matching the diameter of the fastener, just to the depth of the thickness of the fastener. Then widen the hole to allow that fastener to swivel.

After attaching all four fasteners to the legs, flip the top over, center the base on the top and attach the base. Re-member the top is only ⅝"-thick, so don't use screws that are too long!

Extra space for swivel room

I used figure-eight fasteners (Rockler, #21650, 800-279-4441 or rockler. com) to attach the top. These allow the top to move without affecting the base.

THE WRIGHT FINISH

Unlike many of his contemporaries in the early 20th cen-tury, Wright didn't stress too much about the finish on his Prairie furniture. While Gustav Stickley preferred a rather dark, heavy finish on many of his pieces, Wright settled instead on a pleasant, lighter mocha finish for his Prairie furniture pieces.

I found an off-the-shelf stain that adequately matched that philosophy. I wiped on a coat of Olympic Colonial Oak gel stain (available from Lowe's), then wiped off the excess to leave an even, warm-brown color.

A few quick coats of spray lacquer in a can (Deft semi-gloss Clear Wood finish from Lowe's), sanding lightly with #320-grit paper between coats, and the table was finished.

While Wright might not approve of the application I've chosen for his design, I think he'd be happy with the way it looks. Now where is that remote?

THORSEN HOUSE SIDE TABLE

A small project that's big on details.

by David Thiel

I've always appreciated the look of furniture designed by architects Charles and Henry Greene. Though often equated with the Arts & Crafts movement at the beginning of the 20th century, their furniture designs reflect an Asian influence that softens the often hard lines of Arts & Crafts furniture. While looking for a piece to build, I was talking with Robert W. Lang, senior editor for *Popular Woodworking* and author of "Shop Drawings for Greene & Greene Furniture" (Fox Chapel). He suggested adapting a small side table originally made for the Thorsen House in Berkeley, California.

The cutouts on the aprons quickly won me over, but I did make a couple modifications that lightened the look of the table. Rather than a full-width shelf captured between two straight stretchers, I opted to make the stretcher with a top-and-bottom cloudlift design and make the shelf only half the width of the original. I also added some $\frac{1}{16}$" quirk details to the corners of the legs and the edges of the aprons, stretchers and the shelf. These "rabbets" add a simple shadow line to a very pleasant design.

START WITH THE LUMBER

Selecting your lumber for this table is an important step. Because it's such a small piece, wild grain will dramatically change the overall appearance. You want to look for mahogany that is as straight grained as possible. This will become even more critical if you're bookmatching the top piece. And because of the high cost of mahogany, I definitely recommend bookmatching. It allows you to buy 8/4 material and resaw for the top, aprons and stretchers, while still allowing enough thickness to yield the legs and breadboards.

The cloudlifts are subtle curves, not radii. Make a template (bottom) of the curve you like, then transfer that curve to your aprons and stretchers.

A $\frac{3}{8}$" mortising chisel makes quick work of the apron mortises on each leg. One of the stretcher mortises is visible on the leg at the bottom of the photo.

Start by selecting the best wood for the top piece. Pay careful attention to the grain orientation as the piece is almost square and it's easy to get the direction reversed, which will yield a funny-looking top. Resaw the top pieces, then surface and join the two boards, trimming to allow the best grain match possible. Now glue the two (hopefully no more) pieces together to form the top.

While the glue is drying, select the next-best sections of your wood for the aprons and stretchers. Resaw the necessary pieces from your 8/4 material to yield the balance of your pieces. Then surface, plane and saw the stock to final thickness, width and length.

MORTISE & TENON JOINERY

The joinery for the table should start at your mortiser. I chose a ⅜" mortising chisel for all the mortises on this piece. Mark the locations of the mortises on the legs, paying careful attention to the location for the lower stretchers. There are only two stretchers and they will require mortises on only one inside face of each leg. Orient the legs so those faces are on the inside.

The mortises for the aprons are ⅞" deep and 4½" long. They are centered on the legs and start ¾" down from the top of the legs. The two apron mortises will intersect one another in the leg, so be careful while cutting the second mortise to avoid damaging the rather thin interior corner left by the two mortises. The stretcher mortises are ¾" long and start 5⅛" up from the bottom of the legs.

While you're at the mortiser, lay out and cut the ⅞"-deep mortises in the breadboard ends. The middle mortise is 4¾" long and centered on each breadboard. The two outer mortises are 2¼" long and start 1⅜" in from each end. All the breadboard mortises are centered in the thickness of the breadboards.

Remove the top from the clamps and trim it to finished size. I used the table saw to cut the tenons on all the pieces, but you may choose to use a router. In fact, I was a little lazy on the saw and opted to leave the ⅛" blade in rather than switch to a dado to run the tenons. There's also a little logic behind my laziness. By making repeat cuts on the cheek of the tenon my blade leaves slight ridges on the surface. If test fitting my tenon achieves a fit that is too snug, I'm able to come back with a rabbeting plane and trim the tenon to fit. Miter the ends of the tenons to fit the legs.

The tenons are created on the saw by first defining the shoulders both on the thickness (top) and then the width (right) of each tenon. I then simply made repeat cuts on the tenon, nibbling away the waste.

CLOUDLIFTS & QUIRKS

With the tenons cut it's time to add some of the details. Each of the aprons and the two stretchers have what have been coined "cloudlift" designs. This shaped offset is formed on the lower edge of each apron and on both the top and bottom of the two stretchers. The offset is a simple ¼". The location of the offsets can be determined from the scaled patterns for the aprons and stretchers. The transition itself isn't a simple radius, though you could do it that way if you prefer. Rather, the transition can be drawn using ¼" radii, but should then be softened to make the transition more subtle. I made a few test pieces

The quirk detail is created on the legs using the table saw. Essentially, you're creating a ¹⁄₁₆" x ¹⁄₁₆" rabbet on each corner of the leg.

■■ thorsen house side table
■■ INCHES (MILLIMETERS)

REFERENCE	QUANTITY	PART	STOCK	THICKNESS	(mm)	WIDTH	(mm)	LENGTH	(mm)	COMMENTS
A	1	top	mahogany	³/₄	(19)	16³/₄	(425)	15¹/₂	(394)	³/₄" TBE
B	2	breadboard ends	mahogany	1	(25)	1¹/₂	(38)	17	(432)	
C	4	aprons	mahogany	³/₄	(19)	5³/₄	(146)	12¹/₄	(311)	³/₄" TBE
D	4	legs	mahogany	1¹/₄	(32)	1¹/₄	(32)	21¹/₂	(546)	
E	2	stretchers	mahogany	³/₄	(19)	1¹/₄	(32)	12¹/₄	(311)	³/₄" TBE
F	1	shelf	mahogany	¹/₂	(13)	5	(127)	11¹/₄	(285)	
G	32	pegs	ebony	³/₈	(10)	³/₈	(10)	¹/₄	(6)	

TBE= tenon both ends

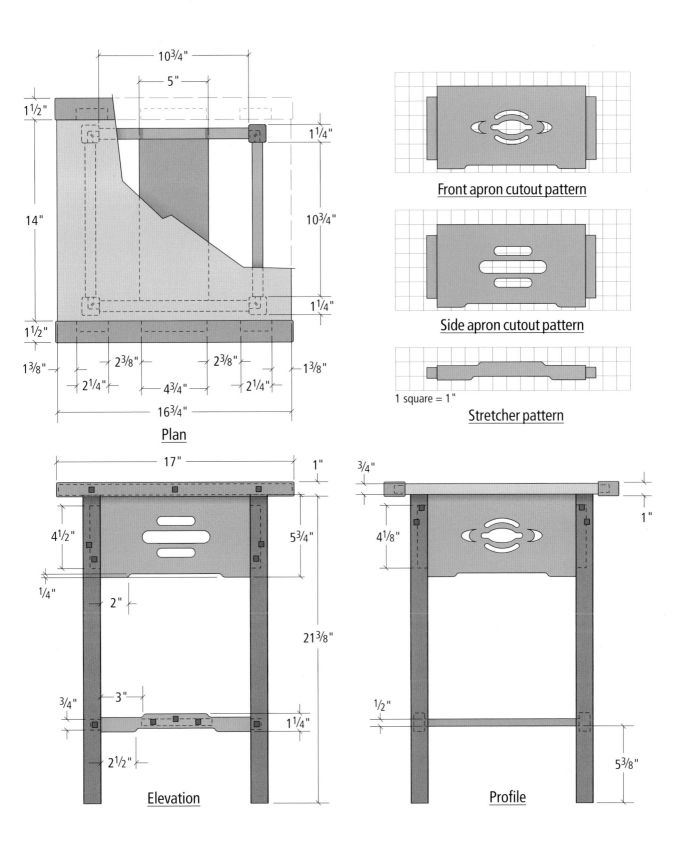

Front apron cutout pattern

Side apron cutout pattern

1 square = 1"

Stretcher pattern

Plan

Elevation

Profile

before I was satisfied with the curve, then used that piece to mark the cloudlift transitions on the actual pieces. With your pieces marked, head to the band saw and make your cloudlift cuts. Use a file and sandpaper to clean up the shapes on all the pieces.

To add another detail, I cut a ¹⁄₁₆" rabbet (or quirk) on the long edges of the legs on the table saw (see picture opposite page), and also on the four long edges of the small shelf. To add the same detail to the lower edge of the aprons and all the edges of the stretchers, I set up a trim router with a bearing guide and a straight bit. The guide allows the bit to follow the cloudlifts without difficulty.

CLOUD LIFTS ON THE BANDSAW

After marking out the cloud lift shapes and locations on each piece, head to the bandsaw. To avoid too much filing and sanding, cut as close as you can to the waste side of the line.

Start each cut by angling into the long horizontal line. Don't try and turn with the radius during the cut. It's too tight to make clean, so just cut in wide and then follow the line.

If the cloud lift is an "inside" cut, it's easier to make the cut in at the far end first, then start from the opposite end and follow across the long line till the piece separates.

To clean up the radii, use the cutting edge of the blade to "nibble" up to the line. This allows a level of precision and control that is impossible when trying to follow a tight radius with the edge of the blade.

The bearing guide shown on this trim router allows the bit to follow the curves of the cloudlifts. You could also install a bearing-guided bit in a router table to make the quirk detail.

Use glue only on the center mortise and tenon of the breadboards. The outer tenons are allowed to freely move to compensate for wood movement.

PATTERNS & EBONY

Before assembly, use your scrollsaw or fretsaw to cut out the patterns on the aprons. Enlarge the scaled patterns to full size (or download the full-size patterns from Magazine Extras our web site) and attach them to the aprons using adhesive spray. Cut the patterns and then use sandpaper and small files to clean them up.

One last step is to make the square holes for the ebony accent pegs. I again used my $\frac{3}{8}$" mortising chisel to make these $\frac{3}{8}$"-deep holes. The locations of the dual pegs on the legs are $\frac{1}{4}$" in from either side and the pegs are $\frac{5}{8}$" apart from one another. The pegs at the tops of the legs start $\frac{3}{4}$" down from the top of the leg. The lower pattern starts $3\frac{1}{8}$" down from the top. The pegs on the stretchers and breadboards are evenly spaced as shown.

ASSEMBLY

Finish sand all the pieces of the table base and assemble the frame. Start with the sides that have the stretchers. Then glue the last two aprons between the two frames. Before gluing up the top, use a $\frac{1}{8}$"-radius router bit to soften the long edges of the top and all the edges of the breadboard pieces. Finally, glue on the breadboards. Screw the shelf in place through two holes in the stretchers that will receive the ebony pegs.

The pegs are next (see photo below). I used ebony, but you could also use walnut.

I attached the top by using my biscuit jointer to cut slots on the inside of the aprons to match the Z-shaped metal mirror fasteners screwed to the top.

The last step is the finish. A coat of boiled linseed oil will leave a lighter finish, allowing the mahogany to darken with age, or you can speed the process by using a stain. A top coat of lacquer and you have a table with unique details.

To make the pegs, carefully rip the accent wood to slightly larger than the mortise size. Round the ends of the "stick" using sandpaper, then carefully trim off the $\frac{1}{4}$"-tall pegs on the band saw. Sand the peg sides at a slight angle (smaller at the bottom) and glue in place just proud of the leg surface.

EASTWOOD-STYLE CHAIR

Use many of the same techniques used in
building a Morris chair to build
Gustav Stickley's favorite place to sit.

By Christopher Schwarz

When Gustav Stickley sat down to read a book in his New York home, this is the chair he favored. "Chair" doesn't really do justice to this project. "Throne" is a lot closer to the truth. With a 27"-wide seat, this white oak Arts & Crafts armchair is the perfect size for a parent and child to curl up with a book.

For the last five years I've collected photos, measurements and auction data on this rare piece — which some Arts & Crafts experts say was built only as a custom order by Stickley's craftsmen.

Using our computer-aided drafting (CAD) software, I was able to generate the construction drawings and cut-

ting list you see here. Then I built the chair and put it in my house.

You might have noticed that the Stickley company now sells a reproduction of this chair, though mine is significantly different. The seat is built in a different way, some of the stretchers are different sizes and Stickley makes the back rails curved instead of straight.

That our two "reproductions" were different came as no surprise to me. During my research I've found that several different versions of this chair are floating out there.

Depending on the price of white oak in your area, plan on spending around $200 to puchase the wood for this chair. The cushions, which are covered in a high-tech vinyl with leather graining, cost $200.

CONSTRUCTION

Many of the same techniques used in building the Shop of the Crafters Morris chair are used in the Eastwood chair, including:
- the mortise-and-tenon work
- the way the seat is built
- the way the angles are cut on the bottom of the legs
- the finish

Here's what's different:

VENEERED LEGS

When gluing up my stock to make the four legs, I glued a piece of quartersawn veneer on the two sides that showed flat-sawn figure. Stickley would commonly do this, and it really can show off the ray flake in the quartered oak.

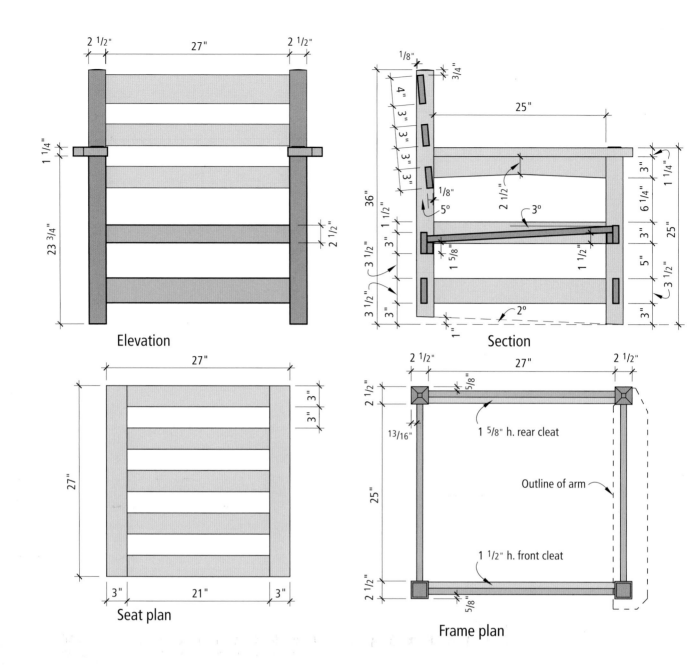

Elevation

2 1/2" 27" 2 1/2"

1 1/4"

23 3/4"

2 1/2"

Section

1/8" 3/4"

4"
3"
3"
3"
3"

25"

36"

3"
1 1/4"

1/8"
5°

2 1/2"

3°

6 1/4"
25"

3 1/2" 1 1/2"

3"

1 5/8"

1 1/2"

5"

3 1/2"
3"

3 1/2"
3"

2°

1"

3"

Seat plan

27"

3" 3"

27"

3" 21" 3"

Frame plan

2 1/2" 27" 2 1/2"

2 1/2"

5/8"

2 1/2"

13/16"

1 5/8" h. rear cleat

Outline of arm

25"

1 1/2" h. front cleat

2 1/2"

5/8"

In order to show quartersawn figure on all four sides of the legs, I veneered the flat-sawn sides with quartersawn veneer. This is the same thing Gustav Stickley did, and many of his legs survive intact. In some, however, the veneer has come loose.

REFERENCE	QUANTITY	PART	STOCK	THICKNESS	(mm)	WIDTH	(mm)	LENGTH	(mm)	COMMENTS
A	2	front legs	white oak	$2^{1}/_{2}$	(64)	$2^{1}/_{2}$	(64)	$25^{5}/_{8}$	(651)	$1^{3}/_{8}$" TOE
B	2	back legs	white oak	$2^{1}/_{2}$	(64)	$2^{1}/_{2}$	(64)	35	(889)	
C	2	lower side stretchers	white oak	$^{7}/_{8}$	(22)	$3^{1}/_{2}$	(89)	27	(686)	1" TBE
D	2	lower stretcher (F and B)	white oak	$^{7}/_{8}$	(22)	$3^{1}/_{2}$	(89)	29	(737)	1" TBE
E	2	side seat stretchers	white oak	$^{7}/_{8}$	(22)	3	(76)	27	(686)	1" TBE
F	1	front seat stretcher	white oak	$^{7}/_{8}$	(22)	$2^{1}/_{2}$	(64)	29	(737)	1" TBE
G	1	back seat stretcher	white oak	$^{7}/_{8}$	(22)	3	(76)	29	(737)	1" TBE
H	2	back rails	white oak	$^{7}/_{8}$	(22)	3	(76)	29	(737)	1" TBE
J	1	back top rail	white oak	$^{7}/_{8}$	(22)	4	(102)	29	(737)	1" TBE
K	2	seat cleats	white oak	$^{7}/_{8}$	(22)	$1^{1}/_{2}$	(38)	27	(686)	screwed to seat rails
L	2	arms	white oak	$1^{1}/_{4}$	(32)	5	(127)	$31^{1}/_{4}$	(794)	screwed to arm supports
M	2	arm supports	white oak	$^{7}/_{8}$	(22)	3	(76)	27	(686)	1" TBE
N	2	seat stiles	white oak	$^{7}/_{8}$	(22)	3	(76)	27	(686)	
P	5	seat rails	white oak	$^{7}/_{8}$	(22)	3	(76)	23	(584)	1" TBE

*TOE=tenon one end; TBE=tenons both ends

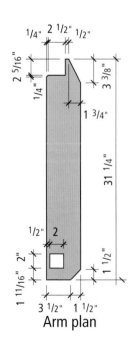

Arm plan

Hate laying out odd angles? Then here's an easy way to lay out the angled mortises on the legs. First cut a piece of scrap wood to $^{7}/_{8}$" wide × 16" long. On the leg face where the mortises will go, mark a line $^{3}/_{4}$" down from the top. Make a second mark $^{1}/_{8}$" in and parallel to the back edge. Then, on the inside edge, mark a line $^{1}/_{8}$" in and parallel to the inside edge. Put your scrap piece on the leg and make all the corners touch the lines you marked. Trace around the scrap. Now you can fill in that rectangle and easily locate all the mortises with simple layout tools.

Cutting mortises at an angle can bend your brain a bit. Here's the trick: tape a 5° wedge to your back leg. If you don't tape the wedge to the leg, you'll find that the angle of cut will change as you move the leg.

front legs via a through-tenon that pokes up ⅛" above each arm.

First cut the tenon on the leg to size, then create a plywood template to cut the mortise. Use the same techniques shown in the Morris chair article for making plywood templates.

Use a plywood template and pattern-cutting bits to cut the mortises in the arms. Start with a short bit with a bearing on top. When you can cut no deeper with that, switch to a longer bit with a bearing on top. When that cuts as far as you can go, use a drill to make a few holes in the bottom of the mortise. Turn the arm over and use a pattern-cutting bit with the bearing on the bottom to clean up the other side. You could make this mortise using template guides and a straight bit, but you're going to find it difficult to cut your template to the perfect size because of the offset between the template guide and template. This method, though it uses more router bits, gets you a super-tight fit on this highly visible joint.

When you've cut all the way through, use a corner chisel to square the corners. I'm partial to the spring-loaded ones that door installers use for squaring the corners of hinge mortises.

Using sandpaper, round over the edges of the tenon that protrude above the arm.

BACK LEG DETAIL

The top of the back legs has a pyramidal shape with a ⅝" square flat in the middle. I set my table saw's blade for 5° and trimmed the top of each leg. If you work toward the top of the pyramid, you won't have to worry about tear out on any of the faces of the leg.

CLEAT POSITION

Finally, you'll want to position the cleat that supports the seat at the back so the seat is angled comfortably. The diagrams show the back at 92° to the seat. You can increase this as you see fit by changing the location of the back rail.

After you're sure the arms fit on the legs, clip the corners of the leg as shown in the plans. Clean up the cuts with a stationary belt sander, then glue the arms in place.

SIX ANGLED MORTISES

All of the mortise-and-tenon work is the same on this chair except the six mortises on the back legs that hold the three back rails. These are angled to slope back 5°. Here's how to set up your mortiser to easily make these cuts.

Mark on each back leg where each mortise stops and starts; use the photo and diagram as a guide. Now take a scrap piece of wood the same thickness as the leg and cut a 17"-long wedge from it at a 5° angle. I made the cut on my band saw and cleaned it up on my jointer. Now tape the wedge to one leg by wrapping it in masking tape. Be careful not to cover your pencil marks.

Now you'll be able to set up your mortiser to easily make this angled cut.

THROUGH-TENONS

The arms are attached to the chair in two ways. After the chair is assembled, screw the arms up through the underside of the arm supports. The arms also are glued to the

Cut the mortises using a plunge router and a pattern-cutting bit. Make the cut in several stages to avoid damaging the bit, and to just make the work easier.

Use a spring-loaded corner chisel to square up the corners. Work from both sides and clean out the middle with a chisel.

FINISHING

This takes some effort, but it is well worth it. The first step is to dye the chair with an alcohol-based aniline dye that's reddish. See the supplies list for ordering information. Then apply one coat of boiled linseed oil to the chair. You can get this at any home center store. Wipe off the excess and let it dry overnight. The linseed oil seals the wood before your final coloring step and helps bring out the ray flake.

Next, we wiped on a thin coat of Behlen's Van Dyke glaze available from Woodworker's Supply. The glaze goes on much like pudding and will penetrate into the pores of the wood adding a depth to the finish. Wipe the excess glaze from the wood's surface until you achieve an even tone. It's easiest to work on one section of the chair at a time to avoid the glaze drying too quickly before wiping off the excess. Allow the glaze to dry overnight, then add a topcoat (three is prefereable) of a clear finish.

SUPPLIES

Moser's Aniline Dye
Woodworker's Supply:
800-645-9292, or woodworker.com
Medium red mahogany, alcohol soluble
• item No. A16701, $16.19 for 1 oz.

Behlen's Van Dyke Shading and Glazing Stain
Woodworker's Supply:
800-645-9292, or woodworker.com
• item No. 916-759, $22.99 for 1 qt.

Prices as of publication date.

MORRIS CHAIR

Almost every woodworker has the skills to build the most comfortable chair in the house.

by Christopher Schwarz

I don't care what they say about dogs, Morris chairs are a man's best friend. The reclining back, wide arms and expansive seat create the perfect place to watch TV, read the Sunday paper or simply contemplate the finer qualities of a beer.

For the last 10 years, I've spent every weekend planted in the original version of this chair, which was built by the Shop of the Crafters in Cincinnati, Ohio, during the heyday of the Arts & Crafts movement. The Shop of the Crafters was founded by German-American businessman Oscar Onken (1858-1948), who ran a successful framing company until he entered the furniture business in 1902, according to Kenneth R. Trapp's history of the company.

Unlike many furniture-makers of the day, Onken didn't want to merely copy the Stickleys of the world. Onken produced an unusual line of Arts & Crafts furniture that was influenced more by German and Hungarian designs than the straight-lined Stickley pieces of the day. In all honesty, a few of Onken's pieces were kind of ugly. Most, however, had a refinement and lightness that rivaled some of the best work of the day.

This Morris chair is an almost exact replica of the one produced by Onken and his company. It differs in only two ways. One, the original chair was constructed using dowels at the major joints. After almost 100 years of use, the front and back rail came loose. This chair is built using pegged mortise-and-tenon joints. Second, I made one change to the chair frame so that furniture historians of the future will know instantly that this not an original piece. I did this to prevent people from passing off these reproductions as originals.

Though this project might look daunting to you, it can be completed by beginners who have just a few projects under their belt. There are only a few principles to learn here: mortising, tenoning and routing with a plywood template. Plus, I'll share with you exactly how I achieved this finish, which has been something we've been working at for several years.

HOW TO SAVE MONEY ON LUMBER

Begin by choosing the right quartersawn white oak for this project. It requires about 10 board feet of 8/4 and 30 board feet of 4/4 lumber. Quartered white oak can be expensive, from $6 to $12 a board foot. If you live in the Midwest, or will pass near east-central Indiana on a vacation, I recommend you check out Frank Miller Lumber Co. in Union City, Ind. (765-964-7705). The company is a huge supplier of quartersawn oak. As a result, prices are reasonable, about $4 to $6 a board foot. Once you buy your lumber, save the pieces with the most ray flake for the arms, legs, front and sides. To save money, use flat-sawn oak for the seat and the adjustable back.

MORTISES: MACHINE OR NO MACHINE?

First cut all your pieces to size according to the cutting list and begin laying out the locations of your mortises using the diagrams. The rule of thumb is that your mortises

should be half the thickness of your tenon's stock. When your stock is ¾" thick, your mortises and tenons should be ⅜" thick. That means the tenons for the beefy back rail should be thicker (⁷⁄₁₆") and those for the side slats should be thinner (¼").

Also remember that except for the tenons on the legs and slats, all the tenons are ¾" long. To ensure your tenons don't bottom out in your mortises, it's always a good idea to make your mortises about ¹⁄₁₆" deeper than your tenons are long.

After you mark the locations of all the mortises, it's time to cut them. There are 38 mortises in this project. You'd be nuts to do these all by hand. Use this project as an excuse to purchase a hollow chisel mortising machine (about $250) or a mortising attachment for your drill press (about $70). If you can't swing the cash, I'd make plywood templates and cut the mortises with a router and a pattern bit. Making plywood templates is something covered later in this story.

One more thing: don't cut the mortises in the arms or the arm buildups until the chair frame is assembled. You'll cut these with a router and a pattern bit after the chair frame is assembled.

TENONS WITH A DADO STACK

Once you get your mortises cut, make tenons that fit snugly into the mortises. You can use a tenoning jig or the fence on your table saw, or you can use a router. I prefer

Make the mortises in the legs before you shape the curve near the bottom or make cutouts on the top.

to use a dado stack and my miter gauge. See the story on page 104 for details on how to do this.

While your dado stack is in your saw, cut the groove in the back piece that holds the seat frame. See the drawing for the location of this groove.

Once you cut your tenons, prepare to assemble the drop-in seat and the adjustable back. To save yourself some grief, sand the edges of the rails that you won't be able to get to after the frames are assembled. Now put glue in all the mortises and clamp up the frames. Set them aside to dry.

morris chair
INCHES (MILLIMETERS)

REFERENCE	QUANTITY	PART	STOCK	THICKNESS	(mm)	WIDTH	(mm)	LENGTH	(mm)	COMMENTS
A	2	front legs	white oak	1⅝	(41)	3¾	(95)	21	(533)	½" TOE
B	2	back legs	white oak	1⅝	(41)	2¼	(57)	21	(533)	½" TOE
C	2	applied sides	white oak	1⅝	(41)	1³⁄₁₆	(30)	4	(102)	
D	1	front rail	white oak	¾	(19)	4¾	(121)	22	(559)	¾" TBE
E	2	side rails	white oak	¾	(19)	4¾	(121)	24	(610)	¾" TBE
F	1	back rail	white oak	⅞	(22)	4¾	(121)	22	(559)	¾" TBE
G	2	side slats	white oak	½	(13)	7⅝	(194)	11⅜	(289)	½" TBE
H	2	arm build-ups	white oak	⅞	(22)	6	(152)	4½	(115)	
I	2	arms	white oak	¾	(19)	6	(152)	35¼	(895)	
J	2	cleats	white oak	¾	(19)	1⅞	(49)	20½	(521)	
K	1	back rod	white oak	¾	(19)	2	(51)	23⁵⁄₁₆	(592)	
L	2	seat stiles	white oak	¾	(19)	2½	(64)	23½	(597)	
M	5	seat rails	white oak	¾	(19)	2½	(64)	17	(432)	¾" TBE
N	2	back stiles	white oak	¾	(19)	1⅞	(49)	28¼	(717)	
O	5	back rails	white oak	¾	(19)	1⅞	(49)	17½	(445)	¾" TBE
P	1	bottom rail	white oak	¾	(19)	3¼	(82)	17½	(445)	¾" TBE

TOE = tenon on one end • TBE = tenon on both ends

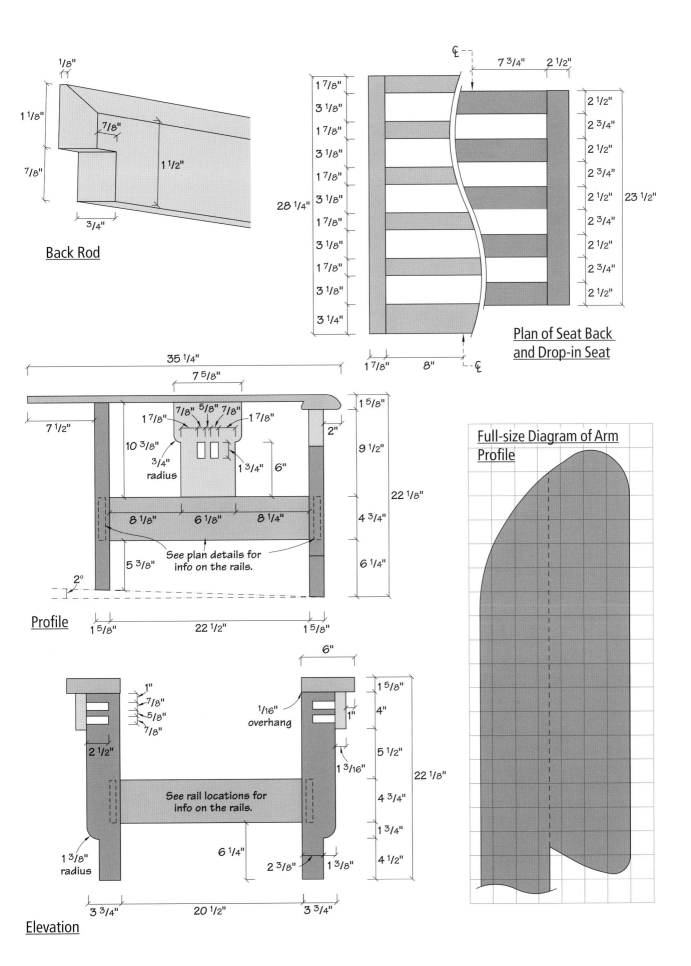

1/8"

1 1/8"

7/8"

7/8"

1 1/2"

3/4"

Back Rod

7 3/4"   2 1/2"

1 7/8"
3 1/8"
1 7/8"
3 1/8"
1 7/8"
3 1/8"   28 1/4"
1 7/8"
3 1/8"
1 7/8"
3 1/8"
3 1/4"

2 1/2"
2 3/4"
2 1/2"
2 3/4"
2 1/2"   23 1/2"
2 3/4"
2 1/2"
2 3/4"
2 1/2"

1 7/8"   8"

Plan of Seat Back
and Drop-in Seat

35 1/4"

7 5/8"

1 5/8"

7 1/2"

7/8" 5/8" 7/8"
1 7/8"   1 7/8"
10 3/8"
3/4"
radius
1 3/4"   6"

2"

9 1/2"

22 1/8"

8 1/8"   6 1/8"   8 1/4"

4 3/4"

See plan details for
info on the rails.

6 1/4"

5 3/8"

2°

Profile

1 5/8"   22 1/2"   1 5/8"

Full-size Diagram of Arm
Profile

6"

1"
7/8"
5/8"
7/8"

1/16"
overhang

1"

1 5/8"
4"

2 1/2"

5 1/2"

1 3/16"

See rail locations for
info on the rails.

22 1/8"

4 3/4"

1 3/4"

1 3/8"
radius

6 1/4"

2 3/8" 1 3/8"

4 1/2"

3 3/4"   20 1/2"   3 3/4"

Elevation

CLIMB-CUTTING TENONS

I own a commercial tenoning jig for my table saw, but I rarely use it. I get better and faster results by cutting tenons using a dado stack and a trick that Contributing Editor Troy Sexton showed me. To avoid tearout on my tenons' shoulders, I "climb cut" the last $^1/_{16}$" or less of the tenon shoulder. You've probably heard of people climb cutting when using a router. Essentially, it's moving the router in the opposite way you normally would to avoid tearout in tricky grain.

That's exactly what you do on your table saw. The final cut on your shoulders is made by pulling the work toward you over the blade and only taking a small cut of material. It sounds awkward, but after a few tenons you get used to it. The risk of kickback is minimal because there's no wood trapped between the blade and the fence. To do this safely, hold your work steady and don't get into a hurry.

Here's how you do it: First install a dado stack into your table saw and set the fence for the finished length of your tenon (almost all of the tenons in this project are $^3/_4$" long). Set the height of your dado stack to the amount you want to thin one side of your tenon (for most of the tenons in this project, that would be $^3/_{16}$"). Then, using your miter gauge, push the work through the dado stack to cut the majority of your tenon.

When this cut is done, slide the work against the fence and pull the miter gauge back toward you to shave the shoulder of the tenon. Flip the work over and do the other side. Then do the edges.

Set your fence so the dado stack will make a $^3/_4$" cut (the length of your tenon). Hold the piece about $^1/_{16}$" from the fence. Push your work through the blade using your miter gauge.

After you finish that first pass, slide the work against the fence and pull it back toward you over the blade to shave the last little bit of the shoulder.

Repeat the same procedure for the edges of the tenon. (If you like a little more shoulder on your edges, increase the height of the blade.) First push the work forward.

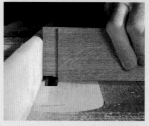

Then slide it against the fence and pull it back toward you to make the final shoulder cut.

When pattern-routing the curve on the legs, make sure you have the work firmly clamped in place. I have the pattern and leg wedged between two pieces of oak (the pattern is on the underside of the leg). Then the leg itself is clamped to the table. You also could perform this operation on a router table with a starting pin for pattern-routing.

Peg the tenons that join the front rail to the front legs and the back rail to the back legs. If you've ever pegged tenons before, you know that dowels can be wildly different sizes than they're supposed to be. Here's a trick. If your dowel is a bit undersized, glue it in place and cut it nearly flush to the surface. Then put several drops of thinned glue on the end grain of the dowel. It wicks in the glue, expands and glues up tight. When the glue is dry, cut the dowel flush.

Be sure to make a full-size mock-up of the legs and sides (left) to determine the angle you need to cut on the bottom of the legs. When you determine that angle, use a grease pencil or magic marker to paint the bottom of the legs. I cut the back and front legs simultaneously. Slowly inch your legs in after each cut until all the color is gone (right).

CURVES AND CUTOUTS

What makes this Morris chair stand out are the curves and cutouts on the legs, arms and slats. Each curve and cutout needs a slightly different strategy.

The large curves on the legs and the small curves on the side slats were cut using a plywood template and a pattern-cutting bit in a router. I made the patterns from ½"-thick Baltic birch plywood. Use the drawings to make your own plywood template using a scroll saw, band saw or coping saw. Smooth all your cuts with sandpaper, then try shaping a couple scraps with your template to make sure your pattern produces the right shape. When satisfied, cut the curves to rough shape on your band saw (about ¹⁄₁₆" shy of your finished line) and clean up the cut with a router and pattern bit. Finish shaping the legs with a chisel.

To produce the large cutouts on the front legs, do what Oscar Onken did: cheat a bit. Make the "cutouts" using a dado stack on your table saw, with the legs on edge. Then glue the applied sides to the legs to cover the open end of the cuts. Instant cutout. While you're at it, cut out the notches on the arm pieces for the rod that adjusts the back.

To complete the legs, you need to cut the bottom of all four legs at a 2° angle so the chair sits flat on the floor. I recommend you make a full-sized mock up (see the photo at left) so you can get the angle exactly right. Cut the angle on a chop saw.

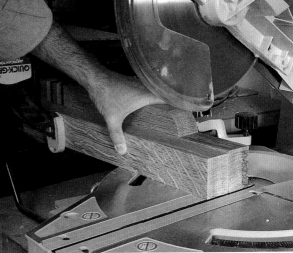

ASSEMBLY

Now you're almost ready to assemble the chair frame. You'll need to first miter the tenons slightly where they meet to fit in the mortises using your table saw. Now finish sand everything. I went to 150 grit using my random-orbit sander and hand sanded the whole piece with 180 grit. Yes, it makes a noticeable difference.

Now glue the front rail between the front legs and the back rail between the back legs. Clamp and allow your glue to dry. Use ¼" dowels to pin the tenons from the inside of the chair. This strengthens the weakest point of this chair. It's at this joint where the original chair came loose.

Glue the side rails between the front and back legs and you can see your chair take shape.

LEARN TO MAKE SQUARE TEMPLATES

Now you need to work on the arms. First glue the arm buildup pieces to the front of the arms. Then get ready to cut the mortises on the arms that will hold the tenons on the legs and side slats. A word of advice here. Mock up an arm out of scrap wood and practice on it first.

To make plywood templates for the mortises, you need to make a square hole in the middle of a piece of ply. The best way to do this is by making plunge cuts into your plywood on your table saw. Refer to the photo above that shows how to do this.

Now cut your mortises. I used a template bit with small cutters on the bottom and a guide bearing on top. It's designed for plunging and is called a "mortising bit" in catalogs. If you don't have a bit with these cutters on the bottom, you can still plunge with a standard straight bit that has a guide bearing. Just plunge slowly and wiggle the router a bit as you go. Cut the mortises in two passes.

After you're sure the arms fit on the legs, cut the curve on the front of the arm. Attach the full-size pattern to your arm and cut the shape on a band saw. Clean up the cuts with a stationary belt sander. Now taper the arms with your band saw and clean up the cut with your jointer. Glue the arms and slats in place.

Now shape the back rod that adjusts

Make cuts in the front edge of the board to check your template against the tenon.

To make a template for the mortises in the arms and the cutouts on the side slats, position your plywood over your table saw and raise the blade into the ply. Move the fence over and repeat. Then turn the pattern 90° and repeat for the other edges of the pattern. Note that I made cuts in the front of the pattern to help me size the pattern to the tenons.

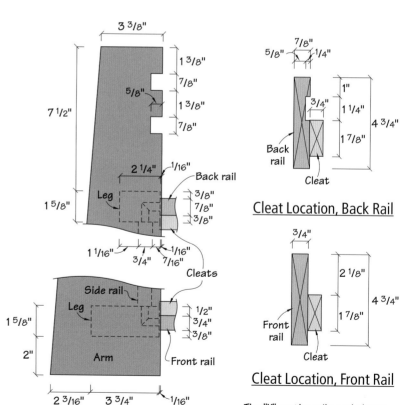

Rail Locations

Cleat Location, Back Rail

Cleat Location, Front Rail

The "X" on the rails and cleats denotes a cross section rather than an end view.

Be sure to make a test arm before you go mortising the real thing. You'll be glad you did.

the seat back angle. Bevel one edge of the rod on your jointer and cut notches on the ends so the rod fits between the arms. Attach the back to the seat frame with a piano hinge. Screw the cleats to the front and back of the frame in the locations shown in the diagram; slip the seat in place.

FINISHING

The finished we used requires mulitple steps with different finishing products, but the final appearance is worth the trouble. First dye the chair with a reddish-hued alcohol-based aniline dye. The dye we used is listed in the supplies box at right. Next apply one coat of boiled linseed oil (available at any home center store) to the chair. Wipe off the excess oil and allow the finish to dry overnight. The linseed oil seals the wood before your final coloring step and helps bring out the ray flake.

Next, we wiped on a thin coat of glaze made by Behlen's. Wipe the glaze until you achieve an even tone. Allow it to dry overnight. Finally, apply three coats of a clear finish.

■■ SUPPLIES
■■

Slotted Piano Hinge
Rockler Woodworking and Hardware:
800-279-4441 or rockler.com
• item No. 19241, $9.99 for 36"

Moser's Aniline Dye
Woodworker's Supply:
800-645-9292, or woodworker.com
Medium red mahogany, alcohol soluble
• item No. A16701, $16.19 for 1 oz.

Behlen's Van Dyke Shading and Glazing Stain
Woodworker's Supply:
800-645-9292, or woodworker.com
• item No. 916-759, $22.99 for 1 qt.

Prices correct as of publication date.

INLAID ROCKER

The wide seat and curved arms of this reproduction make this chair the perfect place to curl up with your child, a good book, or just for an afternoon nap.

By Jim Stack

When I decided to build an Arts & crafts rocker, I wanted something a little lighter in looks than most recognized Arts & Crafts pieces. Many of the chairs can look a little chunky and heavy for my taste. This design was produced by the Limbert Furniture Co. of Grand Rapids, Mich., about 1910. Charles Limbert was a contemporary of Gustav Stickley, but much of his work had a stylized appearance, adding cutouts, sweeps and inlays to separate his work from more austere Arts & Crafts designs.

Start the inlay work on the four legs by using a router with an edge guide to rout the ¼"-wide channels for the inlay.

DESIGN AND LAYOUT

First draw a full-scale side and top view of the chair. The drawings help answer questions about construction and what joints to use. They also let you make mistakes that an eraser can correct. I suggest you take the information from the parts list and the diagrams and make your own full-size elevation and plan view drawings.

BUILDING THE LEGS

Start construction with the legs. The front legs are simple, but remember to orient your wood to show the most attractive face forward. The back legs, with their dog-leg shape, require a routing template. Start by rough-cutting a blank for each leg on the band saw. Next, lay out a ½"-thick plywood template using the dimensions given in the diagrams, then attach it to the blank with flat head screws on the inside of each leg. Put the screws at the mortise locations so the holes won't be seen. Use a router with a template routing bit to shape each leg, and be sure to make one right and one left leg.

ROUTED INLAYS

With the legs shaped to size, lay out the location for the inlays on the front faces of each leg. Start the inlay work by routing the ⅛"-deep by ¼"-wide groove using a straight bit in a plunge router. Next, cut the inlay strips to ¼" × ¼", to fit a little snug in the width for fitting. This also leaves the inlay proud, to be leveled out once the inlay is glued in place. Walnut works well for the inlay. To glue it in place, put glue into the groove, insert the inlay, and then use a caul and clamps to press the inlay into

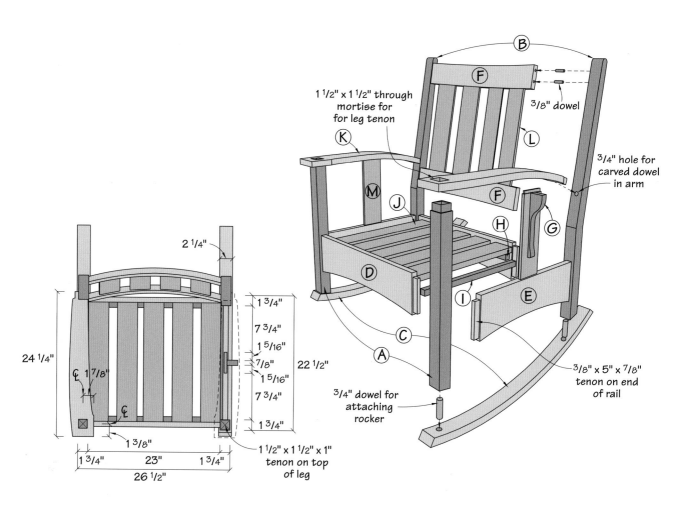

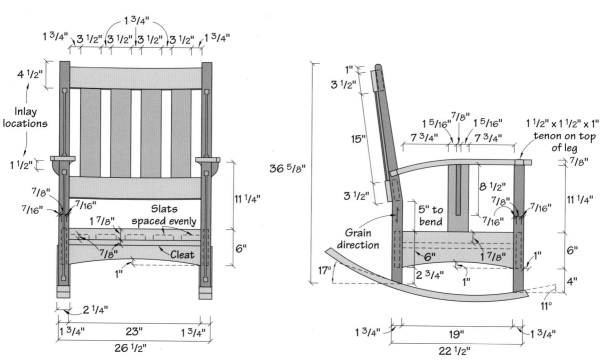

2 1/4"

24 1/4"

1 7/8"

1 3/8"

1 3/4"   23"   1 3/4"
26 1/2"

1 3/4"
7 3/4"
1 5/16"
7/8"
1 5/16"
7 3/4"
1 3/4"

22 1/2"

1 1/2" x 1 1/2" x 1"
tenon on top
of leg

1 1/2" x 1 1/2" through
mortise for
for leg tenon

K

M

J

D

3/8" dowel

3/4" hole for
carved dowel
in arm

L

F

H

G

I

E

C

A

3/4" dowel for
attaching
rocker

3/8" x 5" x 7/8"
tenon on end
of rail

B

F

1 3/4"   3 1/2"   3 1/2"   3 1/2"   3 1/2"   1 3/4"
1 3/4"

4 1/2"

Inlay
locations

1 1/2"

7/8"
7/16"

7/16"

1 7/8"

7/8"

1"

2 1/4"

1 3/4"   23"   1 3/4"
26 1/2"

11 1/4"

6"

Slats
spaced evenly

Cleat

1"
3 1/2"

15"

3 1/2"

17°

Grain
direction

36 5/8"

1 5/16"   7/8"   1 5/16"
7 3/4"   7 3/4"

5" to
bend

6"

2 3/4"

1 7/8"

1"

1 1/2" x 1 1/2" x 1"
tenon on top
of leg

7/8"

8 1/2"

7/8"
7/16"

7/8"
7/16"

11 1/4"

6"

4"

11°

1 3/4"   19"   1 3/4"
22 1/2"

REFERENCE	QUANTITY	PART	STOCK	THICKNESS	(mm)	WIDTH	(mm)	LENGTH	(mm)	COMMENTS
A	2	front legs	white oak	$1^3/_4$	(45)	$1^3/_4$	(45)	$22^1/_4$	(651)	
B	2	back legs	white oak	$1^3/_4$	(45)	5	(127)	$36^5/_8$	(930)	
C	2	rockers	white oak	$1^1/_4$	(32)	$2^1/_4$	(57)	$35^3/_4$	(908)	
D	2	seat rails front and back	white oak	$7/_8$	(22)	6	(152)	$24^3/_4$	(629)	
E	2	side seat rails	white oak	$7/_8$	(22)	6	(152)	$20^3/_4$	(527)	
F	2	back rails	white oak	$7/_8$	(22)	$3^1/_2$	(89)	23	(584)	
G	2	corbels	white oak	$7/_8$	(22)	2	(51)	$8^1/_2$	(216)	
H	2	seat cleats	poplar	$7/_8$	(22)	$7/_8$	(22)	23	(584)	
J	2	seat cleats	poplar	$7/_8$	(22)	$7/_8$	(22)	18	(457)	
K	5	seat slats	poplar	$7/_8$	(22)	$3^1/_2$	(89)	$19^7/_8$	(505)	
L	2	arms	white oak	$7/_8$	(22)	$4^1/_4$	(108)	$24^1/_4$	(616)	
M	4	back slats	white oak	$3/_8$	(10)	$3^1/_2$	(89)	16	(406)	
N	2	side slats	white oak	$3/_8$	(10)	$3^1/_2$	(89)	$12^5/_{16}$	(313)	

The square ends of the inlays can be done with a mortiser, as shown here, or you can use a router with a template and use a chisel to square out the corners.

place. Set these pieces aside to dry for several hours or overnight. After leveling the inlay flush to the leg with a plane, I used a mortiser to create the $\frac{3}{4}$" × $\frac{3}{4}$" square holes to finish the inlay pattern.

LAMINATED BENDING

Now comes the fun part, bending. All the radii are the same, so you have to make only one bending jig for the rockers, arms and back rails. Medium-density fiberboard (MDF) is a stable and affordable material for a bending jig. The longest bent pieces are the rockers, so cut the six $\frac{3}{4}$"-thick jig pieces about 42" long and 8" deep. Next, use a set of trammel points to strike the radius (shown on the diagram) on one of the MDF panels. Rough cut to the outside of the line and then sand to the line. Then use a flush-trim router bit and this first jig part to duplicate the radii on the other five pieces. When the matched layers are placed together, the $4\frac{1}{2}$" width works well for the arms. Layers can be removed as needed to glue up the narrower parts.

Lamination bending is simply bending thin strips of wood over a form and gluing them together. This is a good way to bend wood because the wood remains stable, the grain patterns of the original face remain when bent, and the final lamination is very strong.

Start the lamination process by cutting pieces for the rockers, arms, and back rails. Cut them $\frac{1}{4}$" wider and longer so you can trim them to size after glue-up. Resaw the blanks into strips a little thicker than $\frac{1}{8}$", keeping the pieces in order as they come off the band saw. Next, drum sand or plane the strips to $\frac{1}{8}$" thick.

GLUE UP THE LAMINATION

At glue-up time, have your clamps handy. Be sure to wax or seal all the surfaces on the jig that will come into contact with glue, so the dried glue can be easily removed. With the wood strips in order, apply thinned wood glue to each strip. Then put the whole assembly on the form with a $\frac{1}{2}$"-thick piece of plywood to serve as a caul to even out the clamping pressure. Put the first clamp in the center of the assembly, with the next clamps working out to either end. The clamps should stay in place for *at least* two hours.

In gluing up the laminations, I use a brush to cover every square inch of the wood face. I thin the glue with a little water to make it easier to spread. Thinning will not affect the holding power of the glue. The glue run out on the sides is a good sign that all surfaces are bonding.

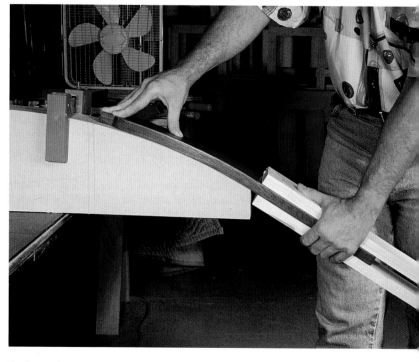

To glue up the arm, the curved end was clamped to the jig while the other half was sandwiched between two straight boards. I found it helpful to glue-up the straight part first, then quickly move the arm to the end of the jig. You may need an assistant to help with this step.

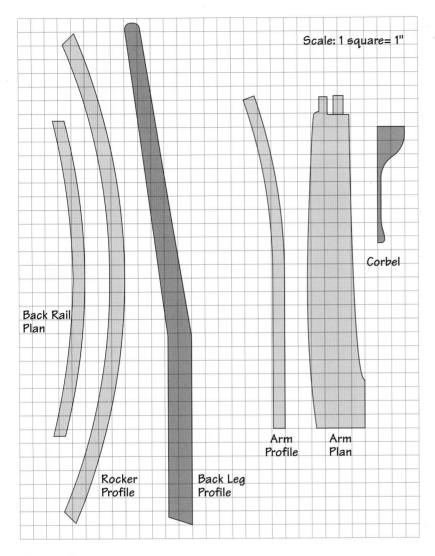

Scale: 1 square= 1"

Back Rail
Plan

Corbel

Arm
Profile

Arm
Plan

Rocker
Profile

Back Leg
Profile

Scaled Patterns

GLUING AND CUTTING THE BACK RAILS

Because the back rails are 3½" wide, I used only five MDF layers for the bending jig. You'll need seven ⅛"-thick strips for each of the rails. Apply glue and put the rail assembly in the center of the jig. When the laminations are dry, scrape the glue off one edge and use a jointer to flatten and square that edge. Then cut the blanks to 3½" wide using the table saw.

GLUING AND CUTTING THE ROCKERS

The rockers are 2¼" wide, so I left four layers in the jig. I used 10 strips for each rocker. Glue the strips as before, and when dry, square and cut them to width. Next, lay the rockers on the full-size drawings and mark the angles on each end. Cut these angles on the table saw using a miter gauge with a 30" wooden fence attached. Hold the rocker on its side, tight against the fence with the curve arching away from your body. Adjust the miter gauge angle until it matches the angle you want to cut on the end of the rock-

er. Do this for both ends of the rockers, then set them aside.

GLUING THE ARMS

Each arm requires seven ⅛" × 4½" strips, and I used all six layers of the bending form. The arms are radiused only on the back half of the arms, so I clamped to only 13" at one end of the radius form (see photo bottom left).

When the arms are dry, scrape the glue off one edge, joint that edge, then cut the blanks to 4¼" wide on the table saw.

SEAT RAILS AND BACK SLATS

The rails and slats are straight, solid wood pieces. Size them as given in the Schedule of Materials. While you're cutting square wood, also machine and cut the seat slats and cleats. The arches on the bottom of the seat rails will be cut after the tenons are cut on the rails.

MORTISES AND TENONS

As with most solid chairs, the secret to longevity is in the joinery. One of the best possible chair joints is a mortise and tenon. Using the diagrams, lay out the ½" × 5" × ¹⁵⁄₁₆"-long mortises for the seat rails on the front and back legs.

Next cut ½" × 5" × ⅞"-long tenons on both ends of the seat rails. Where the tenons meet at the corner of the leg mortises you need to cut a 45-degree bevel on the ends of the tenons.

The back rails are held in place with dowels. To determine the length of the back rails, measure the distance from cheek to cheek on the back seat rail. Then draw a line that same length on a piece of paper. mark the center, then also mark the center of the back rail. Lay the rail on the paper, and square over from the ends of the line. To cut the curved rails, I laid them (convex side down) against the miter gauge fence. I then put a spacer under the rail, (between the blade and the center point of the rail), to support the rail as the cut is made. This cut is safe as long as you adequately support the rail during the cut. Expect a little tear out on the underside of the cut, so take your cut slowly. Turn the rail and cut the other end the same way. Cut the other rail to match the first.

With the back rails cut to length, it's time to lay out the mortises for the slats on the upper and lower back rails. Start by spacing the slats equally along the rail. Because the rails are curved, and the tenons are straight, using a fence as a guide to make the mortises won't work. Draw

¼" × 3¼" mortises centered on the rail, using a 4" wide piece of wood as a straight edge.

To cut the ⁹/₁₆"-deep mortises in the back rails, I again used the mortiser, but without a fence, cutting the mortises free-hand following the straight lines as a guide. The mortise needs to be tight, not pretty, as the shoulder of the slat tenon will hide the mortise.

Using the same dimensions as on the back rail mortises, cut the mortises in the two seat side rails for their side slats. Then cut the tenons on all the back slats and just the bottom tenons on the side slats. The tenons on the tops of the side slats will be cut later.

DRY FITTING THE CHAIR
This is a good point to dry-fit the chair and get a look at how it's all going to go together. The two front legs and front seat rail form a subassembly. The two back legs, the back seat rail, the two back rails and the four slats form another subassembly. These two sub-assemblies are joined to one another with the two side seat rails.

While the chair is clamped together dry, put the back rail/back slat assembly in place between the back legs and clamp it with enough pressure to hold it in place. Adjust the fit of the back slat section to its finished position, and mark the top and bottom back rail locations for the dowels.

DOWELING THE BACK RAILS
Using the marks made on the back legs, mark the two back rails for two ³/₈" dowels in each end. It's probably just as easy to drill the dowel locations in the rails free-hand (rather than making a jig) to keep them perpendicular to the end faces of the rails. Then reassemble the back rail/back slat assembly and use dowel centers to locate the dowel locations in the back legs. Use a drill press to drill the holes in the back legs, then put it all back together again to check the fit.

FITTING THE ARMS
I used a photo in an auction catalog to determine how the arms would fit into the front and back legs. Refer to your working drawings and the diagram of the rear part of the arm to make a full-size paper or cardboard template of the arm. Square over the front of the arms on the table saw, then lay the template square to the front of each arm. Trace the pattern onto the blanks.

Cut out the arms on the band saw leaving the pencil marks, then sand to the pencil marks. Don't cut the tenon and "wraparound" on the back of the arm yet. Instead, just leave the arm about ½" long. By holding the arm blank alongside the front leg and the side of the dry-assembled chair, I was able to mark the arms to length, where they would join the back legs and also draw the angle of the arm at this joint.

With the arm location and angle marked, drill a ¾"

Use a pattern to trace the layout of the arm. The tenon and wrap-around can be made by using the band saw to cut away most of the waste. Use a chisel and file to make the final shape. Check the fit to the back leg as you progress.

hole in each back leg, matching the angle of the arm. Then cut the back end of the arms (see photo at right).

With the chair still dry fit, hold the arms in place allowing the shoulder of the round-tenon joint to flush to the back leg of the chair. Then measure the distance from the back leg to the top of the front leg and transfer this measurement to each arm. Use this location to mark where the through-mortise is to be cut for the front leg's through-tenon.

The top of the front leg serves as a through-tenon for the arm and a ⅛" shoulder is cut on all four sides of the leg, 1" from the top, reducing the thickness of the leg to 1½" at the tenon. But first, make the through-mortise in the arms. Then use the through-mortise to mark the top of the front leg. Set your table saw to cut the top of the leg to fit the mortise. Cutting the peak on the front leg is done on the table saw with the blade set at 7 degrees.

With the chair again dry assembled, fit the arms to the front and back legs. Then mark the underside of the arms for the slat mortises. Cut this ¼" × 3" × ½" deep mortise free-hand as described earlier with the back slats. Then scribe the curve of the arm to the top edge of the side slat, (leaving ½" for the tenon) to the underside of the arm and cut the curve on the band saw. Next, cut the tenon on the table saw to match the curve of the end. Cut out the corbels on the band saw using the template in the diagrams. Then do one more dry fit to check all the parts, and you're ready to start sanding.

I used a router with a guide bushing and a template for making the through-mortise on the arm. Take it slow and make it tight, then use a file to square out the corners.

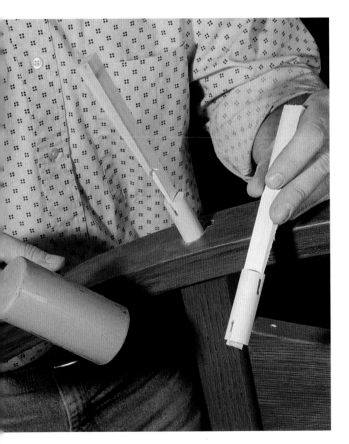

A ¾" dowel with slots and wedges will hold the rockers in place for many years to come.

SANDING AND FINISHING

Sand all parts to 150 grit with a random orbit sander. I chose to finish all the pieces prior to assembly to avoid runs. This gave me a very even and clean-looking finish. I first taped off all the glue joint areas, then applied a gel stain with a predominant red tint, wiping the stain to an even color. I then applied a medium-brown glaze, wiping it to an even color that I liked. I let this all dry for four hours, then sprayed on three coats of lacquer, sanding between coats.

After letting the finish cure overnight, I assembled the chair. To secure the rockers, I used a 2½" × ¾" dowel slotted on both ends at right angles to each other. These slots are for wedges. The first wedge is put into a slot and cut so ⅛" is left sticking out. When the dowel is driven into the hole with the slot and wedge going into the hole first, the wedge will be forced into the slot and will spread the dowel inside the hole in the leg, locking it into place. Another dowel is driven into the other slot and driven home to wedge the rocker in place. (See photo.)

For extra holding power where the arms join the back legs, I drilled a pilot hole and put a screw into the tenon on the arm. I plugged the hole with the same wood that I used for the inlays.

SEAT AND BACK CUSHIONS

The seat is a 6"-thick firm foam pad with a sewn upholstery cover. The back pad measures about 2" thick and is filled with a batting material. The back cushion hangs over the back rail of the chair on straps which button to the back of the cushion to hold it in place.

GREENE BROTHERS HALL BENCH

Arts & Crafts furniture isn't all austere and chunky. This hall bench from the Blacker House shows the movement at its most graceful.

By Jim Stuard

This will upset some of the purists out there, but I think that some of the best designs in the Arts & Crafts style came from the fringes of the movement. Instead of Gustav Stickley's massive and square forms, I prefer art nouveau-influenced furniture from Scotsman Charles Rennie Mackintosh. And instead of the squarish Lifetime furniture, I've always liked the Asian influence in the furniture and architecture of Charles and Henry Greene.

This bench from the brothers Greene was designed and built in 1907 for the Robert R. Blacker house in Pasadena, Calif. The story behind this house is a sad one. As the furniture designed for the house went out of style, most of it was sold at a yard sale in 1947. Then, in 1985, the house was purchased and within three days was stripped of most of its lighting fixtures, stained glass windows and door transoms. These were sold piecemeal to collectors all over the world, quickly recouping the $1 million price of the house. Though new owners have taken possession of the house and a strong effort is being made to reclaim the original pieces, many can only be seen in photos, or as reproductions.

This bench is as faithful to the original as I could manage, including the reed-like design of the back slats that lend a lightness not often seen in the Arts & Crafts style. The construction is a blend of modern and traditional. And while the original was made of teak, I chose cherry.

THE CASE OF THE CHAIR

Because this project is a mix of case construction and chair building, you'll use techniques from both disciplines. Begin construction by cutting the parts according to the cutting list. The most difficult step is getting the joint between the back legs and top rail right. It's a specialized coped-miter that requires patience.

The front legs can be cut from 8/4 material, while the back legs are cut from a laminated blank glued up using scarf joints (see the diagrams for details). I used three pieces of 8/4 cherry for each back leg, with the back section cut from the longest piece to avoid showing a visible

The templates for the slats are provided on the scaled-down grids. After enlarging them, lay out the templates on your wood, cut the tenons on the ends of the boards and band saw the slats to shape.

greene brothers hall bench
INCHES (MILLIMETERS)

REFERENCE	QUANTITY	PART	STOCK	THICKNESS	(mm)	WIDTH	(mm)	LENGTH	(mm)	COMMENTS
A	1	top rail	cherry	$3/4$	(19)	$4^5/8$	(117)	$45^1/2$	(1156)	
B	2	back legs*	cherry	$2^3/4$	(70)	$4^5/8$	(117)	40	(1016)	
C	2	front legs	cherry	$1^3/4$	(44)	$2^1/8$	(55)	$23^3/4$	(603)	
D	2	large slats	cherry	$5/8$	(16)	$4^1/4$	(108)	$18^1/4$	(464)	
E	10	small slats	cherry	$5/8$	(16))	$2^1/4$	(57)	$18^1/4$	(464)	
F	1	center slat	cherry	$5/8$	(16))	$1^1/2$	(38)	$18^1/4$	(464)	
G	2	arms	cherry	$1^3/4$	(45)	2	(51)	$20^1/8$	(511)	
H	2	seat frame ends	cherry	$3/4$	(19)	$4^1/4$	(108)	19	(483)	
I	1	seat frame back*	cherry	$3/4$	(19)	$3^1/2$	(89)	$41^3/8$	(1051)	
J	1	seat frame center	cherry	$3/4$	(19)	$2^1/2$	(64)	$15^1/2$	(394)	
K	4	breadboard ends**	cherry	$3/4$	(19)	$2^1/2$	(64)	$15^1/2$	(394)	
L	2	lids**	cherry	$11/16$	(17)	$15^1/2$	(394)	$14^7/16$	(367)	
M	2	box ends	cherry	$3/4$	(19)	8	(203)	$16^3/16$	(411)	
N	1	box front	cherry	$3/4$	(19)	8	(203)	$46^7/8$	(1191)	
O	1	box back	cherry	$3/4$	(19)	8	(203)	$43^5/8$	(1108)	
P	1	divider	cherry	$3/4$	(19)	$7^1/4$	(184)	17	(432)	
Q	1	divider	plywood	$3/4$	(19)	$17^1/2$	(445)	$48^1/2$	(1232)	

*rough length; **requires fitting after assembly

$5/16$" × $5/16$" × 30" and $7/16$" × $7/16$" × 30" of ebony plug material

1-antique-brass continuous hinge $1^1/2$" × 48" cut in 19" lengths

seam. Start shaping the legs by cutting the profile first. Cut the top radius on the back leg after the back is assembled. Next cut the outside radius of each back leg on the elevation face. Before cutting the curve on the inside edge, lay out and cut the coped miter for the top rail according to the diagram. The straight inside edge gives a better reference for laying out the coped miter. Then rout a ¼" radius on the visible corners of all the legs. Now cut out the arms on the band saw.

To form the storage area, the box ends need a 6° bevel on the front and back edges, and a ¼" × ¼" groove for the bottom that's cut ½" up from the lower inside edge. The same groove is necessary on the front and back box pieces. After making these cuts, mark and cut biscuit slots to attach the front and back legs to the box ends. Make the slots to hold the end panels recessed ½" in from the outside of each leg.

The next step is to cut a ¼" × ¾" tenon on the top end of the boards from which the back slats will be cut. On the bottom end of the boards, cut a 7° bevel to allow the slats to lean to the back, so the long part of the bevel should face forward. Next, cut out the slat shapes on a band saw and use a scroll saw for the centers of the two spade-shaped slats. Then clean up the rough edges with a spokeshave.

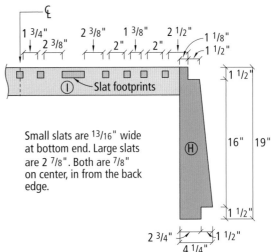

Small slats are 13/16" wide at bottom end. Large slats are 2 7/8". Both are 7/8" on center, in from the back edge.

Plan of seat frame end "H" and slat layout on seat frame back "I"

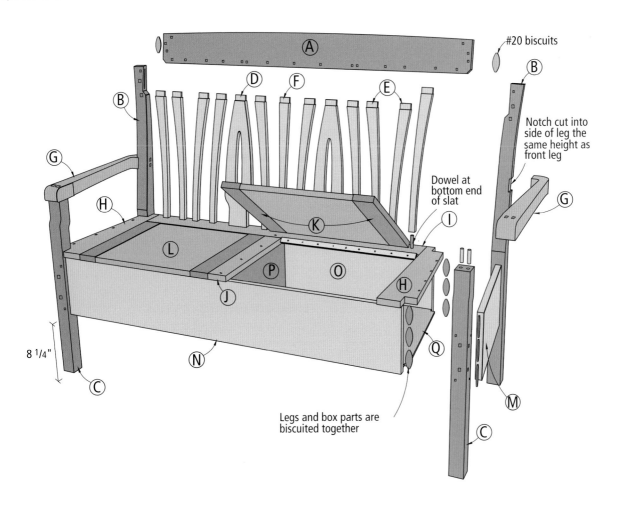

While the slats can be sanded smooth, I find that a spokeshave helps remove irregularities left by the band saw. It also gives the piece a hand-worked appearance.

Notching the back leg to fit the back rail is a little tricky, so take the time to do it right. This joint is one of the most noticed features of the piece.

MAKING ENDS MEET

You're now ready to dry-assemble the bench frame. Use biscuits again to attach the box front and box back between the legs. Make sure the angles are correct and the bottom fits. Then cut the top rail to length and clip the corners at a 45° angle to fit between the legs and biscuit it in place.

The next step is to notch the back legs for the arms. Use the front legs as a guide. The notch is ¼" deep by the size of the arm's end. Mark and drill for dowels to attach the arms to the top of the front leg. Also drill clearance holes in the back legs to screw the rear of the arm to the back leg from the inside of the leg. With the bench still dry-assembled, go ahead and lay out and drill ⅜" dowel holes for the slats.

After resolving any fitting problems, cut a ¼" × ¾" groove into the center of the bottom edge on the top rail. This will hold the slats' tenons. Then glue the bench together for real. Start by nailing the divider in place between the box front and back, holding the top edges flush. Then put glue on the biscuits and fit the legs onto

the box parts, fitting the slats and top rail in place at the same time. There are a lot of pieces to align, but the glue will allow you about five minutes to check the slats before it starts to set.

The next step is to assemble and attach the seat frame. Biscuit the back and center pieces together, and then nail the frame in place to the assembled box. After everything is dry, cut the radius on the top rail and leg ends. Rout a ¼" radius on all the edges of the top rail and smooth it out.

BREADBOARDS AND LIFT LIDS

The last step in assembling the bench is to make the lift lids with breadboard ends. These provide a seat and lid for the storage area below. Begin by gluing up two panels for the lids. Breadboards have been around for hundreds of years as a means of stabilizing a panel as it goes through humidity changes each season. Breadboards can be made in many ways that involve complicated joinery. I chose a method that is simple, and gives an authentic look. Rout three mortises in each breadboard 1" deep by 1½" long using the jig shown on the next page and on page 123.

I made a simple mortising jig to help with the breadboards. Once the three-piece jig is done, a plunge router makes simple work of the mortises.

Use a chisel to square out the mortises. The breadboard ends are a little long so cut them to length after attaching them to the panel with #10 × 3" pan-head screws. When you're happy with the fit of the breadboards, tap the fitted plugs in place with glue. Trim and sand the plugs flush. Attach the lids to the bench with continuous hinges.

PLANTING THE PLUGS

The finishing accent for this piece, and one that is a trademark of the Greene and Greene style, is to add ebony plugs to many of the bench joints. See the box on the previous page for a handy way to do this. Adding color to this bench isn't terribly difficult. First color the wood with Moser's Light Sheraton Mahogany dye (available from Woodworker's Supply 800-645-9292, or woodworker.com, item #844-421). Allow it to dry. Apply one coat of clear finish. Next, we used a brown glaze from Behlen's, also available from Woodworker's Supply, item # 916-759). Wipe the

Cut the tenons on the seat, then cut the mortises in the breadboard ends. Now cut an elongated clearance hole at the bottom of the mortise. Screw the breadboards in place and cap them with the rectangular plugs as shown.

SQUARE PLUGS AND SQUARE HOLES MADE SIMPLE

There doesn't seem to be any rhyme or reason to the plug locations used by Greene and Greene, except that the plugs were symmetrical. Used ostensibly to hide screws, nails and other fasteners, there should be plugs at all of the major joint locations. There are two sizes of plugs, $5/16$" square and $7/16$" square. This is the fastest and easiest way to do this.

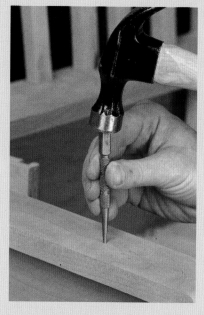

If there's a nail in the location of the plug, set it as deeply as you can.

Now drill a hole (either $3/8$" or $1/4$" in diameter) that's about $3/8$" deep.

Now square the hole. I bought inexpensive steel bar stock from my local home center ($7/16$" square and $5/16$" square). Then I tapered one end on my grinder. Tap the bar stock into your round hole and it will become a square hole.

Put a small dot of glue in the hole and tap your ebony plug in place.

Use a piece of cardboard as a spacer between your work and a flush-cutting saw. Cut the plug and then sand it slightly so there's still a raised bump.

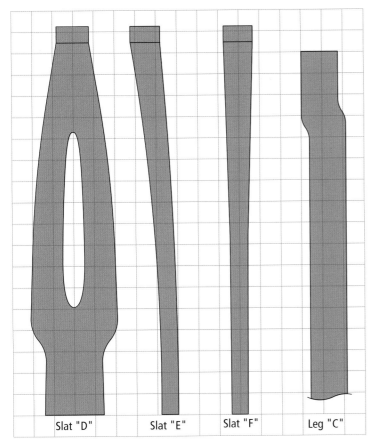

Back slats and leg profile
Each square = 1"

Slat "D"   Slat "E"   Slat "F"   Leg "C"

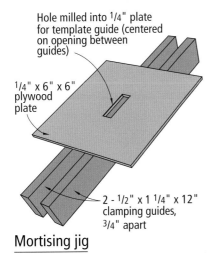

Hole milled into 1/4" plate
for template guide (centered
on opening between
guides)

1/4" x 6" x 6"
plywood
plate

2 - 1/2" x 1 1/4" x 12"
clamping guides,
3/4" apart

Mortising jig

bench with your rag until most of it is colored evenly. Allow
that to dry overnight. Then complete the process with two
coats of a clear finish.

By the way, if you're wondering what a piece like this is
worth these days, we sold this bench on eBay.com in 2000
for $1,200.

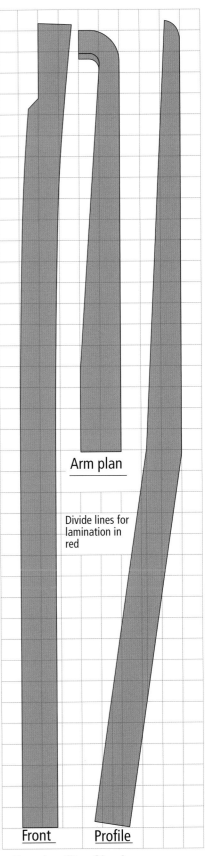

Arm plan

Divide lines for
lamination in
red

Front   Profile

Front/profile of back
leg and arm plan
Each square = 1"

PRAIRIE SPINDLE CHAIR

This Arts & Crafts reproduction will last a lifetime (or more).

By David Thiel

Many Arts & Crafts enthusiasts consider the cube chair the stylistic peak of the Arts & Crafts movement. This version borrows heavily from a chair made by the L. & J.G. Stickley company, but the narrow spindles are characteristic of architect Frank Lloyd Wright's designs. Traditional quartersawn white oak and solid construction techniques make it true to Arts & Crafts principles.

Though the chair isn't complicated, there are a lot of repetitive steps in milling the many mortises and tenons. Begin by cutting the lumber to the sizes given in the parts list.

MORTISES

There are 82 mortise and tenon joints in the chair. A mortiser was my tool of choice, though a plunge router using a ½" straight bit is another option.

Each leg receives two ½" wide × ⅞" deep × 4" long mortises for the stretchers between the legs. These mortises start 10" up from the bottom of each leg, so this is a good time to determine the legs' orientation, making sure the best quartersawn figure faces out where it can be seen. The ½" wide × ⅞" deep × 1½" long apron mortises are next. The rear legs receive apron mortises on the same two faces as the stretcher mortises, while the front legs receive only one apron mortise per leg, located on the side facing the back

legs. These mortises start ¼" down from the top so the aprons will be flush to the leg top.

Once you've completed the leg mortises, move to the side stretchers and aprons and mark each for the 11½" × 1" × ⅝" deep mortises for the spindles. The mortises nearest the legs should be marked starting 1¼" in from each end — a ¾" allowance for the stretcher tenon yet to be cut, plus ¾" spacing between the leg and the first spindle.

A benchtop mortiser makes the repetitive work more manageable.

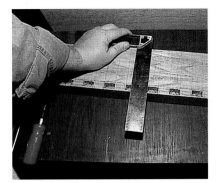

Time spent carefully laying out the mortise locations will pay big dividends during assembly.

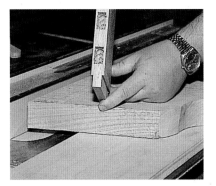

A featherboard provides stability and safety while cutting the tenons.

A simple setup on the miter gauge makes cutting the tenons consistent.

Use a simple stop block n the miter gauge to set the tenn shoulder depth.

Allow a 1" interval between each spindle, and this will provide even spacing.

The back stretcher and apron are marked similarly, but the first mark is made 1¾" in from either end and then every inch. Cutting the through mortises in the arms will be among your final tasks, so you're through with mortises for now.

TENONS

The next step is to make all the tenons. Whichever piece you start with, the stretchers, aprons or slats, the process will be the same steps with just slight dimension adjustments.

I prefer to form the cheeks first and define the shoulder last. This method prevents the saw-kerf from being seen on the shoulder, and prevents a waste piece from being trapped by the blade where it can be thrown back at you. In our case, the waste on most pieces is all sawdust, so there's less risk of throwback, but it's still a good thing to be aware of.

I started with the spindles and set my rip fence for about ⅝" and the blade height for ⁷⁄₁₆". By running the spindle through with one face against the fence, then turning it and running the opposite face against the fence, I

was certain my tenon would be centered.

When the setup was a good fit for the mortise, I attached a guide block to my miter gauge to keep my fingers away from the blade while making sure the slat didn't wobble during the cut. Two passes on each end of each spindle, and I was ready to cut the tenons to width. I readjusted my simple miter gauge jig and completed the cuts.

The final cut on the tenons defines the shoulder of the ½"-long tenons. The shoulder depth is cut using a stop block clamped onto the miter gauge as shown. Again, two passes are made on each end, then the blade depth is reset and the width passes are made. These same steps are used to form the tenons on the stretchers and aprons.

The through tenons on the front legs are made last. Again, the same three steps are used, with the final tenon size being 1½" × 1½" × 1". Before you begin sanding, cut the profile on the corbels, or arm supports, and to cut the arch on the bottom of the side stretchers. Scaled templates are provided for both on page 128. I used a band saw to make the cuts wide of the pencil lines, then I sanded many of the saw marks out with a sanding drum chucked into my drill press. Final sanding for the curved edges is done with a random orbit sander.

Another detail prior to sanding is the 45° bevel on the top front edge of the front stretcher. This attractive detail will keep your legs from going to sleep! I made the cut on the table saw, leaving a ⅜" face on the top edge.

With the sanding done, you're ready to assemble. Start with one set of side aprons and stretchers and 11 slats. Test the tenon fits for any problems, and use a chisel to adjust the fit if necessary. To assemble the side, I clamped the stretcher into my front bench vise and applied glue

The side asemblies should fit snugly, but if you force them, you'll split the wood!

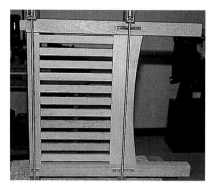

When attaching the legs to the side assembly, the best grain should face outward.

When drilling the peg holes, a piece of tape on the drill bit provides an inexpensive depth gauge.

Keep the saw blade parallel to the leg surface while cutting the peg flush.

Clamp diagonally across the chair frame, to adjust square to perfect.

Gluing on the corbels is fairly simple, but watch for glue squeeze-out.

to all the mortises. Make sure you use enough glue, but remember that too much may keep the tenon from seating all the way in. My tenon fit was tight enough to require just a little persuasion with a dead-blow hammer, but if your tenons require more than a friendly tap, you risk bulging out the thin, ⅛" sides of the mortise.

After all the tenons are seated in the stretcher, remove the piece from the vise and place the apron in the same position, and insert the slat tenons into the apron mortises.

Next, dry-fit the tenons of the assembled side into the mortises on the front and back legs. When the fit is good, glue the mortises, assemble and clamp.

DOWELING THE JOINTS
While the sides dry, drill the legs for pinning the tenons and then insert the pegs. Use masking tape to mark the ⅛" drill bit at a depth of 1½" and drill two holes at each stretcher tenon and one hole at each apron tenon.

Cut the oak pegs to 2" lengths and then sand a chamfer on one end to allow it to slip into the hole easily. After putting a small amount of glue into the peg hole, tap the peg home, making sure the peg's end grain runs opposite the grain of the leg.

A SQUARE CHAIR
After the sides are dry, use the same procedure to assemble the rear slat assembly. Then glue it and the front stretcher between the sides and clamp. You should also check for square at this time, using a clamp to adjust. If your clamps allow it, the corbels can be glued in place at this time. If you've got clamps in the way, wait till the glue on the chair frame is dry and then glue the corbels in place. It's important to center the corbel on the leg and keep the top flush with the leg top on the back leg and the tenon shoulder on the front leg.

THROUGH MORTISES IN THE ARMS
Next cut the through mortises using the router template shown on page 128. Use a table saw to make the template, and simply tack some ¾" × ¾" strips to the underside as indexing guides. These guides provide correct mortise placement, while allowing you to use only one clamp to hold the template in place during routing. (See the Shop Tip for more information on cutting the template.)

Once the template is ready, fit it over one of the arms and mark the location of the mortises. Unless you want to make two templates, you'll have to work from the underside of one of the arms, so pay attention to which side displays

prairie spindle chair
INCHES (MILLIMETERS)

REFERENCE	QUANTITY	PART	STOCK	THICKNESS	(mm)	WIDTH	(mm)	LENGTH	(mm)	COMMENTS
A	2	front legs	white oak	2	(51)	2	(51)	$29^5/_8$	(753)	
B	2	rear legs	white oak	2	(51)	2	(51)	$28^5/_8$	(727)	
C	2	arms	white oak	$^7/_8$	(22)	6	(152)	$29^1/_2$	(750)	miters one end
D	1	back top	white oak	$^7/_8$	(22)	6	(152)	34	(864)	miters both ends
E	2	front and back stretchers	white oak	$^3/_4$	(19)	5	(127)	$24^1/_2$	(623)	TBE
F	2	side stretchers	white oak	$^3/_4$	(19)	5	(127)	$23^1/_2$	(597)	TBE
G	2	side aprons	white oak	$^3/_4$	(19)	2	(51)	$23^1/_2$	(597)	TBE
H	1	back apron	white oak	$^3/_4$	(19)	2	(51)	$24^1/_2$	(623)	TBE
I	33	spindles	white oak	$^5/_8$	(16)	$1^1/_4$	(32)	$13^1/_8$	(333)	TBE
J	6	corbels	white oak	$^3/_4$	(19)	$2^1/_2$	(64)	19	(483)	
K	22	pegs	white oak			$^1/_8$	(3)	2	(51)	dowels
L	4	seat cleats	poplar	1	(25)	1	(25)	22	(559)	
M	2	seat frame pieces	poplar	$^3/_4$	(19)	2	(51)	24	(610)	bridle joint both ends
N	2	seat frame pieces	poplar	$^3/_4$	(19)	2	(51)	23	(584)	bridle joint both ends

TBE = tenons both ends

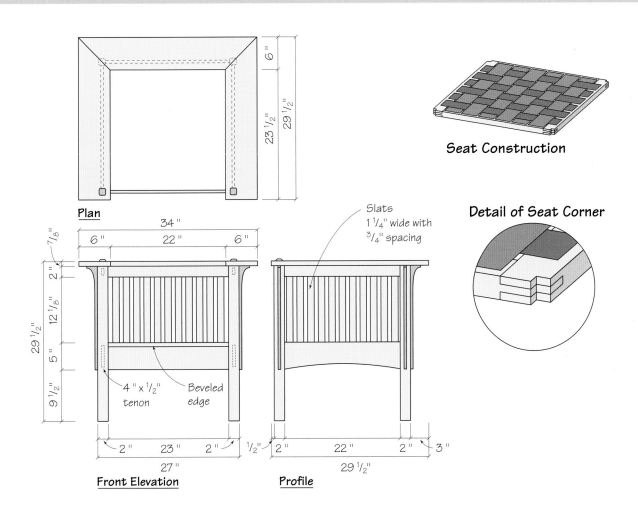

Plan

6 "

23 $^1/_2$" 29 $^1/_2$"

Seat Construction

Detail of Seat Corner

$^7/_8$"

34 "

6 " 22 " 6 "

2 "

12 $^1/_8$"

29 $^1/_2$"

5 "

9 $^1/_2$"

4 " x $^1/_2$"
tenon

Beveled
edge

2 " 23 " 2 "

27 "

Front Elevation

Slats
1 $^1/_4$" wide with
$^3/_4$" spacing

$^1/_2$" 2 " 22 " 2 " 3 "

29 $^1/_2$"

Profile

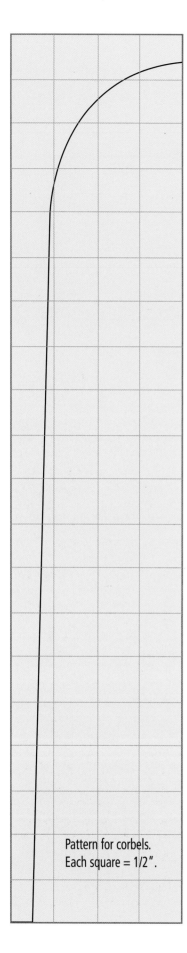

Pattern for corbels.
Each square = 1/2".

the best figure.

Use a 1⅛" boring bit chucked into the drill press to clear away most of the waste from the hole, then rout, and square out the mortises' corners using a chisel.

The 45-degree miter joints at the back corners of the arms are then glued together using biscuits to align and strengthen the joint. But before gluing, gently tap the arms into place over the tenons and mark the height of the arm on the tenon with a pencil. Then carefully remove the arms, and use a biscuit joiner and glue to fasten the mitered arm pieces together.

While these dry, bevel the top of the leg tenon by marking a square centered ⅜" in around the top of the tenon, then use a random orbit sander to form a chamfer around the top of the tenon. This gives the chair an elegant finishing touch.

FINAL ASSEMBLY

Once the arm assembly dries, apply glue to the entire top edge of the chair aprons and corbels and place the arms over the tenons.

A flush-cutting bit makes clean work of the through-mortise in the arms.

To finish the piece in an appropriate style for an Arts & Crafts piece, apply a brown aniline dye to the raw wood, then spray on a coat of lacquer, or shellac. When that has dried, apply a warm brown glaze, wiping off the excess until you have achieved a uniform color. After allowing the glaze to dry overnight, apply finishing coats of lacquer or orange shellac

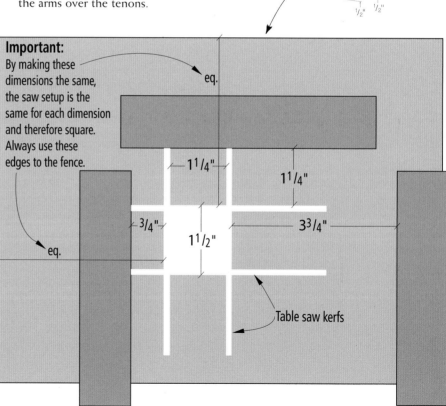

Important:
By making these dimensions the same, the saw setup is the same for each dimension and therefore square. Always use these edges to the fence.

eq.

eq.

1¼"

1¼"

3/4"

3¾"

1½"

Table saw kerfs

1/2" 1/2"

WORKING WITH AN UPHOLSTERER

If you're like most woodworkers, you use a needle only for splinter removal. So unless you're lucky enough to know a seamstress who can make the chair cushions, you'll need the services of an upholsterer.

My upholsterer recommended a web seat, as shown, with a 3"- to 4"-thick foam cushion. He suggested 1-1/2 yards of fabric that I provided, and he provided the batting and webbing material that was mounted to the frame (that I made using bridle joints at the corners for strength. I had allowed a 1/8" space around the frame (for padding and material). The photos below document the assembly of both the seat and back cushions, if you'd like to tackle the process yourself.

1. The seat cushion is shown upside down. Rubber webbing has been stapled in place on the frame. Strips of muslin have been glued to foam, which is 1" larger than the frame size.

2. The muslin has been pulled and stapled in place on the frame bottom. Begin pulling and fastening from the cneter of each side, then work toward the corners for consistency.

3. Right side up, the foam is formed by pulling and fastening muslin to give the cushion its final shape.

4. The upholstery fabric is stapled in place using the same metod as the muslin. A layer of fiberfill is simply placed between the foan and fabric to give the cushion loft and smooth and irregulariteis. Fit the fabric in the corners neatly.

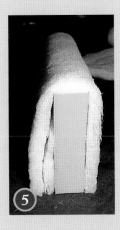

5. The back cushion is rectangluar cut foam wrapped with fiberfill.

6. The zippered back fabric is sewn with separate end pieces to give it the proper angled shape of a bolster.

Gluing the arms in place is another chance to adjust the chair for square.

for a very warm color.

We went to an upholsterer for the seat, using a simple foam cushion mounted on a flat poplar frame. The sizes for the frame are given in the Schedule of Materials. The seat is then simply dropped onto four cleats mounted to the inside of the chair frame. We also had the upholsterer work up a back cushion at the same time.

After that, the chair is ready to put to important work. Ease down, wiggle into a comfortable position and read *Popular Woodworking* while you plan your next project.

SLANT-ARM MORRIS CHAIR

The one piece of furniture most identified with
the Arts & Crafts movement is more than an icon …
it's a very comfortable reading chair!

By David Thiel

Call me lazy, but I'm a sucker for a comfortable chair.
Growing up, it was my Dad's La-Z-Boy. When he wasn't
in it, I was pulling on the handle to recline the back and
relax with a book. It's quite possible that my affinity for
Arts & Crafts furniture stems from that love of a comfortable chair.

About 1900, a number of manufacturers offered reclin-
ing-back chairs called the Morris chair (the predecessor
of the La-Z-Boy) in a variety of designs. The first Morris
chair was produced by British Arts & Crafts designer William Morris' company, Morris Co. But furniture maker and
marketing genius Gustav Stickley brought these chairs
into homes throughout the United States.

Stickley's first design was patented in 1901.
It underwent changes through the years.
Square spindles were added about 1905,
and those spindles turned into broad, flat
slats about 1909.

Stickley's chairs included pegged
through-tenons, steam-bent back rails, a variety of seat designs, and a fumed-oak finish. While
I can appreciate all the hard work that went into those
original chairs, I felt that with the technology we have
today, I could build a chair somewhat more simply, but
still just as attractive and comfortable.

The chair built here includes pegged through-tenons,
but I'll also show you a clever way to get the same (likely
even better) look without all the fuss and without sacrific-
ing strength. I also left some of the back comfort to the
cushion and opted for straight back rails, taking out hours
of work. The cushions are loose, with the seat cushion

supported by a drop-in frame that's criss-crossed with jute
webbing.

As for the finish, fuming can give a great-look-
ing finish to white oak pieces. But it can be
dangerous (toxic fumes), very time
consuming and still cause ir-
regular coloring of the
wood. Instead,
I used a

staining method we've worked on throughout the years, which gives a very good finished look and durability to the piece.

START WITH THE BEST WOOD

One of the secrets to good-looking versus average-looking Arts & Crafts furniture is wood selection. The best pieces use quartersawn white oak that offers amazing cross-grain ray flakes – adding drama and flair to what is essentially a plain furniture design. Quartersawn white oak is more expensive, but I think you'll agree that the results speak for themselves. Also, while this is a pretty large chair, a great amount of wood isn't needed to make the frame. I used about 60 board feet for this chair. That gave me plenty of room to pick the pieces with the best grain and still have lots of scrap for some smaller Arts & Crafts pieces for the future.

When you have your lumber, decide which boards will offer the best grain pattern and mark those for the arms, front and lower side rails, and side slats. Having good grain pattern on the legs is nice too, but I'll show you a trick to make that happen in a second.

If you're working with lumber in the rough and you're having difficulties determining the grain patterns, it may

By first gluing two pieces (cut from the same board) together to form the majority of the leg blank, you get two quartersawn faces. By then adding thick quartersawn veneer (also cut from the same board) to the two plain faces, you've achieved a leg with four quartersawn faces. After carefully planing the legs down to 2" × 2" size, the veneer face will be about $^1/_{16}$" thick, making it almost invisible.

■■ slant-arm morris chair
■■ INCHES (MILLIMETERS)

REFERENCE	QUANTITY	PART	STOCK	THICKNESS	(mm)	WIDTH	(mm)	LENGTH	(mm)	COMMENTS
A	2	front legs	white oak	2	(51)	2	(51)	$23^1/_2$	(597)	$1^1/_4$" × $1^1/_4$" × $^5/_8$" tenon, top
B	2	back legs	white oak	$1^3/_4$	(45)	5	(127)	20	(508)	$1^1/_4$" × 2" × $^5/_8$" tenon, top
C	1	front rail	white oak	$^7/_8$	(22)	$4^1/_2$	(114)	$27^3/_4$	(705)	$^3/_8$" × $3^1/_2$" × $3^1/_4$" TTBE
D	1	back rail	white oak	$^7/_8$	(22)	4	(102)	$27^3/_4$	(705)	$^3/_8$" × $3^1/_2$" × $2^1/_4$" TTBE
E	2	lower side rails	white oak	$^7/_8$	(22)	3	(76)	$29^1/_4$	(743)	$^3/_8$" × 2" × $2^1/_4$" TTBE
F	2	arms	white oak	1	(25)	5	(127)	37	(940)	see diagram for fitting
G	2	upper side rails	white oak	$^7/_8$	(22)	$3^1/_2$	(83)	$26^1/_4$	(667)	see diagram for fitting, $^3/_4$" TBE
H	10	side slats	white oak	$^3/_8$	(10)	$3^1/_8$	(79)	14	(356)	$^1/_4$" × $2^1/_2$" × $^1/_4$" TBE
I	4	corbels	white oak	1	(25)	2	(51)	10	(254)	
J	2	back posts	white oak	$1^1/_8$	(29)	$1^5/_8$	(41)	$29^1/_4$	(743)	
K	1	top back slat	white oak	$^3/_4$	(19)	$3^7/_8$	(98)	$20^1/_2$	(52)	$^1/_2$" × 3" × $^3/_4$"-long TBE
L	4	back slats	white oak	$^3/_8$	(10)	$3^1/_2$	(89)	16	(406)	$^1/_4$" × 2" × $^1/_2$"-long TBE
M	2	seat sides	white oak	$^3/_4$	(19)	$2^3/_4$	(70)	26	(660)	
N	2	seat front and back	white oak	$^3/_4$	(19)	$2^1/_4$	(57)	$20^1/_8$	(511)	$^3/_8$" × $1^1/_2$" × $1^1/_4$"-long TBE
O	2	seat cleats	white oak	$^3/_4$	(19)	$1^1/_4$	(32)	23	(584)	10° bevel on one length
P	2	pivot pins	white oak	$^5/_8$	(16)			$3^1/_4$	(83)	trim to fit after installation
Q	2	back stops	white oak	$^5/_8$	(16)			3	(76)	
R	2	back stops	white oak	1	(25)			$2^1/_4$	(57)	one end rounded
S	2	arm caps	white oak	$1^1/_2$	(38)	$1^1/_2$	(38)	$^1/_2$	(13)	see diagram for fitting
T		dowels/pins	white oak	$^1/_4$	(6)			48	(1219)	cut to fit

TBE=tenon both ends; TTBE=through-tenon both ends; TOE=tenon one end

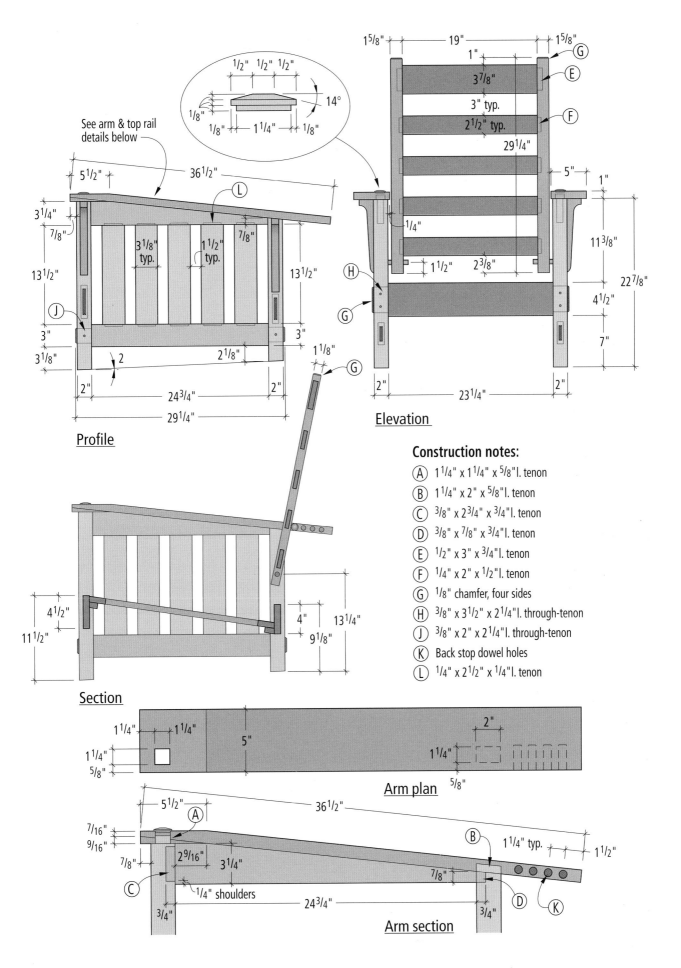

See arm & top rail details below

5 1/2" 36 1/2"
3 1/4"
7/8"
3 1/8" typ.   1 1/2" typ.
7/8"
13 1/2"   13 1/2"
J
3"   3"
3 1/8"
2   2 1/8"
2"   24 3/4"   2"
29 1/4"

1/2" 1/2" 1/2"
14°
1/8"
1/8"   1 1/4"   1/8"

Profile

1 1/8"
G

1 5/8"   19"   1 5/8"
G
1"
3 7/8"
E
3" typ.
2 1/2" typ.
F
29 1/4"
5"   1"
1/4"
11 3/8"
H
22 7/8"
G   1 1/2"   2 3/8"
4 1/2"
7"
2"   23 1/4"   2"

Elevation

4 1/2"
11 1/2"
4"   13 1/4"
9 1/8"

Section

Construction notes:

(A) 1 1/4" x 1 1/4" x 5/8" l. tenon
(B) 1 1/4" x 2" x 5/8" l. tenon
(C) 3/8" x 2 3/4" x 3/4" l. tenon
(D) 3/8" x 7/8" x 3/4" l. tenon
(E) 1/2" x 3" x 3/4" l. tenon
(F) 1/4" x 2" x 1/2" l. tenon
(G) 1/8" chamfer, four sides
(H) 3/8" x 3 1/2" x 2 1/4" l. through-tenon
(J) 3/8" x 2" x 2 1/4" l. through-tenon
(K) Back stop dowel holes
(L) 1/4" x 2 1/2" x 1/4" l. tenon

1 1/4"   1 1/4"
5"   2"
1 1/4"
1 1/4"
5/8"
1 1/4"
5/8"

Arm plan

5 1/2"   36 1/2"
A
7/16"
9/16"   B   1 1/4" typ.   1 1/2"
7/8"
2 9/16"
3 1/4"
7/8"
C   1/4" shoulders
3/4"   24 3/4"   3/4"
D
K

Arm section

A hollow-chisel mortiser makes quick work of the through-mortises. A backing board underneath the legs reduces the tear-out on the exit side of the mortise. While you can use a router to create mortises, a through-mortise of this size will tax a router motor and will require routing from both sides, adding concerns about alignment. A better alternative would be to use a drill press to drill a connected series of holes, then square out the mortise with a sharp chisel.

be beneficial to run the boards through your planer to knock the rough surface off to see the grain more clearly.

LOVE THOSE LEGS

Legs on Morris chairs have been made dozens of ways throughout the years. Because the ray flake only will appear on the quartersawn sides of the board, a square leg will only give two opposing striking sides. To improve this, some people have glued-up the legs from four mitered pieces and joined them with what we would recognize as a lock-miter

joint today. This does a nice job of providing dramatic grain, but if you're planning a true through-tenon in the arms, the mitered version leaves a hollow center.

I chose Stickley's method – veneer. By cutting the legs and the veneer to cover the non-quartersawn sides of the legs from the same section of board, the legs look like they're quartersawn on all four sides – a nice trick.

Start by ripping the two leg-halves slightly over width and length, and glue them together. When the glue has cured, run one glued edge over the jointer, then plane the

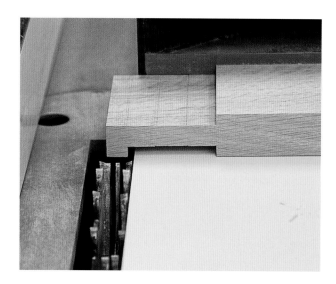

Making the through-tenons is simple, repetitive table-saw work. Using a dado stack and a miter sled, use the rip fence on your first pass to define the shoulder of the tenon. Then simply back the piece away from the fence to nibble off the rest of the cheek cut. Flip the piece (or turn the other cheek) and repeat for the opposite side. Check the tenon's fit in your already-cut mortise to make sure it's a snug fit. It's easier to take a little wood off the tenon than to put it back on. Then do the same on the other end of the rail. To make the shoulder cuts, repeat the process, adjusting the dado height to fit the tenons in the mortises.

Though you can mark the taper on the upper side rails using the information in the diagrams, it's a good idea to check it against the actual chair. This will ensure that the taper ends at the shoulder of the tenon on the back leg.

opposite edge to form, not a square leg, but one that is 1⁷⁄₈" on the non-glue seam face and 2" (or 2⅛") on the glue seam face. Then plane the veneer pieces to ⅛" (or thicker if you're more comfortable that way) and glue those pieces to the seamed faces.

Once again, with the glue cured, head back to the planer and run the leg down to 2" square. Make sure you take evenly from the veneer sides to leave equal amounts of veneer on each side. Then cut the legs to length. Now it's time to do some measuring.

LAYING OUT THE MORTISES

As I mentioned earlier, you can make this chair with true through-tenons or cheat a little – your choice. I did both, making the leg tenons true through-mortises, while the leg/arm tenons are fake. Use the article, "Through-tenon Caps" on the following page to help decide which method you want to use.

Regardless of which method you choose, the locations of the mortises are the same. Use the diagrams to locate the mortises and mark them on the appropriate faces of the legs. While you're at it, mark the locations of the tenons at the tops of the legs as well. The diagrams will help here. Note that the front leg tenon is a complete, four-shouldered tenon, while the back leg tenon is shouldered only on the inside and outside. You could put a shoulder on all four sides, but nobody will see them, and it's a lot of extra work. With

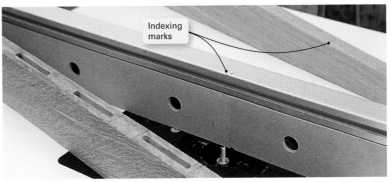

While you could use a mortiser to create the ¼"-wide mortises in the upper and lower rails for the side slats, a router works well and leaves a clean hole. By making indexing marks (indicating the infeed and outfeed sides of the bit) on the router table fence and on the back side of the rails, I'm able to stop and start my plunge cuts accurately. Make your mortises in multiple passes. A ¼" bit is pretty small and any unnecessary stress will send you to the store for a new bit.

I used a combination blade in my table saw to make the relatively short tenons on the back rails. This required three or four passes over the tenon and left a "ridged" appearance on the tenon. I took advantage of this and made the tenons slightly over-thickness, then used a shoulder plane to hand-fit the tenons to the mortises. I guess that's what they call making lemonade out of lemons.

THROUGH-TENON CAPS

Rather than fuss with actual through-tenons, a slightly oversized (1/8") through-tenon cap will give the same look but save time and effort. By using a wood blank and making the cuts shown below on both ends of the blank, caps are made very quickly. This works not only for the leg through-tenons, but also the rail through-tenons in the legs.

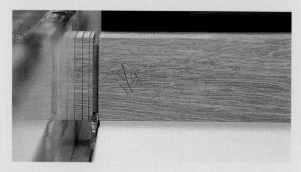

With the blade set to the 1/8" height, define the very bottom of the cap on all four sides.

Shift the rip fence 1/8" to the left to "lengthen" the tenon of the cap.

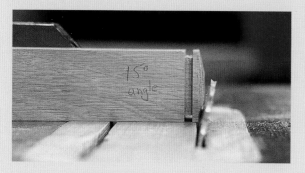

Next, with the rip fence and sled out of the way, set the blade to a 14° bevel and bevel the top of the cap to leave an 1/8" side.

Finally part the cap from the blank. Watch your fall-off so it falls clear of the blade!

everything marked, check them again. This isn't a place you want to make a mistake.

Note that the upper side rails don't have through-tenons, only blind tenons. The mortise needs to be only 1/16" deeper than the tenon length to allow for glue space and to make sure the tenon doesn't bottom out before the shoulder is tight against the leg.

I used a 3/8" hollow-chisel mortiser to make my mortises. If you don't have a hollow-chisel mortiser you can use a drill press to bore out most of the waste material. Simply clean up the edges with a sharp chisel.

THROUGH-TENONS

Next, grab one of the legs and head to the table saw. To cut the tenons on the rails I used a dado stack, a miter sled and a rip fence. By cutting the cheeks of the tenon oversized to start, I was able to edge up to the appropriate thickness, checking the tenon in the actual mortise as I went.

When your first tenon is the correct thickness, go ahead and cut the rest of them, then reset the saw to trim the tenons to width, again checking the fit as you go. Use the same technique to form the tenons on the tops of the front and rear legs.

If you don't have a dado stack, you also can use a standard combination blade in your saw and make repeated passes to remove the material. It's slower, but still works. I actually have found the ribbed face left on the tenon by a single blade can make fitting the tenon very easy. Cut the tenon over-size then simply plane the high points off the ridges with a shoulder plane to fine-fit the tenon.

PUTTING A SLANT ON THINGS

You're almost done with the rails, but before you can actually fit the upper side rails, you need to cut a taper on each upper side rail. First dry-fit the chair except for the upper side rails, clamping the chair frame to pull the joints tight.

With the chair dry-assembled (right) you get a good look at the through-tenons and a good sense of the structure of the chair. To finish off the look of the through-tenons, I first marked how much the tenon protruded from the mortise (this should be $1/4$" in all cases) then marked an $1/8$" line around the end of each tenon. I then used a file to simply chamfer the ends of the tenon (below) at an approximate 45° angle. Push towards the end of the tenon on all four sides to avoid tear-out or splintering.

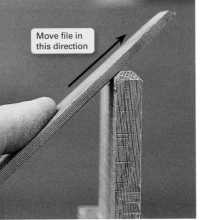

Move file in this direction

Here's very clever way to make the slanted arm. The arm at right has had the wedge cut from the front of the arm on the band saw. The arm on the left shows the wedge moved to the underside of the arm, completing the slant. You'll lose a $1/16$" of thickness at the front of the arm, but it's hardly noticeable and the finished arms have a nearly seamless grain match.

Then slip the upper side rail into the front mortise (if possible) and use the diagrams on page 51 and a straight edge to lay out the taper. Then cut the taper on the band saw and you can go ahead and fit the rear tenons.

You're still not done with the frame. The next step is to mark and make the mortises for the side slats. Because the side slats are $3/8$" thick, that leaves room for only a thin ($1/4$") tenon. These tenons don't need to be very long. I used my router table to make the mortise in the upper and lower side rails, marking the stop and start locations on both the pieces and the fence of the router table.

With the mortises complete, it's time to head back to the saw for a few minutes to cut the tenons on the side slats. To do this, use the same technique you did for the upper side rails.

To make the back, use the diagrams to mark the mortise locations, then go ahead and cut the mortises and tenons.

CAPS OR THE REAL THING?

If you've opted for real through-tenons, mark the tenons where they exit the mortises, then mark and file the bevels to finish off the through-tenons. Otherwise, look at the story "Through-tenon Caps" at left to make the tenon caps and dry-fit them in the legs.

SLICK SLANT ARMS

Stickley used three types of arms on his Morris chairs: a flat arm, a bowed arm (making a gentle arch over the chair side) and the slant arm. For some reason the slant arm always struck me as most comfortable. Besides, the slope is just slight enough that you can still balance a cool drink on the arm.

The way the arm is cut to form the slant is Stickley traditional. The arm is formed from a single piece of wood. A wedge shape is marked out on the side of the top of the arm, then it is cut away on the band saw. That same wedge is then reglued in place underneath the arm, forming the slant.

You lose a little thickness in the front part of the arm, but a good blade in your band saw will make this fairly simple. The joint practically disappears and the wood transition on the top of the arm is seamless. It's a cool trick. Use the photo above to help you lay out the wedge shape on the arm.

With the arms slanted, it's time to make mortises in the arm. Mark the tenon location on the top of the arms using the diagrams.

The through-mortises are made by first using a $1/2$" drill bit to make clearance holes at two opposing corners. Then simply use a jigsaw to connect the dots.

After marking the through-mortise location on the arms, I used a ½" drill bit to make access holes through the arm at opposite corners of the mortise location (left). Then I used a jigsaw to connect the holes, making a reasonably square and clean hole (right). Happily, because I was using tenon caps to face the through-tenon look, the mortise only needs to fit the stub tenon and not be perfect when viewed from the top of the arm.

The rear blind mortise is easily located by slipping the front mortise over the front tenon, then clamping the arm in place, holding the overhang spaced correctly to the inside of the arm. Then use a pencil to mark the exact location of the mortise.

I used a plunge router free-hand to cut out the rear mortises. I'm very comfortable with a router and this free-hand operation wasn't difficult, but you can also use an edge guide to ensure an accurate cut.

NO GLUE YET!

While I know you're antsy to glue something together, you're not ready yet. You need to disassemble the frame and

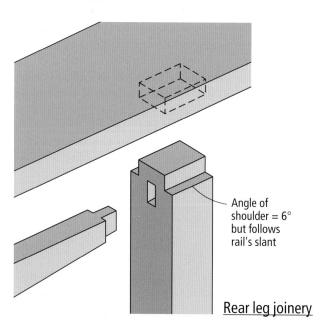

Angle of
shoulder = 6°
but follows
rail's slant

Rear leg joinery

mark the locations on the two rear legs for the pivot holes for the back. Also mark the pivot location on the back posts, then head to the drill press and use a Forstner bit to drill the holes. While you're at the drill press, use the diagrams to mark the locations on the arms for the back stop holes and drill them as well. You should be able to dry-assemble the chair and slip a couple of dowels into the back now and get a good look at how everything's fitting together.

PUTTING ON THE GLUE

If everything seems to be fitting fine, you're almost ready to glue things up. But first, before you disassemble the chair, mark the angle on each of the leg bottoms that is keeping the chair from sitting flat. It should be no more that an ⅛" offset and should only require a 2° trim on the table saw.

Disassemble the chair, then head to the saw and trim the leg bottoms. Pay attention to the length of the front legs (which should be the same) and the back legs (which should be the same).

With the legs trimmed you're in for some sanding. But do it now, because it's a lot more difficult once everything is assembled. I worked up through 150-grit sandpaper, then got things organized for gluing up the chair.

Start with the two sides, first gluing the slats between the upper and lower side rails. Clamp across the rails, then go ahead and insert the rail assembly into the leg mortises. As you clamp up each side, align the upper side rail with the tenon shoulders on the front and rear legs. This will allow gluing contact along the full length of the underside of the arm. Glue both sides, then set them aside.

While the glue is curing, cut the frame pieces for the seat, and cut mortises and tenons to assemble the frame.

With the arm slipped in place over the front leg tenon, I clamped the arm in position with the appropriate interior overhang and marked the actual location of the rear tenon. I then routed the oversized mortise (using multiple depth-settings to achieve final depth) just short of the pencil lines and used a chisel to clean up the edges (below right).

Rout oversize to accommodate tenon angle

You could make the frame with a more simple joint, but honestly this is where a lot of your weight will be focused so making a strong frame is a good idea.

Take the side assemblies out of the clamps, but keep them handy. Glue the front and rear rails between the two sides. Measure between the legs at the top and bottom of the legs to make sure everything is square. If you've got a couple extra clamps, go ahead and glue up the back frame at this time as well.

While the glue is curing, slip the arms in place on the leg tenons and then go ahead and make the arm caps, fitting them in place in the arms. After sanding the arms, glue the caps in place, too.

You're now ready to fit the seat into the frame. The seat rests on two cleats mounted to the inside of the front and back rails. Both cleats are cut longways at a 10° angle, then screwed in place on the rails. The rear cleat is mounted flush to the bottom of the back rail, while the front cleat is held down ⅞" from the top of the rail to allow space for the seat frame, and a little extra room.

With the seat frame free of the clamps and sanded, the front and rear edges also should be trimmed at a 10° angle and fit onto the cleat to produce an easy fit.

FINAL DETAILS

You're almost down to the wire. There are a couple final details to finish, including the corbels (the arm supports) and the back support pegs. Use the diagram at right to cut and shape the corbels from some ¾"-thick stock. A band saw and oscillating spindle sander make quick work of these pieces.

With the arms clamped in place on the chair, fit the corbels to the legs (the rear corbels need to be beveled to match the slope of the arm), then glue the corbels to the leg, making sure their top edge is flush to the leg tenon shoulder and the underside of the arm.

You might be tempted to glue the arms on at this point, but the chair is much easier to finish with the arms loose.

Turn to the back stops and use the diagrams to cut and drill the 1"- and ⅝"-diameter dowels to form the stops. Round over the end using a sander or by hand sanding. While you're working with the ⅝" dowel stock, mark and cut the two dowels that will make the pivots for the back. The dowels should finish flush, or slightly recessed in the holes in the back, with ¼" of space on either side of the back, between the arms. The back also should stay loose, again to make finishing easier.

As a last step, drill and cut lengths of ¼" dowel rod to peg the through-tenons on the frame. I used two pegs on the front and rear of the legs for each joint, and a single peg in each of the side joints. Make sure you drill through past the tenon, but not all the way through the leg. To make it easier to get the pegs all the way into the holes, I used an electric pencil sharpener to chamfer the leading end of each dowel. Add some glue, then pound the pegs home. Use a flush-set trim saw to cut the pegs flush to the legs. Sanding finishes the job.

READY FOR FINISHING

With everything finish-sanded, it's time to stain. As I mentioned earlier, Stickley used ammonia to fume his furniture. We've come very close to his finish using aniline dye, brown glaze and a topcoat of lacquer.

I used a water-based amber maple dye from J.E. Moser to put the first layer of color on the chair. Because the dye is water-based, I first wet a rag with water and wiped the entire chair down, just dampening the surface. After the water had evaporated, I went back over the chair with 220-grit sandpaper to knock down the raised grain. By pre-wetting the chair, the grain is raised hardly at all when the dye is applied.

Before dying, take some masking tape and cover the locations on the arms where glue still needs to be applied. This tape

Here you can see the essence of the "reclining" chair. The four evenly spaced holes in the rear of the arm allow you to move the back stop to whatever location is most comfortable for your sitting needs. It can't get much simpler than that.

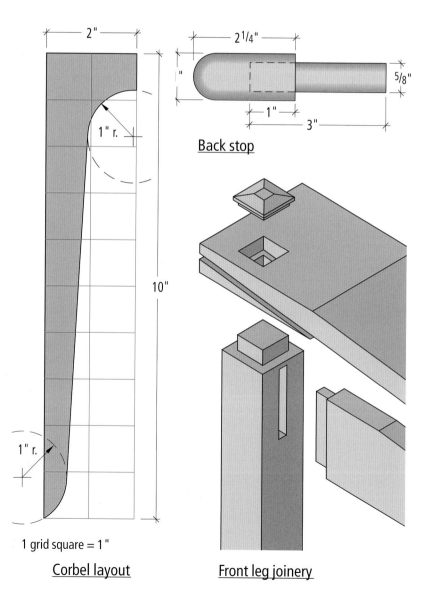

Back stop

1 grid square = 1"

Corbel layout   **Front leg joinery**

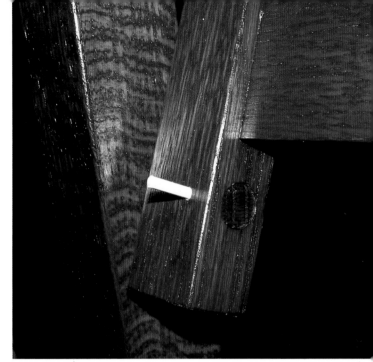

Pegging the through-tenon joints adds a nice expressed-joinery look to the piece, but also adds extra strength to the joint itself. The pegs are hammered home into the hole, then cut flush to the surface of the leg. By using a saw with little or no set to the teeth, you avoid scratching the face of the leg too much. If you don't have such a saw, slip a piece of paper between the leg and the saw. It'll save you some frustrating sanding.

To assemble the back to the chair, drill a hole through the back post and into the pivot dowel. Next a $1/8$" dowel pin is glued in place. The dowel at right was cut to the exact length of the hole and is just started in the hole. When slid all the way in, it will be flush to the surface of the post and a brown marker will blend the end of the dowel to match the post. If the back ever needs to be removed, the pin can be drilled out, and the pivot dowel easily removed.

will stay in place until after the final finish coat. Once removed, the arms can be glued in place with a sure bond unaffected by the finish.

After the dye has dried overnight, apply the brown glaze, letting the color infuse the grain and slightly color the chair, but wipe off the excess glaze or it will hide the grain. Again, let the piece dry overnight, then you're ready for a couple coats of lacquer.

Conveniently, because all the surfaces on the chair are fairly small in surface area, I was able to use a commercially available lacquer in a spray can to finish the chair. While you still need a well-ventilated finishing area, no other equipment but the spray cans are necessary.

With the finish complete, strip the tape off and glue the arms in place. Be careful clamping across the finish. It can take days for the lacquer to cure completely.

Next, put the back in place and slide the pivot dowels into the holes. The back should be located to allow $1/4$" clearance on either side. To fix the back location, drill a single $1/8$"-diameter hole through the inside surface of each back post, pegging the dowel. While this is a simple way to fix the back, it's invisible once the cushion is in place, and if necessary, it can be drilled out to remove the back at a later date.

Slip the back stops in place and the chair is nearly done.

COMFY CUSHIONS
Depending on your comfort level with a needle and thread or a sewing machine, you may want to opt for a professional

Interwoven jute webbing, nailed to the seat frame with upholstery tacks, serves to support the seat cushion.

upholsterer to add the loose seat and back cushions. To support the seat cushion, I attached interwoven lengths of jute webbing to the seat frame using upholstery tacks (see above). The cushions are boxed-corner pillows and can be made at home. The back pillow has loops attached at the top that slip over the top of the back posts to hold the cushion in place.

That's all there is to building the comfiest reading chair I know. It's also one of the most stylish chairs I own, and I can stare at the amazing grain for hours. Enjoy.

STICKLEY OTTOMAN

After half a dozen Morris chair plans, we decided it was time to help you put your feet up and relax.

By David Thiel

A Morris chair (heck, almost any chair) just isn't complete without an ottoman to prop your feet on. Sadly, by the time you finish building the chair you're usually so glad to have completed the project that the ottoman gets delayed until later. Well, now is the time!

Over the years we've published a number of plans for Morris chairs in *Popular Woodworking* in varying styles and by several designers. After looking at dozens of comparable ottomans, we selected a traditional and simple design from Gustav Stickley.

The #300 ottoman we used as a model is one of Stickley's earlier pieces. Originally offered with a hard leather seat, it sold for $7.50 in the 1912 catalog. Recent auctions have seen this simple piece sell for as much as $800.

The dimensions on our project match Stickley's, but we've updated the seat material to adjust the cost (as well as to make it a little more comfortable).

HOW TO BUILD IT

As far as furniture projects go, this one is basic. But it does give you a chance to work on a hallmark joint of Arts & Crafts furniture — the mortise and tenon.

There are four mortises per leg, but for the first-time builder the construction method used is very forgiving. The blind tenons, including the ones in the top rail joints (which ultimately are hidden by the upholstery) easy.

If you opt for "one-piece" legs without adding veneer, choose the best grain pattern to face "forward." Take a close look at the grain on the pieces for your legs and mark the tops to offer the best look.

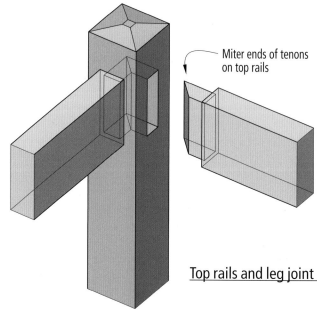

Miter ends of tenons on top rails

Top rails and leg joint

The simplicity of the mortise-and-tenon joint is spruced up a little on this piece with the addition of pegs, which make the joints more solid and add a nice decorative touch.

The more significant step only sharp-eyed woodworkers will notice at first is to make the legs from multiple pieces of wood. By doing so, the highly figured quartersawn white oak shows on all four sides. Mother Nature hasn't figured out how to do this yet, but we have.

Also, if upholstery is something that has kept you from trying this type of project before, don't sweat it. I'm hardly an upholsterer myself, and everyone who has seen my ottoman seems to think it turned out pretty well, so we've included a short story about the upholstery (see "Upholstery Made Easy" on page 147).

FOUR-FACED LEGS

Quartersawn white oak is one of the features that dresses up the plain styling of Arts & Crafts furniture. Cut from the center of the log out to the bark, the orientation of the growth rings runs almost perfectly perpendicular to the face of the board. This reveals splashes of "ray flake" that are beautiful to behold, but they only happen on the perpendicular faces.

There are a couple of good ways to give the legs this ray flake on all four faces, but Stickley chose to simply add quartersawn veneer to the two flatsawn faces, which I copied.

Start making the legs by cutting eight leg halves that are $7/8$" × 2" × 16". The $7/8$" thickness will require you to start with 4/4 rough lumber, but ultimately the oversized dimensions will be to your benefit, as you'll see.

First, glue each of the four leg pairs together, face-to-face, orienting the best quartersawn grain pattern to the outside. When the glue has dried, square one corner of each piece on the jointer, then size each leg (using your table saw, then your jointer for a final pass) to $1 5/8$" (across the face that shows a seam) × $1 3/8$" or slightly larger (across the quartersawn face).

These dimensions will allow you to add $1/8$"-thick veneer to the two layered faces, then run the entire leg down to $1 1/2$" square, leaving an almost invisible veneer face on two sides.

Next, run eight veneer pieces to $1/8$" × $1 3/4$" × 16". If $1/8$" is thinner than you're comfortable running on your planer, leave it at $1/4$" — just know that you'll have to plane more off those faces after glue-up. Glue the veneer pieces to the leg blanks, making sure the veneer extends over all the edges.

After the glue has dried, trim the veneer pieces flush to the leg centers (I used a No. 3 hand plane). Then run the veneer faces through the planer (alternating sides on each

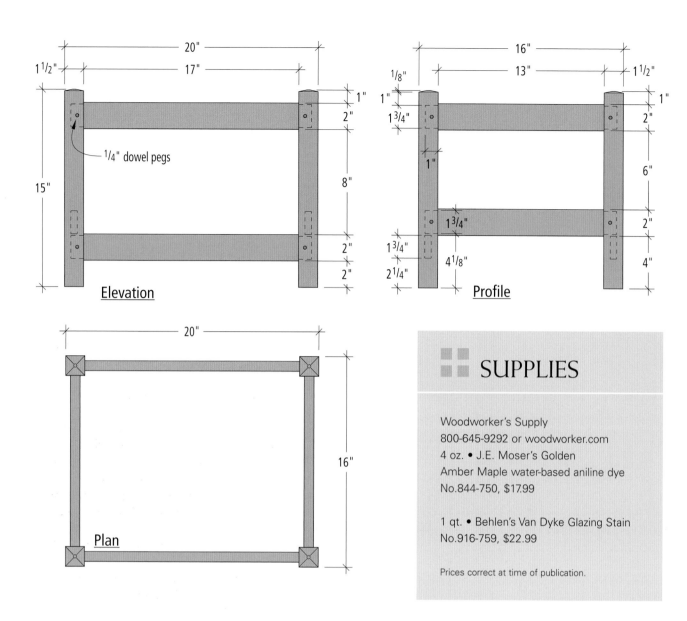

Elevation

Profile

Plan

pass) until the leg is 1½" square. Trim the legs to length for a four-faced leg.

MAKING THE HOLES

The next step is to find where you want the mortises to be on the legs. First determine the orientation of the legs (best faces out), then use the illustrations above to mark the mortise locations.

The mortises can be ⅜" wide, and that's fine, but to be honest with you, I had a ½" mortise chisel in my mortiser, so that's where they ended up. I cut the mortises 1¹⁄₁₆" deep to allow an extra ¹⁄₁₆" for glue squeeze-out. Cut the mortises, then be sure to clean the chips out of the bottoms so the tenons will seat properly.

FILLING THE HOLES

I cut my tenons on the table saw with a single combination blade. If you have a dado stack on hand, use it. A dado stack will allow you to cut your tenons faster.

Because my mortises are ½" wide, all of the shoulders on my tenons are ⅛". This makes it unnecessary to change the blade height when moving from face to edge shoulders.

Because the top rails are all at the same height on the legs, the tenons will bump into each other before fully seating against the leg. Take a minute to miter the ends of the tenons on the top rails so they can meet without interfering with the fit. Because the lower rails are staggered in height, this isn't a problem.

With all the tenons cut, test-fit the ottoman. Assemble both ends, then insert the longer rails between the two assemblies. The tenons should require a little wiggling to slip all the way into the mortises, but you shouldn't have to bang on them with a hammer. Check to be sure that all the shoulders fit flush against the legs without any gaps. When all the joints are acceptable, go ahead and disassemble the frame.

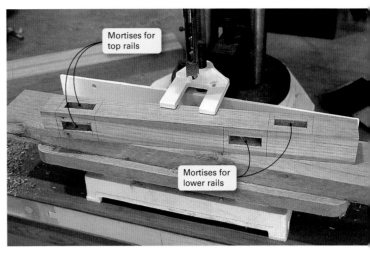

Mortises for top rails

Mortises for lower rails

To offer four faces with quartersawn white oak on each leg, the leg centers are glued then planed to 1⅝" × 1⅜". Then the ⅛" or ¼" oversize "skins" of quartersawn veneer are glued to the flat-sawn faces. After the glue dries, plane the legs to their finished 1½" × 1½" dimension.

The mortises for the top rails are on adjacent inside faces and intersect in the middle of the leg. The mortises for the lower rails are staggered to fit one on top of the other. I used a benchtop hollow-chisel mortiser to make quick work of the mortises, but a router (or even a chisel and mallet) will work just as well.

TOPPING THE LEGS

When laying out the mortise locations on the legs, you will probably notice that the top rails will sit 1" short of the tops of the legs. Don't freak out – you didn't do anything wrong. This extra space leaves room for the upholstery material and space for you to bevel the tops to dress them up a little.

Dig through your toolbox for a combination square or other similar tool that will help you mark a line ⅛" down from the top of the leg on all four faces.

Then set your disc sander's table to a 12° angle and, using a miter gauge on the sander, slowly bevel the tops of the legs on all four sides. This will leave a ¼" × ¼" square at the top. This bevel is a great detail.

STEEL EDGE OR MINERAL GRIT?

Now is the appropriate time to smooth the wood to the surface finish that you prefer. While we'll often just tell

you to sand using 100 to 220 grits, there is another option here.

Because of the possible dramatic effect of the grain in the quartersawn white oak, preparing the wood to best present the grain is important. When you sand wood you effectively tear the ends of the fibers to smooth the wood surface. This leaves a feathery end to the grain structure and can obscure the grain pattern and affect the way the wood takes a stain.

A better method for this project is to cut the ends of the fibers using a hand scraper or scraper plane. With a little extra effort (and a lot less dust) you can leave crisp ends on the fibers that will really let the ray flake pop when you add the finish.

READY FOR ASSEMBLY

With all the pieces test-fit and sanded (or scraped), you're ready to put the ottoman together.

stickley ottoman
INCHES (MILLIMETERS)

REFERENCE	QUANTITY	PART	STOCK	THICKNESS	(mm)	WIDTH	(mm)	LENGTH	(mm)	COMMENTS
A	4	legs	white oak	1½	(38)	1½	(38)	15	(381)	For solid legs. For build-up dimensions, see page 143.
B	2	lower rails	white oak	¾	(19)	2	(51)	19	(483)	1" TBE
C	2	lower rails	white oak	¾	(19)	2	(51)	15	(381)	1" TBE
D	2	top rails	poplar	¾	(19)	2	(51)	19	(483)	1" TBE, mitered
E	2	top rails	poplar	¾	(19)	2	(51)	15	(381)	1" TBE, mitered

TBE = tenons both ends

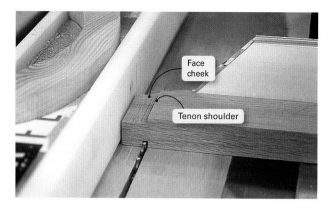

The shoulders for all the rail tenons are made with little fuss on the table saw. Define the shoulder on the first pass using a miter gauge for support, then nibble the rest of the material away, backing the piece away from the rip fence.

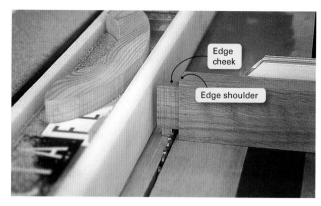

Cut the adjacent shoulders and cheeks in the same manner. I'm using a combination blade here, which leaves a corduroy-like finish on the cheeks. Because of that, I've left the tenons oversized and will use a shoulder plane to pare them to fit.

Just as with the test run, assemble the ends first, applying glue to the inside of the mortises, lightly covering all four walls. Applying the glue to the mortise rather than the tenon will keep glue squeeze-out (and clean up) to a minimum.

With the ends assembled and clamped, go ahead and insert the long rails and clamp them as well. You're nearly done.

A BUNCH OF PEGS

The last detail before finishing is to peg all the tenons. I use ¼" red oak dowel stock for this step. You can use white oak, but the white oak dowels are harder to find at the store, and the red oak makes the pegs stand out a bit more on the leg once color is applied.

Chuck a ¼"-diameter bit into your drill and use a drill stop collar or a piece of tape to make the 1" depth neces-

One of the most visible details on the ottoman is the shallow bevel on the leg tops. You could make the cuts using a table saw or miter saw, but I took advantage of a benchtop disc sander that let me fine-tune the bevels as I went.

sary to drill through the tenon and into the opposite wall of the mortise.

Mark all the peg locations, then start drilling. You can peg the holes as you go (add the glue to the hole, not the peg) or wait until all the holes are drilled before starting to glue.

Cut all the pegs ¼" longer than the depth of your holes. Then, when the peg is fully seated in the hole, trim the excess with a flush-cut saw with little or no set to the teeth. If you don't have such a saw, slide a piece of cardboard under the blade to keep from scratching the face of the leg. Do a little more sanding or scraping around the pegs and you're ready to break out the dye.

COLOR ME NUTTY BROWN

As mentioned, quartersawn white oak can be amazing to look at, but a finish designed to enhance the wood helps a lot.

I use a water-based aniline dye to put the first layer of color on the wood. Because the dye is water-based, it will raise the grain when applied. So to prepare the wood for finishing, I first wipe down the entire piece with a damp cloth (just water) then hand-sand the piece with 220-grit paper to knock off the burrs.

Next, add the aniline dye and let it dry overnight. Then it's time for a coat of brown glaze. The glaze is a stain, but it's the consistency of thin pudding and will lay on the wood and fill the grain slightly. Let the color infuse the grain, but be sure to wipe off the excess or it will hide the wood.

Let the glaze dry overnight again, then you're ready for your favorite clear, protective top coat. With a project this size, I often use lacquer in a spray can with good results. The rest is upholstery. Use the story opposite to help you through these steps.

Then you're ready to put your feet up and relax.

UPHOLSTERY MADE EASY

If you've been waiting to tackle a first upholstery project, this is a simple one. All you need are a few yards of black muslin (or similar material), some foam block, batting and a finished cover of your choice.

You can find all the materials you need to upholster furniture at your local craft-supply store or fabric store. I bought all of my materials at a local Michael's.

As you can see, I used my pneumatic stapler (a wide-crown is great if you have one, but narrow-crown will work in a pinch), but you can use standard upholstery tacks as well. The photos walk you through all the steps except the finished cover, which is the same process as used in attaching the last batting layer (shown in photo 4).

Start by mitering the corners of the muslin around the legs and tacking the edges to the inside of the rails, tightening the material as you go.

Cut out the corners of the batting sheet and wrap it around the legs and rails, tightening as you go. Tack the batting to the inside of the rails.

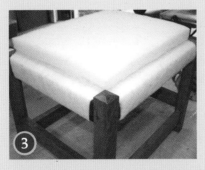

A layer of 2" foam will add cushion. The piece should be cut to fit just inside the rails and will lay in place on the first batting layer.

A second layer of batting holds the foam in place. It is cut and attached exactly as the first layer, but keep tightening the material to maintain a uniform look.

A top layer of muslin covers the batting and foam. The corners are miter-cut, then folded around the legs to avoid loose strings and unraveling.

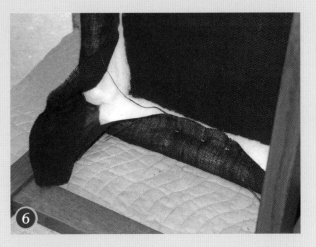

The final muslin layer is tucked around the rail and tacked at the center. Then work out towards the legs, rolling and tacking as necessary. Trim any excess.

ARTS & CRAFTS BRIDAL CHEST

Contrasting woods highlight the elegant lines of this Gustav Stickley-designed classic.

By Robert W. Lang

In days gone by, a chest similar to this would contain a bride's dowry. The form goes back to Gothic times, but this is an adaptation of a Gustav Stickley piece from 1901. Admiring the lines of this piece, I was curious to see how the design would look with contrasting materials, not the usual Craftsman dark oak. The panels are quilted bird's eye maple, and the other parts are Jatoba, also known as Brazilian cherry.

The original was made of quartersawn white oak with wrought-iron braces on the corners. What makes this unusual for a Stickley design are the decorative corbels on the panels. These also appeared on a few dining room case pieces made in the early 1900s.

Decorative curved elements in Stickley furniture are usually associated with Harvey Ellis, who worked for Stickley in 1903. This design appeared well before Ellis worked for Stickley, and before Stickley wrote against using purely decorative elements in his furniture catalogs.

Stickley doesn't always get the credit he deserves as a furniture designer. Building this bridal chest with non-traditional materials takes his design out of the Craftsman context, and shows Stickley's remarkable sense of line, proportion and texture.

In many of the original bridal chests I have seen, the center panels have cracked. I think the corbels are the culprits, keeping the solid-wood panels from expanding and contracting in the grooves of the stiles. To avoid this problem, I decided to use veneered panels. The veneer is on a core of ½"-thick medium-density fiberboard (MDF), and the backing veneer is sycamore, a less-expensive alternative to the figured faces.

The veneer on the wider center and end panels is bookmatched. I pressed the panels one at a time in a simple shop-made cold press, and worked on the chest's solid-wood components while the glue on the panels was curing.

If you think of this chest as a simple box, most of the work is in the five paneled assemblies: the front and back, two ends and the top. The panel assemblies are joined with mortises and tenons, and each of the four legs is really two stiles with the long edges mitered together.

I fabricated all of the stiles and rails, and then dry-fit each of the panel assemblies before cutting and assembling the miter joints that connect the legs.

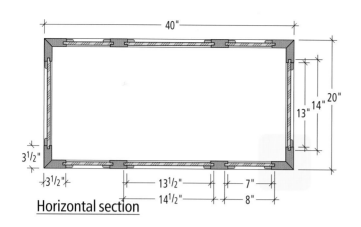

Horizontal section

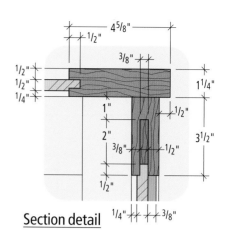

Section detail

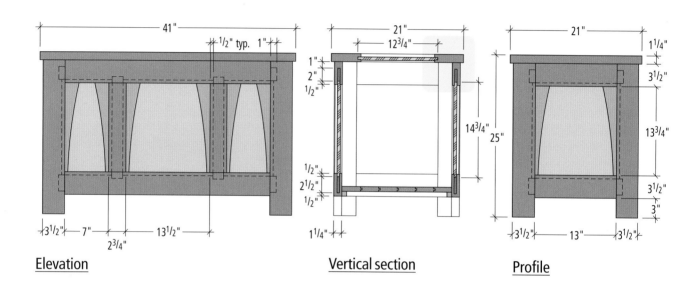

Elevation

Vertical section

Profile

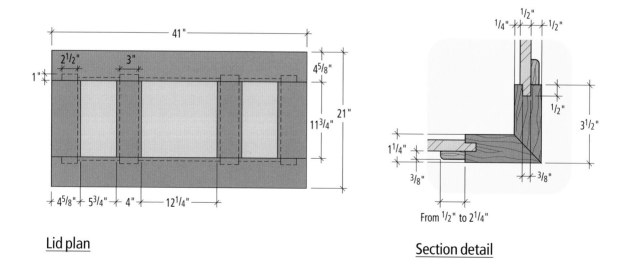

Lid plan

Section detail

From 1/2" to 2 1/4"

MANAGING BITS AND PIECES

This isn't really a difficult project to build; the hardest part is keeping track of what piece goes where. The applied corbels make it necessary for the panel grooves to be off-center on the edges of the stiles and rails. As I cut the parts I decided where they would go in the finished chest, and marked each one with a lumber crayon. As I worked on the joints I paid close attention to which face of each part was the outside piece.

After cutting the panel parts to size, I grouped four of the leg pieces together and marked them out as left-handed pieces, using a story pole to transfer the measurements. I then laid out the other four leg pieces as right-handed, marking the locations of the grooves for the panels and the mortises that hold the stiles and rails together.

The mortises are the same width as, and in line with, the grooves that capture the panels. These ⅜"-wide grooves are set ½" back from the outside face of the stiles and rails, so I had to be careful to keep all the parts oriented correctly as I milled the grooves.

I cut the stopped grooves with a stack dado set on the table saw, carefully lowering and raising the legs on and off the cutters. Because the mortises fall in the ends of the grooves, the exact length of the grooves isn't critical. The grooves in the rails and in the intermediate stiles run the full length of those parts. After milling all the grooves, I began making mortises with my hollow-chisel mortiser,

The mortiser is set with the chisel flush with the panel groove. Plunge the bit and chisel to make distinct holes, then come back and clean up the waste in between.

setting the distance from the fence to the chisel to match the location of the groove.

The tenons were cut with a stack dado set on the table saw, and then trimmed to a piston fit with a shoulder plane. With the individual panels dry-assembled, I made sure that the faces of the joints were flush with a few swipes of my smoothing plane.

GETTING READY TO ASSEMBLE

I cut the veneered panels to their final size, and then milled a rabbet on the back of each panel using the router

arts & crafts bridal chest
INCHES (MILLIMETERS)

REFERENCE	QUANTITY	PART	STOCK	THICKNESS	(mm)	WIDTH	(mm)	LENGTH	(mm)	COMMENTS
A	2	top stiles	jatoba	1¼	(32)	4⅝	(117)	41	(1041)	
B	2	top end rails	jatoba	1¼	(32)	4⅝	(117)	13¾	(349)	11¾" between tenons, 1" TBE
C	2	top center rails	jatoba	1¼	(32)	4	(102)	13¾	(349)	11¾" between tenons, 1" TBE
D	2	top end panels	maple	½	(13)	6¾	(171)	12¾	(324)	⅜" × ½" tongue around edge
E	1	top center panel	maple	½	(13)	13¼	(337)	12¾	(324)	⅜" × ½" tongue around edge
F	8	legs	jatoba	1¼	(32)	3½	(89)	23¾	(603)	33" between tenons, 1" TBE
G	4	f and b, top & bottom rails	jatoba	1¼	(32)	3½	(89)	35	(889)	13¾" between tenons, 1" TBE
H	4	f and b, center stiles	jatoba	1¼	(32)	2¾	(70)	15¾	(400)	⅜" × ½" tongue around edge
J	2	f and b, end panels	maple	½	(13)	8	(203)	14¾	(375)	⅜" × ½" tongue around edge
K	2	f and b, center panels	maple	½	(13)	14½	(368)	14¾	(375)	13" between tenons, 1" TBE
L	4	side, top and bottom rails	jatoba	1¼	(32)	3½	(89)	15	(381)	⅜" × ½" tongue around edge
M	2	side panels	maple	½	(13)	14	(356)	14¾	(375)	Cut to pattern
N	16	corbels	jatoba	⅜	(10)	2¼	(57)	13¾	(349)	
O	2	bottom cleats	jatoba	¾	(19)	¾	(19)	37½	(953)	
P	2	bottom cleats	jatoba	¾	(19)	¾	(19)	16	(406)	
Q	5	bottom planks	cedar	¾	(19)	3³⁄₁₆	(81)	37½	(953)	¼" × ¼" tongue and groove
R	1	bottom plank	cedar	¾	(19)	2⁵⁄₁₆	(59)	37½	(953)	¼" × ¼" tongue and groove

TBE: tenon both ends

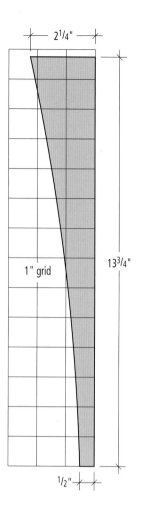

← 2¼" →

1" grid

13¾"

½"

Corbel pattern

Story pole

With the dimensions marked on a story pole, the locations for the mortises are marked on the legs as a group.

table. With a slot-cutting bit set just under ⅜" above the table surface, I made a tongue that slipped in the grooves of the stiles and rails. This is a good technique when working with plywood panels of inconsistent thickness as the fixed distance between the table and cutter will produce a consistent part that matches the width of the groove. I then sanded the veneered panels to 220 grit to prepare things for assembly.

Before assembling any of the panels, I cut 45° bevels on the long edge of each

leg that didn't have the groove for the panels. I glued pairs of legs together, clamping them with a combination of clear packing tape and clamps. After letting the glue on these joints dry overnight, I glued together the front- and back-panel assemblies. The two end-panel assemblies are put together as the entire case is assembled.

With the back panel lying face down on the bench, I assembled the rails and panels for the sides. Once they were in place, I put glue on the tenons and

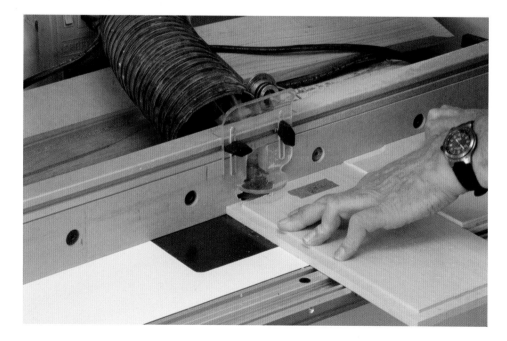

Setting the cutter above the table surface cuts a consistently sized tongue on the back of the panels.

Each of the tenons is planed to fit snugly in its mortise. A batten across the bench eliminates the need to clamp the parts while fitting.

dropped the front panel assembly in place. I then set the chest upright on my bench and clamped across the ends, checking for square.

After the glue on the solid parts had dried, I sanded the outside of the chest with a random-orbit sander, working from 100 grit up to 220, followed by a hand sanding with 280 grit. The top panel was then put together and sanded.

Strips of clear packing tape across the joint let the miters fold together. More tape and additional clamps provide a tight, strong joint.

Rails and panels for the sides are slipped into the already-assembled back panel.

Assembling the front and back panels first simplifies the final assembly — putting the sides together results in a completed case.

ADDING THE CORBELS

I made the ⅜"-thick corbels by resawing some of the 1¼"-thick stock left over from making the rest of the chest. After planing them to thickness, I stacked four pieces together with double-faced carpet tape holding the layers together. I made a pattern of the corbel shape from ½" MDF, and traced the outline on the top layer of the stack.

Using stock a few inches longer than I needed, and interlocking the patterns, I was able to get eight corbels from each stack. I cut the pieces on the band saw, and sanded the curved edges on the spindle sander before taking the stacks apart. With a ⅛"-radius roundover bit in my laminate trimmer, I eased the curved edges before sanding the corbels.

The corbels are glued to the panels and edges of the stiles. I used a couple ¾"-long 23-gauge headless pins to fasten the wider part of the corbels to the panels, filling the nail holes with some sawdust and cyanoacrylate glue. I hand sanded the entire cabinet, and applied three coats of Waterlox wiping varnish before hinging the lid and putting in the tongue-and-groove bottom.

I used four 2½"-long, no-mortise hinges for the lid, spacing them evenly along the

The assembled chest is flipped upright, the corners are checked for square and the case is clamped.

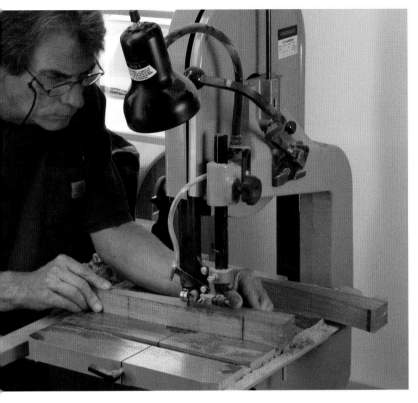

A stack of four blanks held together with double-sided tape yields eight matching corbels.

The difference in thickness between the corbel and the adjacent stile and rail adds visual interest.

top rail of the back of the chest. To hold the lid in the open position, I used a pair of toy-box supports. Because the chest was still bottomless, I could lay it on its back on my bench, and reach inside to position the supports.

GETTING TO THE BOTTOM

I don't have a daughter, so this chest will live at the foot of our bed, holding extra blankets. I placed ¾" by ¾" cleats around the perimeter of the bottom, flush with the bottom edge of the rails. The bottom planks are ¾"-thick aromatic cedar, held together with simple tongue-and-groove joints. I nailed the bottom planks to the cleats at the edges and ends. The cedar is left unfinished.

In the end, this chest has a clean, contemporary look with classic proportions. Changing the material may have disguised its origin, but the strength of the design shines through. Good design, after all, is timeless.

After cutting, the edges are sanded with the stack still stuck together.

∷ SUPPLIES

Rockler
800-279-4441 or rockler.com
2 pair • bronze no-mortise hinges
No.28696, $1.99/pair
1 • RH lid support
No.26229, $5.19 ea.
1 • LH lid support
No.26195, $5.19 ea.

Prices correct at time of publication.

GUSTAV STICKLEY'S NO. 72 MAGAZINE CABINET

Harvey Ellis designed these Arts & Crafts shelves with subtly tapered legs and arched top rails that make it stylish.

By Christopher Schwarz

If you had been shopping for a magazine cabinet in 1910 and came across this piece in Gustav Stickley's catalog, chances are you would have turned the page with barely a glance.

The photo of the No. 72 Magazine Cabinet in the 1910 catalog is horrible. Someone in Gustav Stickley's art department mangled the picture, and it bears almost no resemblance to the real thing. The legs look both spindly and lumpy. The shelves don't look sturdy at all.

In real life, this piece of furniture is impressive. It was one of several pieces of furniture designed by Harvey Ellis, an architect, painter and designer. Ellis's short stint with Gustav Stickley's company before Ellis' death in 1904 was remarkably fruitful. Under his talented pen, a fair number of Stickley's massive and overbuilt furniture forms became lighter and a bit more graceful.

The No. 72 Magazine Cabinet is a good example of this period. The curved top rails and tapered legs all conspire to make this piece look more delicate than it is.

Like most Arts & Crafts projects, this one is straightforward to build. I used about 15 board feet of 4/4 mahogany, four board feet of 5/4, and six board feet of 8/4 — I had a little wood left over, but that always beats a second trip to the lumberyard. The plans for this project were developed by Robert W. Lang for his new book "More Shop Drawings for Craftsman Furniture" (Cambium Press, 800-238-7724). This is Lang's second book of Craftsman furniture plans, and it features measured drawings for 30 pieces of museum-quality classics. If you are an Arts & Crafts fan, this book is required reading.

START WITH THE SIDES

Most of the work on this project is in the two assemblies that make up the sides of the cabinet. And the heart of these side assemblies is the side panels.

These two panels have a tongue on the two long edges that are glued into a groove in the legs. Dados in the panels hold the shelves in place. And the rails are tenoned into mortises in the legs. Finally, the top is screwed down to the cabinet using cleats.

The first task is to prepare the side panels to be glued between the legs. I used a traditional tongue-and-groove

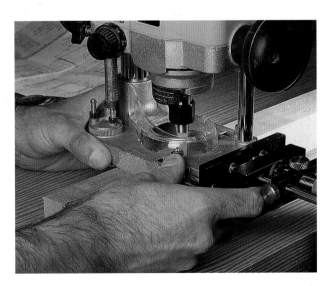

There are a variety of ways to cut the groove in the legs: A router table and a plow plane come to mind. I prefer to use a straight bit in a router with an edge guide. This allows me to see my cut at all times.

WHO WAS HARVEY ELLIS?

Though Harvey Ellis worked for Gustav Stickley for only about a year until he died in 1904, Ellis's work left an indelible impression on Stickley's furniture. Chunky forms became lighter. Rails became curved. Legs became tapered on the sides. And — perhaps most significantly — some furniture became inlaid.

Before Ellis's stint with Stickley, Ellis led an itinerant life as an avant-garde painter, graphic designer, draftsman and sometimes architect, according to scholars. Born in Rochester, N.Y., in 1852, Ellis displayed an early knack for art as a child. His father decided he needed more discipline and sent him to West Point in 1871, according to the Harvey Ellis papers at the University of Rochester. Ellis was discharged from the military school for "tardiness, personal untidiness and gross neglect in his French assignments," according to the papers. There also were rumors of an affair with an actress.

Ellis went to New York to study art at the National Academy of Design, but he ended up as an architectural draftsman for Arthur Gilman instead. He returned to Rochester in 1877 and set up an architectural office with his brother, and together they designed many public buildings. After seven years or so Ellis left the firm and designed houses and public structures for cities across the Midwest. He rejoined his brother's firm in 1894 and also started designing interiors and becoming interested in the Arts & Crafts movement.

After separating from his wife, Ellis joined the staff of Stickley's magazine, *The Craftsman*, and began designing furniture and writing stories for the influential publication. He died in January 1904 at the age of 52, in part due to acute alcoholism, according to the university papers.

SUPPLIES

Frame Mortise and Tenon Jig
Leigh Industries Ltd.
P.O. Box 357
104-1585 Broadway St.
Port Coquitlam, BC, Canada
V3C 4K6
800-663-8932
leighjigs.com

Lie-Nielsen Small
Bronze Spokeshave
Lie-Nielsen Toolworks
P.O. Box 9
Warren, ME 04864-0009
800-327-2520
lie-nielsen.com

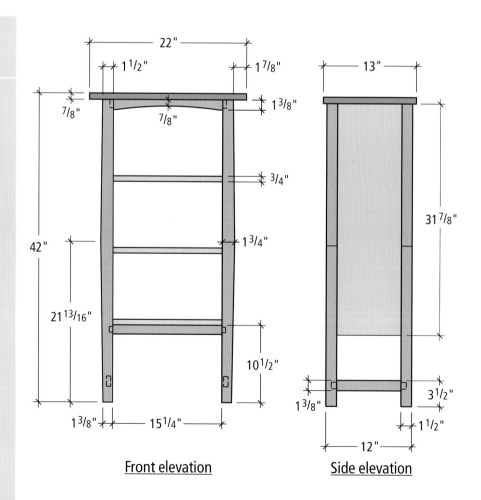

Front elevation   Side elevation

gustav stickley's no. 72 magazine cabinet
INCHES (MILLIMETERS)

REFERENCE	QUANTITY	PART	STOCK	THICKNESS	(mm)	WIDTH	(mm)	LENGTH	(mm)	COMMENTS
A	4	legs	mahogany	$1^{1}/_2$	(38)	$1^{3}/_4$	(45)	$41^{1}/_8$	(1044)	
B	2	side stretchers	mahogany	$^{5}/_8$	(16)	$1^{3}/_8$	(35)	$10^{1}/_2$	(267)	$^{3}/_4$"TBE
C	2	side panels	mahogany	$^{3}/_4$	(19)	$9^{3}/_4$	(248)	$31^{7}/_8$	(809)	$^{3}/_8$" tongue, 2 edges
D	2	bottom rails	mahogany	$^{3}/_4$	(19)	$1^{1}/_4$	(32)	$16^{3}/_4$	(425)	$^{3}/_4$"TBE
E	2	arched top rails	mahogany	$^{3}/_4$	(19)	$1^{3}/_8$	(35)	$16^{3}/_4$	(425)	$^{3}/_4$"TBE
F	3	shelves	mahogany	$^{3}/_4$	(19)	$11^{3}/_4$	(298)	$15^{3}/_4$	(100)	
G	1	top	mahogany	$^{7}/_8$	(22)	13	(330)	22	(559)	
H	2	cleats	mahogany	$^{1}/_2$	(13)	$^{1}/_2$	(13)	8	(203)	attach top to sides

TBE = tenon both ends

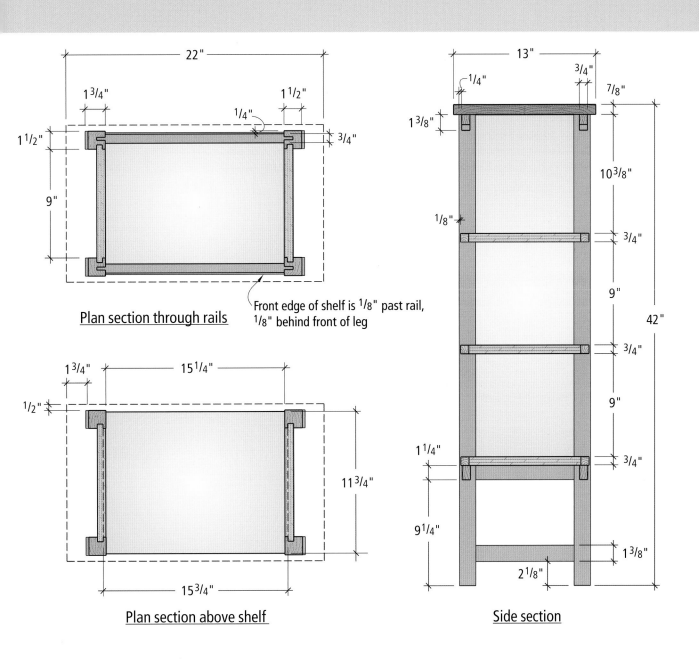

Plan section through rails

Front edge of shelf is $^{1}/_8$" past rail, $^{1}/_8$" behind front of leg

Plan section above shelf

Side section

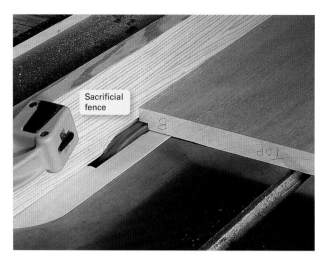

Cut the tongues on the edges of the side panels using a dado stack in your table saw (plus a sacrificial fence). You also could use a rabbeting bit in your router table.

When your grooves and tongues are complete, they should fit snugly as shown. If you're not up to this task, you could simply glue the panel to the legs without any joinery. Just make sure you keep everything lined up so you're certain you'll achieve a tight joint.

joint. It's more elaborate than simply gluing the panel between the legs without joinery. However, it also guarantees you will have no visible gap between the legs and panel.

If you want to do things in this more traditional way, begin by milling a ½"-wide, ⅜"-deep and 31¾"-long stopped groove on the leg in the location shown in the diagram. Square out the groove where it stops using a chisel.

Now cut a matching tongue on the two long edges of your panel.

To keep things neat, I used a backsaw to cut a small shoulder on the bottom corners of the panel that conceals where the groove ends (see the photo below).

Before you can glue the side panel between the legs, you need to cut the ¼"-deep by ¾"-wide dados that hold the shelves. Use the diagrams at right to lay out the locations of the dados, then cut them using your dado stack as shown in the photo.

If all this seems complicated, the sides can be simplified. Make your side panels 9" wide instead of 9¾" and don't cut the tongues and grooves. Cut the dados for the shelves and then simply glue the panels between the legs.

The long-grain joint between the side panel and legs is stronger than the wood itself — you'll just have to be careful about lining everything up and making sure your stock is milled perfectly to avoid any gaps between the legs and

You'll need to notch the bottom of the side panel to fit in the leg groove. A backsaw makes quick work of this simple operation (above). Clean up the cut with a sharp chisel and you're ready to move on (right).

Cut the dados in the side panels using this setup on your table saw or a straight edge and a hand-held router. The gauge block on the right of the blade keeps the panel from getting caught between the fence and the blade.

the side panels.

Before you glue anything up, however, you're going to want to first cut the mortises in the legs. So set your parts aside and fit the shelves in their dados.

THE SHELVES ARE SIMPLE

Cut the shelves to finished size and mark out the notch that needs to be cut in the corner of each shelf. This notch allows the shelves to wrap around the legs. You can rig up some fancy setup with your router table to do this, but I prefer using a backsaw for such a simple task (see the bottom photo at right).

Now fit your shelves in the dados and make any adjustments necessary using a block plane or chisel. When everything is fitting nice and snug, it's time to cut the mortise-and-tenon joints that hold everything together.

I usually cut my tenons using a dado stack or a tenon

saw. When it comes to mortises, I usually choose to drill them out on the drill press or fire up the hollow-chisel mortising machine.

For this project, I used the Leigh Frame Mortise and Tenon Jig. This jig is a precise joint-cutting system.

DETAILS LIGHTEN THE LOAD

With the tenons and mortises milled, it's time to make a few cuts that will visually slim this chunky box a bit.

The first order of business is cutting the curve on the top rails. Mark the curve using the diagrams and a flexible piece of scrap wood. Cut the curve using a coping saw and clean up the saw marks using a spokeshave or sandpaper.

Now cut the tapers on the legs using the diagrams as a guide. I cut the tapers using my band saw and cleaned up

To prevent tearout where the dado stack exits the side panel, put down a couple pieces of masking tape to support the wood fibers. This really works.

Sure, you could set up your router table or table saw to cut the notches in the shelves. But a sharp backsaw works just as well.

the cuts with a smoothing plane. Keep the offcuts because they are useful when gluing the case together at the end of the project.

Now sand or plane down all your parts and glue up the side assemblies. In order to attach the top, screw the cleats to the top edge of your side assemblies and bore a couple holes through the cleats. Break all the edges of your parts with 120-grit sandpaper.

Now comes an important decision. You can go ahead and assemble the case and then finish it. Or you can tape off the joints, finish the individual parts and then assemble the case. I took the latter course.

I kept the finish simple on this piece. I wiped on Minwax's Red Mahogany 225 stain on all the parts. This stain is available at most home-center stores; 8 ounces will cost you less than $3. Allow the stain to dry overnight.

The next day, apply a few coats of your finish of choice. I sprayed M.L. Campbell's Magnalac precatalyzed lacquer (satin sheen) using a HVLP spray system. Sand between the second and third coats with 320-grit stearated sandpaper. Remove the tape from the tenons and then glue up the individual parts of the cabinet. Use the falloff pieces from cutting the leg tapers to clamp the lower part of the case squarely.

Now fit your parts together and tune up the notches in the shelves with a sharp chisel so you get a tight fit between the sides and the shelves.

If you haven't figured it out yet, magazine cabinets aren't much good for storing modern magazines (unless you stacked them flat). But they do make handy bookshelves — especially for antique volumes.

Once I set the cabinet in place next to my fireplace and loaded it up with books, I took a second look at the picture of the original in the 1910 Gustav Stickley catalog. Someone in his art department should have been fired for butchering that photo. This is a nice piece.

A spokeshave cleans up your saw cuts on the top rails quickly. After working with the fancy Leigh jig, it's a relief to pick up a tool that's simpler than I am.

Most people don't notice the tapers on the legs. (My wife didn't, and she has a sharp enough eye to always find my car keys.) The tapers are critical, however. You would definitely notice their absence.

"DRAWINGS FOR CRAFTSMAN FURNITURE"

Author (and *Popular Woodworking* editor) Robert W. Lang has published *More Shop Drawings for Craftsman Furniture* that includes 30 shop drawings of some of the most well-designed Craftsman furniture from this important artistic and cultural movement. You get measured drawings of the plan, profile and elevation (usually called a three-view in design circles) and at least a couple of exploded 3D drawings (called isometrics). Plus there's a cut list. Intermediate woodworkers will be able to go straight to work. For the beginners, there's a section in the front of each book that explains basic construction techniques. However, first-timers would do well to get a couple of simpler projects under their belts first.

For more details on these books, visit the publisher's web site: cambiumbooks.com. You can order these books direct from the publisher by calling 800-238-7724. Each book costs $22.95 plus shipping.

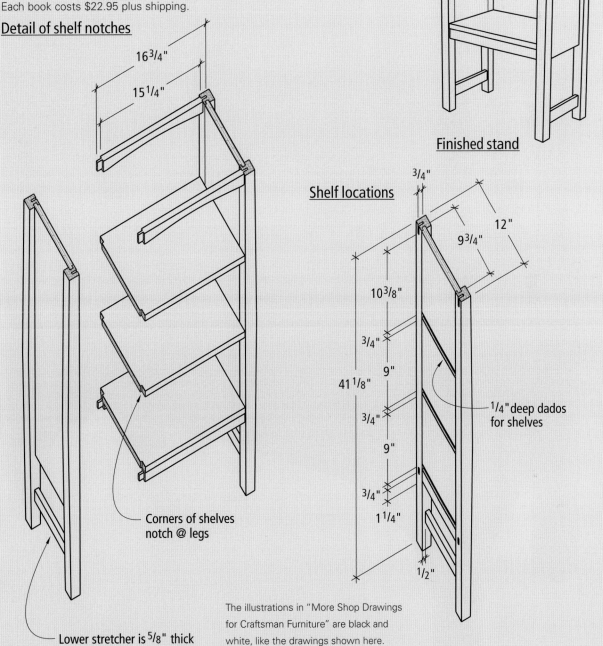

Detail of shelf notches

16³/₄"

15¹/₄"

Finished stand

Shelf locations

3/4"

12"

9³/₄"

10³/₈"

3/4"

9"

41¹/₈"

¹/₄" deep dados
for shelves

3/4"

9"

3/4"

1¹/₄"

Corners of shelves
notch @ legs

Lower stretcher is ⁵/₈" thick

1/2"

The illustrations in "More Shop Drawings for Craftsman Furniture" are black and white, like the drawings shown here.

BYRDCLIFFE LINEN PRESS

Recreating a classic cabinet that breaks the rules of Arts & Crafts.

By Robert W. Lang

The history of most pieces of furniture can be traced back to one individual — usually the designer, the maker or the client. The roots of this linen press spread to include a fascinating group of people at an early 20th-century art colony known as Byrdcliffe, located near Woodstock, N.Y.

With its carved door panels and distinctive colors, this unusual cabinet is one of the finest examples of the Arts & Crafts period. The basic form can be traced back to English designs of the period, but the stylized carving and overall proportions make it unique. The original is part of the collection of the Metropolitan Museum of Art in New York.

Fewer than 50 pieces of furniture were made at Byrdcliffe between 1903 and 1905. Fewer than half of those found buyers; the remaining pieces were found in various buildings at the colony after the 1976 death of the founder's son. Many of these had been left unfinished, the idea being that the buyer could choose a color when purchasing.

THE CAST OF CHARACTERS

Byrdcliffe was founded and financed by Englishman Ralph Radcliffe Whitehead. He inherited the family's felt fortune at age 32, and was a follower of John Ruskin. Although not an artistic man himself, he married a painter, and enjoyed the company of many prominent artists and intellectuals.

In the early 1890s, he wrote about an idealized community of artists, but didn't act on these plans until the birth of his two sons gave him a desire to do something useful with his fortune. He purchased 1,300 acres of land, built about 30 buildings, including a well-equipped woodshop and surrounded himself with a talented group of artists and writers.

Although Whitehead held artists in high esteem, he had a rather low opinion of craftsmen. In his written plan for his community he stated: "Now, in order to have anything good made in stuff, or in hard material, we must seek out the artist to provide us with a design, and then a workman to carry it out as mechanically as possible, because we know that if he puts any of his coarser self into it he will spoil it."

Who actually made and carved the furniture produced at Byrdcliffe is not known. Apparently there were several different cabinetmakers, as the quality of construction varies from piece to piece. Although Byrdcliffe was intended to be self-supporting, Whitehead was wealthy enough to abandon the furniture-making part of his plan after a little more than a year of dealing with the "coarser" workmen.

Many of the artists in residence created furniture designs. Apparently Whitehead selected a general form, and drawings were made by individual artists. Decorative panels were a common feature, although most were painted, not carved. Among the most talented designers at Byrdcliffe were Edna Walker and Zulma Steele. This piece was designed by Walker.

The designs by Walker and Steele are the most beautifully proportioned and distinctive pieces of Byrdcliffe furniture. This cabinet in particular is a refreshing break from the mass and machismo of many Arts & Crafts pieces.

100 YEARS LATER

Usually when I make a reproduction of an existing piece I try to stay as close as possible to the original. In building this cabinet, however, I had to make some guesses, and

REFERENCE	QUANTITY	PART	STOCK	THICKNESS	(mm)	WIDTH	(mm)	LENGTH	(mm)	COMMENTS
A	8	leg fronts and backs	QWO	1	(25)	$2^1/_2$	(64)	$54^1/_4$	(1378)	miter long edges
B	8	side stretchers	QWO	$1^1/_8$	(29)	$2^1/_2$	(64)	$54^1/_4$	(1378)	miter and rabbet long edges
C	4	side panel stiles	QWO	$^3/_4$	(19)	$3^1/_2$	(89)	$44^1/_2$	(1131)	
D	2	side panel top rails	QWO	$^3/_4$	(19)	$6^1/_2$	(165)	$8^3/_8$	(213)	$1^1/_4$" TBE
E	2	side panel mid rails	QWO	$^3/_4$	(19)	$5^1/_8$	(130)	$8^3/_8$	(213)	$1^1/_4$" TBE
F	2	side panel bottom rails	QWO	$^3/_4$	(19)	$3^5/_8$	(92)	$8^3/_8$	(213)	$1^1/_4$" TBE
G	2	lower arched rails	QWO	$^7/_8$	(22)	$5^1/_8$	(130)	$8^3/_8$	(213)	$1^1/_4$" TBE
H	2	top side panels	QWO	$^5/_8$	(16)	$6^7/_8$	(174)	13	(330)	$^1/_2$" TAS
I	2	bottom side panels	QWO	$^5/_8$	(16)	$6^7/_8$	(174)	$18^1/_4$	(463)	$^1/_2$" TAS
J	1	top	QWO	$^3/_4$	(19)	$18^3/_4$	(476)	41	(1041)	
K	1	front top rail	QWO	$^7/_8$	(22)	$2^5/_8$	(67)	$34^3/_4$	(885)	1" TBE
L	2	drawer rails	QWO	$^7/_8$	(22)	$1^1/_4$	(32)	$34^3/_4$	(885)	1" TBE
M	1	bottom front rail	QWO	$^7/_8$	(22)	$1^3/_8$	(35)	$34^3/_4$	(885)	1" TBE
N	1	bottom apron	QWO	$^3/_4$	(19)	$6^3/_4$	(171)	$34^3/_4$	(885)	1" TBE
O	2	stiles at doors	QWO	$^3/_4$	(19)	$2^3/_{16}$	(56)	$19^3/_4$	(502)	
P	2	stiles at top drawer	QWO	$^3/_4$	(19)	$2^3/_{16}$	(56))	$7^1/_2$	(191)	
Q	2	stiles at bottom drawer	QWO	$^3/_4$	(19)	$2^3/_{16}$	(56)	$8^1/_2$	(216)	
R	1	drawer rail support	QWO	$^3/_4$	(19)	$1^3/_8$	(35)	$32^3/_4$	(832)	
S	2	fill behind crown	QWO	$^3/_8$	(10)	$1^5/_{16}$	(33)	$12^1/_8$	(308)	
T	1	fill behind crown	QWO	$^1/_4$	(6)	$1^5/_{16}$	(33)	$32^3/_4$	(832)	
U	6	web frame stiles	poplar	$^3/_4$	(19)	$2^1/_2$	(64)	$35^1/_2$	(902)	
V	9	web frame rails	poplar	$^3/_4$	(19)	$2^1/_2$	(64)	$10^7/_8$	(276)	$^3/_4$" TBE
W	4	web frame panels	plywood	$^3/_4$	(19)	$10^3/_8$	(264)	$14^3/_4$	(375)	
X	2	crown moulding	QWO	1	(25)	2	(51)	48	(1219)	
Y	2	door hinge stiles	QWO	$^3/_4$	(19)	$3^7/_8$	(98)	$19^3/_4$	(502)	
Z	1	left lock stile	QWO	$^3/_4$	(19)	$3^7/_8$	(98)	$19^3/_4$	(502)	
AA	1	right lock stile	QWO	$^3/_4$	(19)	$4^1/_8$	(105)	$19^3/_4$	(502)	
BB	2	door top rails	QWO	$^3/_4$	(19)	$3^7/_8$	(98)	$9^3/_4$	(248)	1" TBE
CC	2	door bottom rails	QWO	$^3/_4$	(19)	$3^7/_8$	(98)	$9^3/_4$	(248)	1" TBE
DD	2	door panels	basswood	$^5/_8$	(16)	$8^3/_4$	(222)	13	(330)	$^1/_2$" TAS
EE	1	top drawer front	QWO	$^3/_4$	(19)	$7^1/_2$	(64)	$31^1/_4$	(793)	trim to fit
FF	1	bottom drawer front	QWO	$^3/_4$	(19)	$8^1/_2$	(216)	$31^1/_4$	(793)	trim to fit
GG	2	drawer sides	maple	$^3/_4$	(19)	$7^1/_2$	(64)	$14^1/_4$	(362)	dovetailed to front
HH	2	drawer sides	maple	$^3/_4$	(19)	$8^1/_2$	(216)	$14^1/_4$	(362)	dovetailed to front
II	1	drawer back	maple	$^3/_4$	(19)	$7^1/_2$	(64)	$32^3/_4$	(832)	in dado in sides
JJ	1	drawer back	maple	$^3/_4$	(19)	$8^1/_2$	(216)	$32^3/_4$	(832)	in dado in sides
KK	2	drawer bottoms	plywood	$^1/_4$	(6)	$14^1/_2$	(369)	$30^3/_8$	(772)	
LL	4	drawer runners	QWO	1	(25)	$1^1/_2$	(35)	$14^1/_4$	(362)	$^3/_4$" TOE
MM	3	back frame rails	poplar	$^3/_4$	(19)	$2^1/_2$	(64)	30	(762)	$^3/_4$" TBE
NN	3	back frame stiles	poplar	$^3/_4$	(19)	$2^1/_2$	(64)	$43^3/_8$	(1102)	
OO	2	back planks	poplar	$^1/_2$	(13)	$4^7/_8$	(124)	$43^3/_8$	(1102)	$^1/_4$" rabbet both edges
PP	4	back planks	poplar	$^1/_2$	(13)	$4^7/_8$	(124)	$43^3/_8$	(1102)	$^1/_4$" rabbet both edges

TBE = tenon both ends; TAS = tenons all sides; TOE = tenon one end

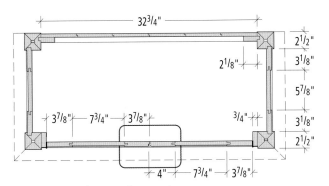

Plan section at doors

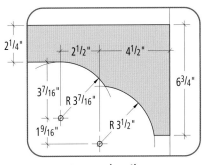

Door stile detail

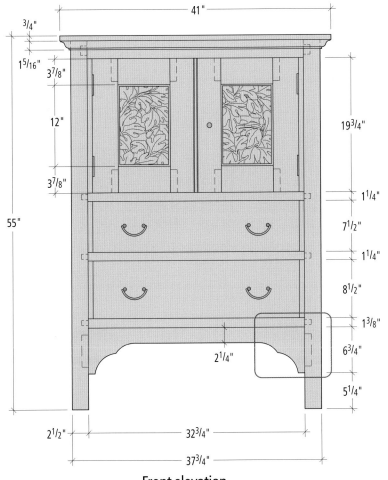

Front elevation

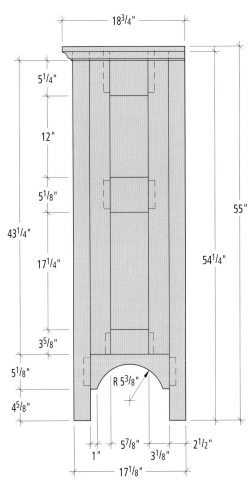

Side elevation

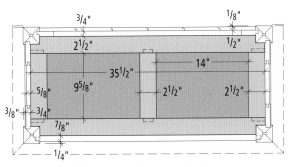

Web frame & dust panel plan

Apron detail

DOORS CARVED, THEN COLORED

The completed carving is given a wash coat of shellac, then colors are applied with watercolor pencils.

The colors are blended with an artist's brush dipped in water.

After tracing the pattern on the basswood panels, the design of sassafras leaves is carved.

After the coloring is complete, the panels are allowed to dry several days before being finished with amber shellac.

I made a few changes to suit my own taste. I had only a photograph of the front of the cabinet and overall dimensions to work with, so the layout of the side panels and the details of construction are my best guesses.

In the original, the carvings are very flat. They are simply outlines of leaves and branches with the edges rounded over. I originally carved the panels this way, but just wasn't happy with the effect. I thought they seemed rather lifeless and static, so I recarved the panels and added more relief.

Additionally, the crown moulding on the original comes flush to the bottom edge of the top, apparently attached to the edges. The closest router bit I could find (Freud 99-406) had a small fillet at the top. I thought this looked nicer, and rather than wrap the crown around the perimeter of the top, I set it below, letting the top overhang by ⅛". This added one more shadow line, and if the top expands or contracts, then the joint between the moulding and the top won't show.

The third change was to the color. The oranges and reds on the panels are the same as the original, but the green stain is darker and deeper in color. The finish on the

A group of stiles for the web frame is clamped together to lay out the joints. Leaving the stack clamped together provides a stable base for the router used to cut the mortises.

The side panels are assembled as a unit, then fit in a groove in the leg, and butted at the bottom to the thicker arched rail.

back of the cabinet. The dust panels are birch plywood.

I brought the rough white oak into the shop and let it acclimate while I worked on carving the panels (far left). I'm a decent carver, but not a fast one, so the oak had plenty of time to adjust. Full-size patterns for the panels are available in pdf format from our web site, popularwood-working.com. Click on "Magazine Extras" at the very bottom of the home page.

I gave the completed panels a thin coat of blonde shellac before coloring them with watercolor pencils, available from any artist's supply store. The colors are applied dry, then blended with an artist's brush dipped in water. I let the panels dry for several days, then gave them two coats of amber shellac to seal in the color and warm up the background.

original varies in color, and I suspect that it may have faded or been refinished at some point. I decided to use a richer forest green, similar to a color that can be seen in another Byrdcliffe piece, a fall-front desk designed by Steele.

OAK AND (NOT) SASSAFRAS

Like the original, the visible parts of this cabinet are made of quartersawn white oak. The carved panels are often described as being made from sassafras, but they are obviously not. The carving depicts the leaves of a sassafras tree and in the original the panels are either poplar or basswood. I used basswood for the carvings, soft maple for the drawer boxes, and poplar for the interior web frames and

THE REAL WORK BEGINS

I milled all of the oak parts slightly oversized, and let them sit for a few days before planing them to finished dimensions. Absolutely straight stock is essential for a project like this. The side panels are all joined with mortises and tenons. Once these were assembled, I cut a rabbet on the long

The web frames are notched around the legs and attached to the side rails with pocket screws. The front and back edges will be glued to the rails as they are assembled.

Several joints must be fit at one time as the second panel and leg assembly is put in place. Get some help so both sides can be fit and clamped at the same time.

MAKING THE LEGS

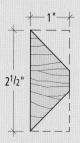

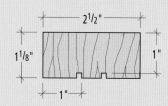

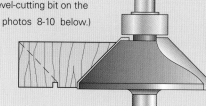

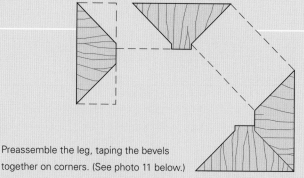

First, bevel the edges of the thinner piece without reducing the width. (See photos 1 and 2 below.)

Second, cut grooves in the bottom of the thicker piece. (See photos 3-7 below.)

Third, after rough-cutting the bevels, trim as shown with bevel-cutting bit on the router table. (See photos 8-10 below.)

Preassemble the leg, taping the bevels together on corners. (See photo 11 below.)

The assembled leg shows quartersawn figure on all four faces. (See photo 12 below.)

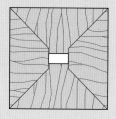

After ripping all the parts to finished width, cut a 45° bevel on both long edges of the thinner parts. Cutting the second bevel brings the part to its finished width.

Be careful ripping the second bevel. After the leading edge clears the blade, use a push stick centered in the stock's width to move the material past the saw blade without tilting it.

Set up to cut the grooves in the bottom of the thick pieces. With a thin piece of scrap against a thicker one, draw a line to indicate the difference in thickness. Flip the thicker piece over and use the pencil line to set the height of the saw blade.

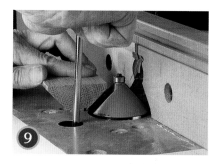

With the blade height and fence settings adjusted, cut two grooves in the back of the thicker leg parts.

After the grooves are cut, the saw is again tilted to 45° and the waste is removed. Leave about ¼" of flat on the edge to ride against the router table fence.

The 45° bevel bit is set to intersect the corner of the groove and the edge of the workpiece. The goal is to create the bevel without reducing the width on the face of the piece.

edge of each panel so that the faces of the stiles fit in a stopped groove cut in the legs as seen at right (next page). This makes the sides of the case very strong, and if the stiles shrink in width over time, the joints won't open up.

The web frames and dust panels are also mortise-and-tenon construction. I clamped the stiles together to lay out the mortises and then realized that leaving them clamped together would provide a stable base for the small plunge router I used to cut the mortises (page 168).

IMPOSSIBLE LEGS

Like a lot of Arts & Crafts furniture, the legs are an important element. The problem with quartersawn oak in this situation is two-fold: Thick stock usually isn't available, and the edge grain is ugly compared to the face grain. There are several ways to work around this, and the method I developed shows quartersawn figure on all four faces of the legs, and is relatively simple to mill and assemble.

I could have laminated the legs from thinner stock and then veneered the edges, but I have seen too many old pieces constructed this way that have cracks in the veneer. Quartersawn wood moves more in thickness than in width, so there's a good chance that this method will eventually fail.

Mitering four pieces together is a logical alternative, but without some way to keep the pieces from sliding during glue-up, assembly can be very difficult. In the early 1900s, Leopold Stickley developed a method that used rabbeted miters to form what he called a quadralinear leg. It's a good method, but without the custom-made shaper cutters he used it is difficult to mill.

Looking for a simpler method, I realized that by making the front and back pieces of the legs a different thickness than the sides, I could make two of the pieces with simple miters, and use a small rabbet on the thicker pieces to keep the parts from sliding during assembly. The photos on these pages show the steps I took.

When I had the legs assembled, I used a plunge router with a fence to cut the stopped grooves for the side and back panels, then laid out and cut the mortises in the front legs for the rails at the front of the carcase.

The side panel assembly is placed in the groove in the

(4) Set the distance from the blade to the fence by lining up the edge of a thin piece of stock to the left side of the blade. I use the saw cut in the table saw's zero-clearance insert as a guide.

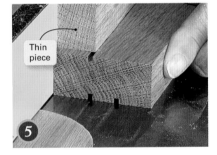

(5) Make some test cuts in scrap. Check the width of the groove by placing the edge of the scrap against the fence, and a thin piece of scrap on top. When the corner of the thin piece meets the far edge of the groove, the fence is set correctly.

(6) Check the depth of the groove by placing a thin piece on the saw table, and butt the thicker piece against it. The face of the thin piece should meet the bottom of the groove.

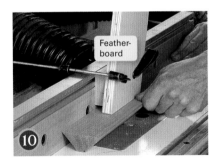

(10) After making some test cuts and fine tuning the router table setup, the edges are beveled. The block behind the featherboard holds it away from the fence, so it is pushing down on the narrow flat left between the two bevels.

(11) After all the parts are milled, I assemble the corners and hold them together with packing tape. All but the last corner is taped before gluing. I then flip the taped parts over, put glue on the edges, then fold the parts back together, taping the last corner.

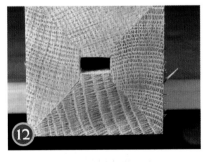

(12) The completed legs have a small rectangular hollow in the center, and show quartersawn figure on all four sides. This is a stable assembly, relatively quick to make and easy to assemble.

leg, and the arched bottom rail is placed in its mortise. The two pieces are then glued and butted together where they meet before the second leg is put in place. With the left and right leg and panel sides together, the entire carcase can be assembled.

With one side panel and leg asssembly face down on some horses, I notched the corners of the web frames around the legs, and held them in place with pocket screws. The back frame was then put in the groove in the rear leg, followed by the front rails in their mortises. The butt joints between the rails and the front edge of the frames were glued and clamped at this time, as were the joints between the web frames and the back frame.

Putting the second leg and panel assembly on is straightforward, but there are a lot of parts that need to come precisely together. I made a dry run, and then got some help to fit it all together and apply the clamps.

NOT DONE YET

Usually, getting the carcase assembled means that the end is in sight, but this cabinet contains several details that require additional work. Much of the interest of this design comes from the varying setbacks of the faces of the parts, particularly those on the front elevation.

The side panels are set back ⅜" from the face of the legs, and the arched rail below it is ⅛" thicker. On the front of the cabinet, the rails are back ¼" from the legs. At the top of

The drawers and drawer fronts are fit before finishing the cabinet. After hanging the doors, I mark where the right door overlaps the left before cutting the rabbet.

The drawer runners have a tenon on the front end that fits in a mortise in the stile. These are placed in position before the stile is glued in place.

The back of the drawer runner is screwed to the back leg after being squared to the front of the cabinet. A groove in the side of the drawer box lets the drawers slide nicely.

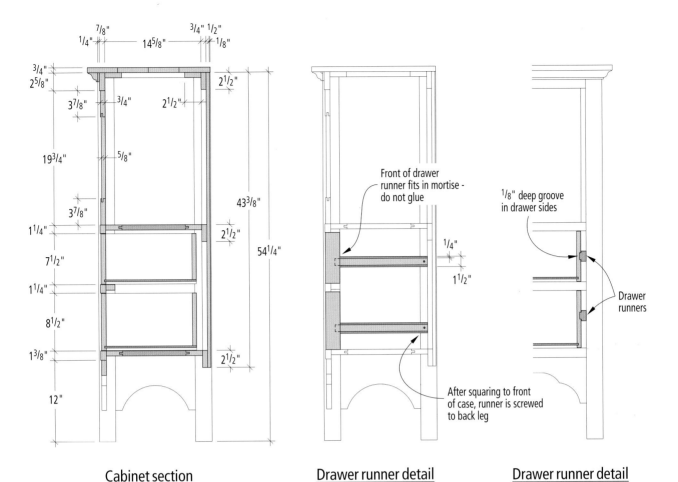

Cabinet section

Drawer runner detail

Front of drawer
runner fits in mortise -
do not glue

After squaring to front
of case, runner is screwed
to back leg

Drawer runner detail

1/8" deep groove
in drawer sides

Drawer
runners

the cabinet, filler strips were glued on so the back of the crown moulding would be flush with the outside edges of the legs.

The lower front rail and the stiles for the door hinges are $\frac{1}{16}$" back from the rails, as are the vertical pieces beside the drawers.

The hinge stiles allow the doors to swing clear of the legs, and this detail is seen in many pieces of Arts & Crafts furniture. The doors and drawer fronts are $\frac{1}{16}$" back from the front edge of the stiles. On the doors this offset is accomplished when locating the hinges. The placement of the stopped groove in the side of the drawer boxes locates the face of the drawer fronts.

The stiles for the hinges were cut and put in place, and the doors were assembled without glue so that all of the cutting for the hinge mortises could be done conveniently. Once I was satisfied with the fit of the doors, I marked where the right door overlaps the left, took everything apart and then glued the hinge stiles in place.

DRAWER RUNNERS

The drawers are rather wide, so I decided to use wood runners to guide them in and out without the bottoms of the drawer box sides rubbing on the web frames or the front rails of the cabinet. At the front of the cabinet, the runners fit loosely in mortises in the stiles beside the drawers. At the back, the runner is held to the back leg with a screw. This method allows minor adjustments to be sure that the runner is square to the face of the cabinet.

After securing the runners, I used a plunge router with a fence attached to cut the grooves in the sides of the drawer boxes. Squaring the ends of the grooves with a chisel and some test fitting allowed me to fit the drawer fronts precisely. I rubbed a pencil on the edges of the runners and moved the drawers in and out several times. This marked any high spots on the runners and the grooves. I used a shoulder plane to fine-tune the fit of the drawers and runners. I then rubbed a

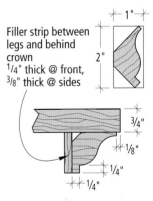

Filler strip between
legs and behind
crown
$\frac{1}{4}$" thick @ front,
$\frac{3}{8}$" thick @ sides

Crown moulding

block of paraffin on the runners to let the drawers move effortlessly.

I fit and mitered the three pieces of crown moulding together and attached them as a unit to the cabinet. I glued the front edge in place, and attached the returns to the sides of the cabinet with a few 23-gauge pins. The top is attached to the cabinet with pan head screws through the web frame in oversized holes from below. With everything complete and fitted, I hand sanded the entire cabinet to 150 grit before staining.

IT'S NOT EASY BEING GREEN

At the art supply store, I picked up two 1.25 oz. tubes of artist's oil color; one phthalo blue and one chrome yellow. To make the green stain, I mixed half of each tube together with a pallet knife on a scrap of wood and added this to a pint of natural Watco Danish Oil, an oil/varnish blend. While stirring the mixture I added one-third of a pint of mineral spirits. This turned out to be twice as much liquid as I needed, but it's better to have too much than to run out halfway through.

I applied this stain to the cabinet, saturating the surface. After letting it sit for 15 minutes, I wiped off the excess with a clean rag and allowed the stain to dry overnight. I dissasembled the doors and stained the stiles and rails separately before gluing them together so that I wouldn't get any stain on the finished panel.

The stain dries to a rich deep color and leaves some pigment in the open pores of the oak. The stain was followed with a coat of natural Watco. This coat was rubbed on sparingly with a rag. This tends to float the color off the harder, smoother areas, changing the color to more of an olive tone and highlighting the flakes and rays of the quartersawn oak. This coat was allowed to dry on the surface for 48 hours, and then the cabinet was scuffed with a Scotch-brite pad.

Some areas were a little too green, so I used some medium walnut Watco in those areas, carefully blending the color. This was allowed to dry on the surface overnight, and once dry these areas were scuffed with the abrasive pad. The entire cabinet was then given two additional coats of natural Watco, followed by a coat of paste wax.

SUPPLIES

Whitechapel Ltd.
800-468-534 or
whitechapel-ltd.com
4 • 3" x 1⅝" butt hinges
    No.205H1, $6.21 ea.
4 • polished rosette pulls
    No.5PR14, $14.24 ea.
1 • hollow brass knob
    No.97KSB5P, $9.12 ea.

Lee Valley
800-871-8158 or
leevalley.com
2 • ball catches
    No.00W12.01, $1.80 ea.
Prices correct at time of publication.

Further Readng
Cornell University
www.museum.cornell.edu/byrd-cliffe/
• Byrdcliffe: An American
  Arts & Crafts Colony,
  online exhibition

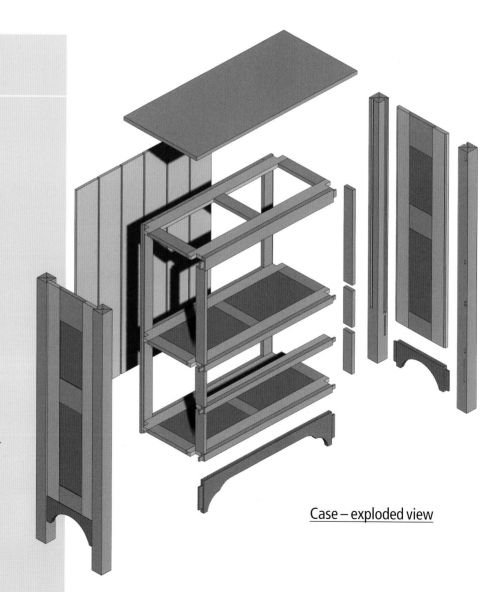

Case – exploded view

After staining, the wood is a rich green color and the open pores of the wood are filled with pigment.

The stain, a mixture of artist's oil colors and Watco Danish Oil is liberally applied. After letting it soak into the surface for 15 minutes the surface is wiped dry.

I finished the inside of the cabinet with shellac, then installed the shiplapped back planks, screwing them at top and bottom to the cross rails of the back frame.

I wanted the hardware to look old, so I soaked it in lacquer thinner and scrubbed the finish off with a nylon abrasive pad. I then put the parts in a plastic container along with a smaller container. I poured some ammonia into the smaller container, and put the lid on the larger one. Fumes from the ammonia oxidized the hardware in a few hours, giving me the patina I wanted.

I hung the doors on the cabinet, used a pair of ball catches at the top to keep them closed, and installed the pulls and knob.

POST SCRIPT

As a commercial enterprise, the furniture made at Byrdcliffe was a dismal failure. As examples of fine design, however, they were a tremendous success. In making this piece, I wanted to add the finest craftsmanship I could to this wonderful design, paying some respect to the anonymous craftsmen that Ralph Whitehead assumed would spoil the work if left unattended.

I knew I had succeeded when I showed my wife the finished cabinet. She looked at it for a while and then said, "It's like looking through pine trees on the edge of a forest on a perfect day in the fall." When craftsmanship evokes poetry, it's been a pretty good day.

The stain is followed by a coat of natural color Watco, which lightens the color and highlights the figure of the quartersawn wood.

ARTS & CRAFTS TOOL CABINET

The goal: The maximum tools in the minimum space.

By Christopher Schwarz

While sawing the 60th dovetail for a drawer side, when my patience was as thin as the veneer facing on cheap plywood, a familiar feeling crept into my body. I began to experience an understandable lust for my biscuit joiner.

It sat patiently on a shelf, and I knew that its chattering, rattling teeth would make everything about this tool cabinet go much faster. But I resisted, because I had the words of a Victorian social reformer, art critic and part-time madman ringing in my head.

The writings of Englishman John Ruskin (1819-1900) were a cornerstone of the American Arts & Crafts movement. Ruskin decried the worst parts of 19th-century industrialism. He promoted craft, pensions and public education when there was little of those things for the poor.

And in his book the *Seven Lamps of Architecture, The Lamp of Memory*, which was published in 1849, he wrote a passage that all woodworkers should read. It's a bit long and a bit dramatic, but it has stuck with me just the same.

"When we build, let us think that we build forever. Let it not be for present delight nor for present use alone. Let it be such work as our descendants will thank us for; and let us think, as we lay stone on stone, that a time is to come when those stones will be held sacred because our hands have touched them, and that men will say, as they look upon the labor and wrought substance on them, 'See! This our father did for us.'"

The biscuit joiner stayed on the shelf. I continued to saw, chop, pare and fit for another four or five hours. Ruskin, I hoped, would have approved.

FROM THE BOOK OF TOLPIN

While Ruskin kept me going through this long and difficult project, I really have a 20th-century craftsman and author to thank (or blame) for my obsession with building a fine tool cabinet. Since it was first published in 1995, *The Toolbox Book* (Taunton Press) by Jim Tolpin has become the most-thumbed book in my library. I've studied every page, toolbox and drawing between its maroon cover boards (the dust jacket is long gone).

Years ago, I resolved to build myself a cabinet that might rival some of the examples in *The Toolbox Book*. This year, I gave it my best shot. Since early 2004 I've spent many spare moments doodling on graph paper and on my computer to come up with a design that satisfied the three things I wanted from a cabinet: It had to hold a lot of tools, look good and be built to last. After studying my work habits, measuring all my tools and paging through thousands of examples of Arts & Crafts casework, this is what I came up with.

It's small but spacious. Have you ever ridden in an old Volkswagen Beetle? They are surprisingly roomy, and especially generous with the headroom. Somehow, the Beetle violates the laws of space and physics, and it is roomy but can also be parked between two oversized Hummers. This cabinet is designed to function the same way. The interior is a mere $11\frac{1}{4}$"- deep, $22\frac{1}{2}$" wide and $31\frac{1}{2}$" tall. Yet, thanks to good planning, it holds every hand tool I need.

The cubbyholes and shelf for hand planes are carefully sized for all the planes needed in a modern shop. The drawers are loaded with trays of tools. Each tray contains

Tools need to be protected, organized and easily retrieved. That's a tall order.

Here are some of the problems I've run into over the years: Hanging tools on a wall keeps them organized and close at hand, but unprotected. Keeping them in a traditional sliding tool till in a chest keeps them protected and organized, but you dig around for them endlessly. Drawers under a bench keep them protected and close at hand, but most drawers end up a jumbled mess.

Here's my solution, and so far it works well. The cubbyholes are sized exactly to hold a full complement of hand planes. Finding the right plane and getting it down for use has never been easier.

The chisel rack puts my most-used sizes out where I can get them. And the rack is designed to hold the tools even when the door is accidentally slammed.

The saw till on the right door is the same way. These two saws do 80 percent of my work and they're always handy.

The real feature is the drawers. The smaller drawers hold tools for a specific operation. In the larger drawers, the interchangeable trays stack inside the drawers and also hold tools for a specific operation. Whenever I dovetail, I grab the top right drawer. No more making mounds of tools on the bench.

Chisel Rack

This simple L-shaped bracket holds the five chisels I use most, plus my drawbore pins. Don't use a magnetic strip; it will magnetize your tools, which makes them difficult to sharpen.

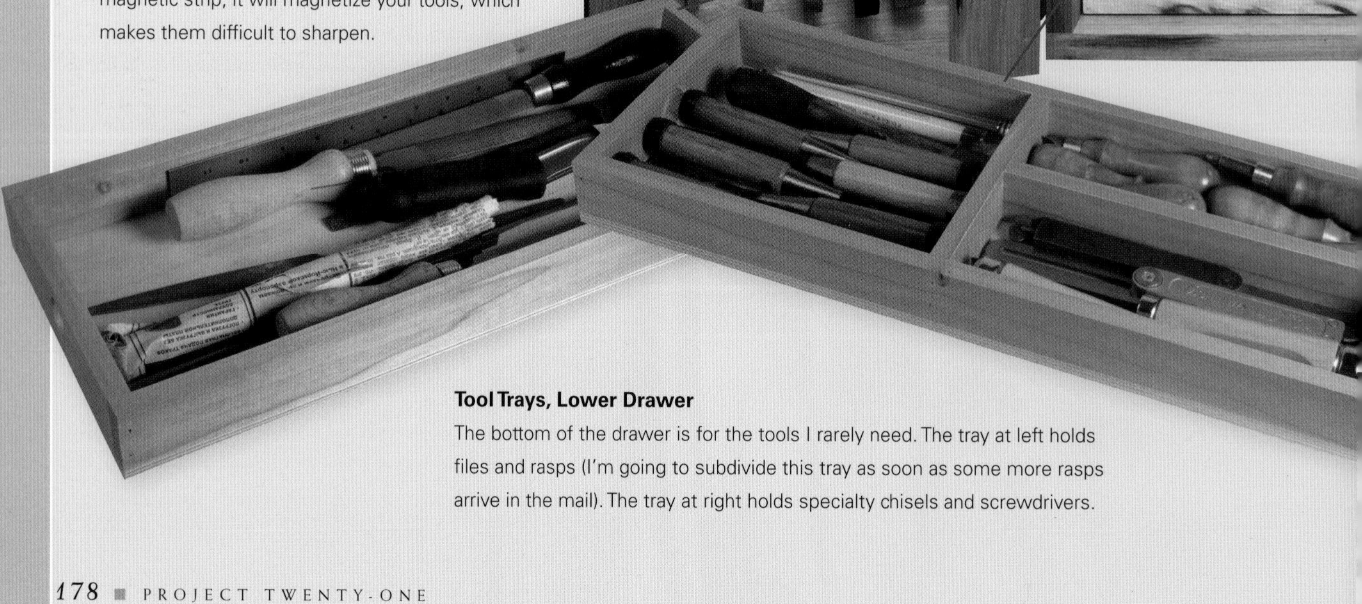

Tool Trays, Lower Drawer

The bottom of the drawer is for the tools I rarely need. The tray at left holds files and rasps (I'm going to subdivide this tray as soon as some more rasps arrive in the mail). The tray at right holds specialty chisels and screwdrivers.

Top Shelf Plane Cubby

This area isn't just what's left over from the remainder of the cabinet. It is carefully sized at $22\frac{1}{2}$" wide × $5\frac{3}{4}$" high to hold a No. 7 jointer plane (a constant companion in my shop), plus a jack plane, panel plane and scraper plane.

Small Plane Cubbies

The cubbyholes are a magic size: $6\frac{1}{4}$" high, about $3\frac{5}{16}$" wide and $10\frac{1}{2}$" deep. This size holds all my joinery planes, my scrub plane, smoothing planes and miter plane.

Saw Till

My saw till holds the two most useful joinery saws – a dovetail saw and a carcase saw. My full-size saws reside on pegs below the cabinet.

Four Upper Drawers

Each of the four drawers holds all the tools for a common operation: one is for dovetailing, the second is for trimming and squaring assemblies, the third is for marking and measuring, and the fourth is for nailing and screwing.

Tool Tray, Middle Drawer

The lower section of the drawer holds waterstones and honing guides (make sure the stones are bone dry before putting them back in the drawer). The tray shown above holds my four spokeshaves and some specialty sharpening equipment.

When sawing the tails, clamp the two sides together and cut them at the same time. This saves time and effort and prevents layout errors.

all the tools for a routine function, such as dovetailing, sharpening or shaping curved surfaces.

The cabinet looks pretty good. I spent months thumbing through old Art & Crafts furniture catalogs and contemporary hardware catalogs for inspiration. This cabinet and its lines are a little bit Gustav Stickley, a little Harvey Ellis and a little of myself.

The cabinet will endure. No compromises were made in selecting the joints. Every major component (with the exception of the changeable, nailed-together trays) are built to withstand heavy use. Of course, when you discuss durable joints, you are usually talking dovetails, which is where we'll begin construction.

A CASE THAT TAKES A BEATING

When this cabinet is fully loaded, my best guess is that it weighs more than any single member of our staff at the magazine (modesty prevents me from revealing what that upper limit might be). To ensure the bottom and top pieces can withstand this weight, I joined them to the side pieces with through-dovetails.

One interesting variation worth noting here is that instead of using one solid top piece, I substituted two 3"-wide rails and dovetailed them into the sides to save

If your rabbets for the back are perfectly square, your case is much more likely to end up square, too. Clean up any imperfections with a rabbeting plane, such as this bullnose rabbet plane.

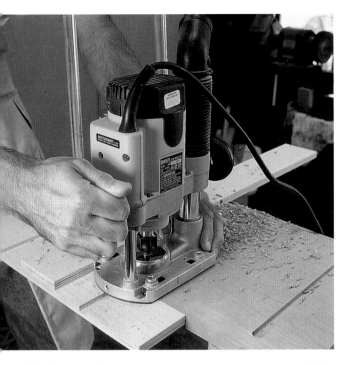

The shop-made T-square jig and a plunge router make quick work of the dados.

Here you can see how you use the dado cut into the jig to line up the jig with your layout lines. Using a router with a flat side on its base is more accurate than using a router with a round base.

a little weight. Because I cut these dovetails by hand, it was simple to lay out this unusual arrangement. If you plan to use a dovetail jig, you will save yourself a headache by forgetting the rails and making your top one solid piece instead.

If you're cutting the dovetails by hand, it's faster and more accurate to clamp your two sides together and saw the tails on the side pieces simultaneously. For years I resisted this technique because it seemed more difficult, but now I know better.

A second feature of the case to note is that the rabbet for the back is a hefty 1" wide. This allows room for the ½"-thick shiplapped back, plus a ½"-thick French cleat that will park the cabinet on the wall and keep it there.

Fitting the dividers is easy with a hand plane. I merely make sure the dividers are surfaced a few thousandths of an inch thicker than where I want them to be. Then I thin them down with a smoothing plane until they slide in with just a little persuasion.

After gluing the sides to the bottom and top rails, trim the dovetails flush with a block plane. Soak the end grain with a little bit of mineral spirits to make it easier to cut. Here you can also see how I supported the case as I worked on it. The big slab holding up the side is an offcut from an old door that's clamped to my bench.

the same router jig, but with the plunge router set to make only an $\frac{1}{8}$"-deep cut. Laying out the locations of these parts for the hand plane cubbyholes might seem daunting. If you want the openings evenly spaced, they should each be 3.333" wide. I don't have any infinite numbers on my ruler. But it's actually child's play to lay out the cubbyholes with a pair of dividers (they look like a school compass but with two pointy tips — no pencil). You can tweak these tools until they step off the cubbyholes as precisely as you please. Dividers are one of my secret weapons.

With all these parts cut and fit, make the back of the case. I used ambrosia maple. It's cheap and looks a bit like the spalted maple I used in the doors and drawers. The back boards are joined by a $\frac{1}{4}$"-deep × $\frac{3}{8}$"-wide shiplap on each long edge.

The top cap is easy. Cut the wide chamfer on the underside using your table saw. Clean up the cut with a block plane. Attach the top to the rails with screws.

You are now at a critical juncture. You can go ahead and get some quick gratification and assemble the whole case. But good luck when you go to finish it. Getting those cubbyholes finished right will be murder. The better solution is to glue up only the sides, bottom and top rails. Tape off the exposed joints and finish all the case parts (I used two coats of a satin spray lacquer). Then assemble the case. I know it sounds like a pain (it is). But the end result is worth it.

Finish the back pieces and top cap while you're at it. Now you can screw the back in place and the top cap. You are ready for the doors and drawers.

EASIER THAN THEY LOOK

The doors aren't too bad. The mullions and muntins that form the four lights in each door appear difficult, but thanks to a little legerdemain, it's no problem.

And then there are the stopped dados. These $\frac{1}{4}$"-deep joints in the side pieces hold all the dividers. Cutting these joints is simple work with three tools: a plunge router, a bearing-guided straight bit and a shop-made T-square jig that guides the whole shebang. Lay out all the locations of your dados on the sides. Park the jig so it lines up with your layout lines. Cut the dados in two passes.

Fitting all the horizontal dividers to fit the dados is easy. The $\frac{1}{2}$"-thick dividers simply need a small notch at the front to fit over the rounded end of the dado created by the round straight bit. A sharp backsaw is just the tool here.

The $\frac{3}{4}$"-thick horizontal divider needs a bit more work to fit in the $\frac{1}{2}$"-wide dado. A $\frac{1}{4}$" × $\frac{1}{4}$" end-rabbet is the answer.

The through-dados that hold the vertical dividers use

But before getting mired in those details, you need to assemble the doors. Here's how they work: The stiles and rails are joined using mortise-and-tenon joints. For mid-size doors such as these, I use ⅜"-thick by 1"-long tenons.

Cut your tenons and your mortises, then mill a ¼"-wide by ⅜"-deep groove in the rails and stiles to hold the door panel. I generally make this groove on the router table using a straight bit and featherboards. It's the easiest way to make the groove start and stop in the right place in the stiles.

The door panel needs a rabbet on its back to fit in the groove. But before you mill the panel, you should know a bit about spalted maple. Its black spidery lines are caused by the spalt fungus, which attacks the tree after it's been felled. In short, it's partly rotted.

It's always best to wear a respirator when dealing with spalted wood. There are numerous accounts of people who have had respiratory problems after breathing in the dust.

Once you fit the panel, assemble the doors — the mullions and muntins are added after assembly. Once the glue cures, cut a ¼"-wide by ½"-deep rabbet on the backside of the opening for the glass. This rabbet will hold the narrow backing strips that are built up into the mullions and muntins.

This technique was explained fully by Glen Huey in our August 2002 issue

Cut the rabbet on the backside of the door using a rabbeting bit in your router table. With a large tabletop such as this, it's simple work.

Glue one backing strip into the rabbet in the door on edge. Then flip the door over and glue a mullion onto the backing strip. Then use spring clamps to hold everything while the glue dries.

Install the horizontal muntins the same way. First glue a backing strip into the rabbet on the backside of the door. Then flip the door over and glue the muntin to that.

REFERENCE	QUANTITY	PART	STOCK	THICKNESS	(mm)	WIDTH	(mm)	LENGTH	(mm)	COMMENTS
A	2	sides	cherry	$3/4$	(19)	$12^1/4$	(311)	33	(838)	$3/8$"-deep × 1"-wide rabbet at back
B	2	top rails	cherry	$3/4$	(19)	3	(76)	24	(610)	dovetailed into sides
C	1	bottom	cherry	$3/4$	(19)	$11^1/4$	(285)	24	(610)	dovetailed into sides
D	1	top cap	cherry	1	(25)	17	(432)	32	(813)	$1/2$"-deep × 3"-wide bevel
E		shiplapped back	maple	$1/2$	(13)	$23^1/4$	(590)	33	(838)	$1/4$" × -$1/4$" shiplaps
F	1	major horizontal divider	cherry	$3/4$	(19)	$10^1/2$	(267)	23	(584)	in $1/4$"-deep × $1/2$"-wide dados
G	1	thin horizontal dividers	cherry	$1/2$	(13)	$10^1/2$	(267)	23	(584)	in $1/4$"-deep × $1/2$"-wide dados
H	3	thin horizontal dividers	cherry	$1/2$	(13)	$9^1/4$	(235)	23	(584)	in $1/4$"-deep × $1/2$"-wide dados
I	5	vertical dividers	cherry	$1/2$	(13)	10	(254)	$6^1/2$	(165)	in $1/8$"-deep × $1/2$"-wide dados
J	2	small vertical divideres	cherry	$1/2$	(13)	$9^1/4$	(235)	23	(584)	in $1/8$"-deep × $1/2$"-wide dados
K	2	large door stiles	cherry	$3/4$	(19)	$2^3/4$	(70)	33	(838)	
L	2	small door stiles	cherry	$3/4$	(19)	$1^1/4$	(32)	33	(838)	
M	2	top door rails	cherry	$3/4$	(19)	$2^3/4$	(70)	10	(254)	1" TBE
N	2	intermediate door rails	cherry	$3/4$	(19)	$2^1/4$	(57)	10	(254)	1" TBE
O	2	lower door rails	cherry	$3/4$	(19)	$3^3/4$	(95)	10	(254)	1" TBE
P	2	door panels	maple	$1/2$	(13)	$8^1/2$	(216)	$16^3/4$	(425)	in $1/4$"-wide × $1/2$"-deep groove
Q	2	vertical door muntins	cherry	$1/4$	(6)	$1/2$	(13)	8	(203)	
R	4	horizontal door muntins	cherry	$1/4$	(6)	$1/2$	(13)	$3^3/4$	(95)	
S	2	backing strips	cherry	$1/4$	(6)	$1/2$	(13)	$8^1/2$	(216)	in $1/4$"-wide × $1/2$"-deep rabbet, glued to vertical muntin
T	4	small backing strips	cherry	$1/4$	(6)	$1/2$	(13)	$4^1/8$	(105)	glued to horizontal muntin
U	4	small drawer fronts	maple	$3/4$*	(19)	$2^1/2$	(64)	11	(279)	in $1/4$"-deep × $1/2$"-wide rabbet on bottom edge
V	8	small drawer sides	poplar	$1/2$	(13)	$2^1/2$	(64)	9	(229)	in $1/4$"-deep × $1/4$"-wide rabbet on bottom edge
W	4	small drawer backs	poplar	$1/2$	(13)	$2^1/2$	(64)	11	(279)	
X	4	small drawer bottoms	plywood	$1/4$	(6)	$10^1/2$	(267)	9	(229)	screwed to drawer box
Y	1	medium drawer front	maple	$3/4$*	(19)	5	(127)	$22^1/2$	(572)	in $1/4$"-deep × $1/4$"-wide groove for bottom
Z	2	medium drawer sides	poplar	$1/2$	(13)	5	(127)	9	(229)	in $1/4$"-deep × $1/4$"-wide groove for bottom
AA	1	medium drawer back	poplar	$1/2$	(13)	$4^1/2$	(115)	$22^1/2$	(572)	
BB	1	medium drawer bottom	plywood	$1/2$	(13)	$8^3/4$	(222)	22	(559)	in $1/4$"-deep × $1/2$"-wide rabbet on bottome edge
CC	1	large drawer front	maple	$3/4$*	(19)	$6^3/4$	(171)	$22^1/2$	(572)	in $1/4$"-deep × $1/4$"-wide groove for bottom
DD	2	large drawer sides	poplar	$1/2$	(13)	$6^3/4$	(171)	9	(229)	in $1/4$"-deep × $1/4$"-wide groove for bottom
EE	1	larger drawer back	poplar	$1/2$	(13)	$6^1/2$	(165)	$22^1/2$	(572)	
FF	1	large drawer bottom	plywood	$1/2$	(13)	$8^3/4$	(222)	22	(559)	in $1/4$"-deep × $1/2$"-wide rabbet on bottome edge

* Finished dimension, laminated from two pieces of wood; TBE= tenon, both ends

("Simple Divided-light Glass Doors"). But the photos on page 183 explain it better than words can. Essentially, you create the T-shaped moulding that makes the mullions and muntins by gluing together $1/4$"-thick × $1/2$"-wide strips of wood. It's simple work.

What's not so simple is mounting the doors with the strap hinges. These hinges are inexpensive, beautiful and handmade. As a result, they need a bit of tweaking and bending and hammering and cursing to get them just right to hang a door.

Here's my best tip: Screw the hinges in place with the cabinet on its back. Then stand it up, loosen the hinge screws and make your final adjustments. I used a block plane to make some adjustments, and a mallet for others. Let your frustration level be your guide.

GETTING A HANDLE ON DRAWERS
The drawers are a long slog. Even though I'm a fair dovetailer, it took me three solid days of work to get the drawers assembled and fit. But before you start listening to that

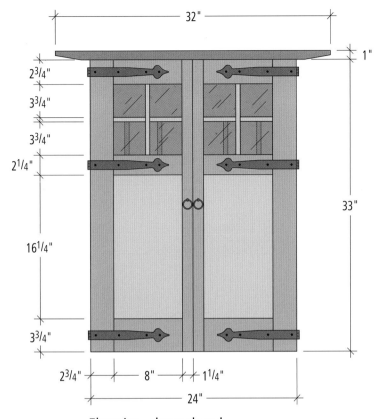

32"

1"

2³/4"

3³/4"

3³/4"

2¹/4"

33"

16¹/4"

3³/4"

2³/4"   8"   1¹/4"

24"

Elevation - doors closed

17"

3"   3"

3"

10¹/2"

5³/4"

6¹/4"

2¹/2"

2¹/2"

5"

9¹/4"

6³/4"

12¹/4"

13"

Profile

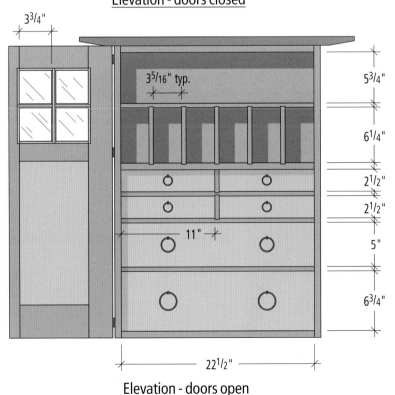

3³/4"

3⁵/16" typ.

5³/4"

6¹/4"

2¹/2"

2¹/2"

11"

5"

6³/4"

22¹/2"

Elevation - doors open

SUPPLIES

Lee Valley Tools
800-871-8158 or leevalley.com

6 • 28mm ring pulls, 01A61.28, $1.85
   each

2 • 40mm ring pulls, 01A61.40, $2.80
   each

2 • 50mm ring pulls, 01A61.50, $3.50
   each

6 • Unequal strap hinges, 9¹/2" × 5",
   01H21.39, $9.70 each

4 • Magnetic catches, 00S16.01, $1.20
   each

7 • #6 × ⁵/8" black pyramid-head screws
   (bags of 10), 01X38.65, $1.60 a bag

Prices correct as of publication date.

Build the drawers with through-dovetails. Then glue a piece of ¼"-thick veneer to the front.

Here you can see the two different ways of installing the drawer bottoms. The bottom in the top drawer rests in a rabbet in the sides. The drawer bottom for the larger drawers slides into a groove.

lock-miter router bit whispering in your ear, remember this: The drawers are going to hold a tremendous amount of steel. And when you open the drawers during a future project, you'll never be disappointed to see dovetails.

To make things a tad easier, I built all the drawers using through-dovetails and ½"-thick material for the front, sides and back. Then, with the drawer glued up, I glued on a ¼"-thick piece of spalted maple to the front piece. This trick also allowed me to stretch my supply of spalted maple.

The four small drawers are built a little differently than the two larger ones. Because the small drawers are shallow, I wanted to use every bit of space. So the bottom is ¼"-thick plywood that's nailed into a ¼" × ¼" rabbet on the drawer's underside.

The larger drawers are more conventional. Plow a ¼" × ¼" groove in the sides and front pieces to hold a ½"-thick bottom, which is rabbeted to fit in the groove.

Install the dividers in the drawers so they can be easily removed in the future. A 23-gauge pinner is an excellent tool for this job.

Once everything is finished, install the glass using small strips of cherry ($\frac{1}{8}$" and $\frac{1}{4}$" thick). A few dabs of clear silicone and a couple small pins do the trick.

Build all the drawers to fit their openings exactly, then use a jack plane to shave the sides until the drawer slides like a piston. Finish the doors and drawers, then it's time for the fun part: dividing up the drawers, building trays for the tools and tweaking the hardware so everything works just right.

As you divide up the drawers and trays, one word of advice: Don't fasten any of the dividers permanently. Your tool set will change, and you want to be able to easily alter the dividers. I fit mine in place with friction and a couple 23-gauge headless pins. The dividers can be wrenched free when I need room for a new tool.

When you hang the cabinet, use wide cleats — mine were each 5" wide. This allows you to get more screws into the cabinet and into the studs. Also, for extra insurance, I rested the bottom of the cabinet on a 2"-wide ledger that also was screwed into the studs.

With the project complete, the voice of Ruskin was finally silenced for a short time as I assessed my work. (I for one was happy for the silence; Ruskin vacillated between madness and lucidity during the last years of his life.) I scolded myself for a few things: the reveals around the drawers on the left edge of the cabinet are a tad wider than the reveals on the right side. And in a couple of the dovetails at the rear of the drawers, there are a couple small gaps. It's not perfect.

But before I got too down on myself, I remembered one more quote from Ruskin that relates to handwork and the pursuit of perfection. This one deserves as much ink as the first.

"No good work whatever can be perfect," he writes, "and the demand for perfection is always a sign of a misunderstanding of the ends of art."

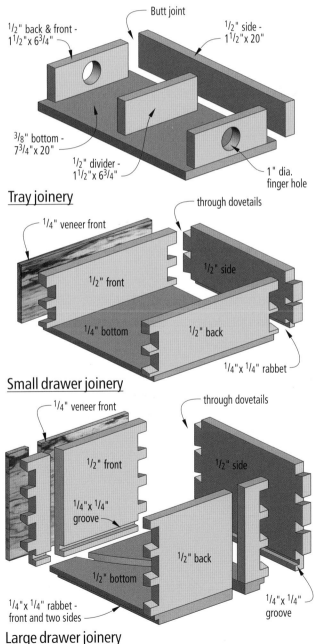

Tray joinery

$\frac{1}{2}$" back & front - $1\frac{1}{2}$" x $6\frac{3}{4}$"

Butt joint

$\frac{1}{2}$" side - $1\frac{1}{2}$" x 20"

$\frac{3}{8}$" bottom - $7\frac{3}{4}$" x 20"

$\frac{1}{2}$" divider - $1\frac{1}{2}$" x $6\frac{3}{4}$"

1" dia. finger hole

Small drawer joinery

$\frac{1}{4}$" veneer front

through dovetails

$\frac{1}{2}$" front

$\frac{1}{2}$" side

$\frac{1}{4}$" bottom

$\frac{1}{2}$" back

$\frac{1}{4}$" x $\frac{1}{4}$" rabbet

Large drawer joinery

$\frac{1}{4}$" veneer front

through dovetails

$\frac{1}{2}$" front

$\frac{1}{2}$" side

$\frac{1}{4}$" x $\frac{1}{4}$" groove

$\frac{1}{2}$" bottom

$\frac{1}{2}$" back

$\frac{1}{4}$" x $\frac{1}{4}$" rabbet - front and two sides

$\frac{1}{4}$" x $\frac{1}{4}$" groove

ARTS & CRAFTS SIDEBOARD

By David Thiel

When the Arts & Crafts movement swept America in the early 1900s, furniture scale was anything but diminutive. Houses had 10'-high ceilings, and even the "modest" bungalows of the time had larger spaces for living (but much smaller spaces for sleeping) than today's typical tract houses. Common sizes for sideboards at that time were 38" to the top, 24" deep and anywhere from 40" to 80" in length. In today's 12' × 12' dining area that's just too large. I scaled mine down to 34" to the top, 19" in depth and 66" in length. Some of the construction has been updated as well, using biscuits where appropriate and plywood panels.

As with most Arts & Crafts pieces, wood selection and hardware are the features that bring the simple construction to life. The material for the legs, top, sides, drawer faces and doors should be carefully selected from quarter-sawn white oak to provide the largest and most uniform ray flake possible.

START CONSTRUCTION WITH THE SIDE PANELS

After choosing your lumber for the most dramatic effect, begin construction by cutting the legs to size and marking the locations of the ½" × 2" × ¾"-deep mortises for the three 3"-wide rails. In addition, the back legs get a ¼" × ¼" groove on the inside face for the backs to slip into. The side panels are assembled using tongue-and-groove construction. Set your table saw to run a ½"-deep center groove down the inside edge of the stiles and rails. Make the groove wide enough to allow your ¼" panels to fit snugly without forcing. Then reset your saw to cut ¼" × ½" tongues on both ends of the top side rails, and the bottom of each stile.

The final step on the lower rails is to draw an arch 1" up from the bottom of the rail, running from side-to-side. Cut the arches on both lower rails using a jigsaw, then sand the edge smooth. Next, cut the panels to size (leave ¹⁄₁₆" clearance all the way around the panels so they won't interfere with assembly). Prior to assembling the sides, finish sand both sides of the panels and the inside edges of the stiles and rails. Then glue up the parts, putting only a spot of glue on the panels.

ATTACHING THE RAILS

The next step is to cut and prepare the rails that will divide the drawers and run between the two side panels. The long rails (one oak and two poplar) are the same size and can be cut and tenoned at the same time. Once the tenons are complete, the front rail gets a 1" arch as on the sides. The two back rails each get a ½" × ½" rabbet to hold the back pieces and partitions.

I made the rest of the rails and the two center partitions out of plywood with a 1" solid oak front edge. With the rails and partitions edged, cut notches in the front edge of the two partitions and the back edge of the long drawer rail to form a bridle joint. This provides strength

REFERENCE	QUANTITY	PART	STOCK	THICKNESS	(mm)	WIDTH	(mm)	LENGTH	(mm)	COMMENTS
A	1	top	white oak	1	(25)	19	(483)	66	(1676)	
B	4	legs	white oak	$1^3/_4$	(45)	$1^3/_4$	(45)	33	(838)	
C	4	side stiles	white oak	1	(25)	3	(76)	$26^1/_2$	(673)	$^1/_2$" TOE
D	2	side rails	white oak	1	(25)	3	(76)	8	(203)	$^1/_2$" TBE
E	2	side rails	white oak	1	(25)	3	(76)	13	(330)	
F	2	side panels	white oak ply	$^1/_4$	(6)	8	(203)	24	(610)	
G	2	partitions	white oak ply	$^3/_4$	(19)	$15^1/_4$	(387)	26	(660)	
H	1	front rail	white oak	1	(25)	3	(76)	$61^1/_2$	(1562)	$^3/_4$" TBE
I	2	rear rails	poplar	1	(25)	3	(76)	$61^1/_2$	(1562)	$^3/_4$" TBE
J	1	drawer rail	white oak ply	$^3/_4$	(19))	3	(76)	60	(1524)	
K	2	drawer rails	white oak ply	$^3/_4$	(19)	3	(76)	$28^1/_4$	(717)	
L	1	bottom	plywood	$^3/_4$	(19)	$13^1/_4$	(349)	60	(1524)	
M	2	posts	white oak	$1^3/_4$	(45)	$1^3/_4$	(45)	$5^3/_4$	(146)	20-degree pyramidical bevel at top
N	1	plate rail	white oak	$^3/_4$	(19)	$3^1/_2$	(89)	60	(1524)	
O	1	front rail	white oak	$^5/_8$	(16)	$1^1/_4$	(32)	$63^1/_8$	(1610)	
P	2	rail spacers	white oak	$^5/_8$	(16)	1	(25)	$^7/_8$	(22)	
Q	2	backs	white oak ply	$^1/_4$	(6)	$15^1/_8$	(384)	24	(610)	
R	1	back	plywood	$^1/_4$	(6)	29	(737)	24	(610)	
S	2	shelves	white oak ply	$^3/_4$	(19)	15	(381)	14	(356)	
T	12	drawer runners	white oak	$^3/_8$	(10)	$^1/_2$	(13)	13	(330)	
U	4	door stiles	white oak	$^3/_4$	(19)	3	(76)	$20^1/_8$	(512)	
V	4	door rails	white oak	$^3/_4$	(19)	3	(76)	$10^1/_2$	(267)	$^3/_4$" TBE
W	2	door panels	white oak ply	$^1/_4$	(6)	$10^1/_2$	(267)	$15^5/_8$	(397)	
X	2	drawer fronts	white oak	$^3/_4$	(19)	$4^7/_8$	(124)	15	(381)	
Y	1	drawer front	white oak	$^3/_4$	(19)	$4^7/_8$	(124)	$28^1/_8$	(714)	
Z	6	drawer sides	poplar	$^9/_{16}$	(14)	$4^7/_8$	(124)	14	(356)	
AA	2	drawer backs	poplar	$^3/_4$	(19)	$4^3/_8$	(112)	15	(381)	
BB	1	drawer back	poplar	$^3/_4$	(19)	$4^3/_8$	(112)	$28^1/_8$	(714)	
CC	1	drawer front	white oak	$^3/_4$	(19)	$5^1/_2$	(140)	$28^1/_8$	(714)	
DD	2	drawer sides	poplar	$^9/_{16}$	(14)	$5^1/_2$	(140)	14	(356)	
EE	1	drawer back	poplar	$^3/_4$	(19)	5	(127)	$28^1/_8$	(714)	
FF	1	drawer front	white oak	$^3/_4$	(19)	$5^7/_8$	(149)	$28^1/_8$	(714)	
GG	2	drawer sides	poplar	$^9/_{16}$	(14)	$5^7/_8$	(149)	$28^1/_8$	(714)	
HH	1	drawer back	poplar	$^3/_4$	(19	$5^3/_8$	(137)	$28^1/_8$	(714)	
II	1	drawer front	white oak	$^3/_4$	(19	7	(178)	$28^1/_8$	(714)	
JJ	2	drawer sides	poplar	$^9/_{16}$	(14)	7	(178)	14	(356)	
KK	1	drawer back	poplar	$^3/_4$	(19	$6^1/_2$	(165)	$28^1/_8$	(714)	
LL	2	drawer bottoms	plywood	$^1/_4$	(6)	$14^1/_8$	(359)	$14^5/_{16}$	(364)	
MM	4	drawer bottoms	plywood	$^1/_4$	(6)	$14^1/_8$	(359)	$27^7/_{16}$	(697)	

TBE = tenons both ends; TOE = tenon one end

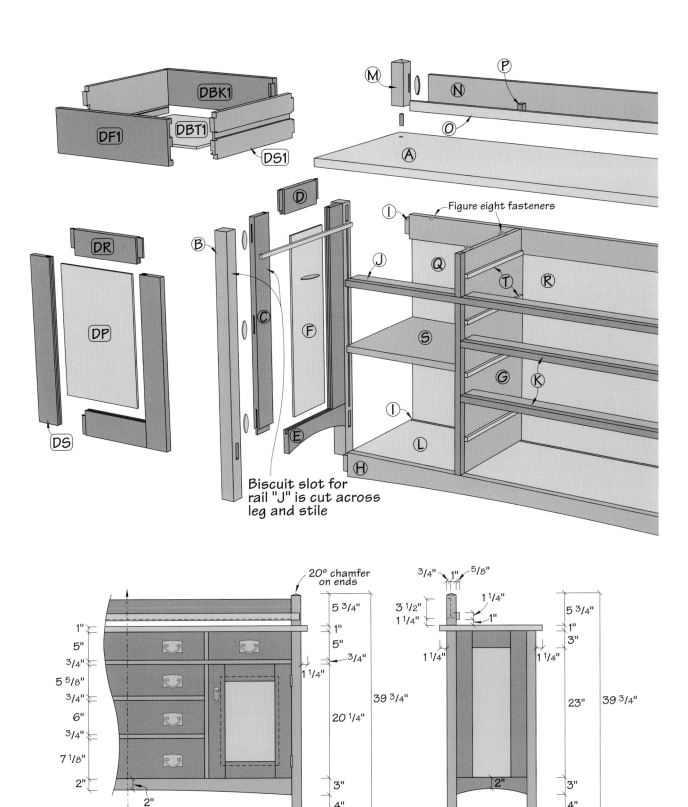

DBK1

DF1

DBT1

DS1

M

N

P

O

A

DR

DS

DP

B

D

C

F

E

Biscuit slot for
rail "J" is cut across
leg and stile

I

J

Q

T

R

Figure eight fasteners

S

G

K

I

L

H

Elevation

20° chamfer
on ends

5 3/4"

1"

5"

3/4"

1 1/4"

1"

5"

3/4"

5 5/8"

3/4"

6"

3/4"

7 1/8"

2"

2"

C_L

39 3/4"

20 1/4"

3"

4"

14 1/8"

3/4"

15 1/8"

1 3/4"

31 3/4"

Profile

3/4" 1" 5/8"

3 1/2"

1 1/4"

1 1/4"

1"

5 3/4"

1"

3"

1 1/4"

1 1/4"

23"

39 3/4"

2"

3"

4"

1 3/4" 3" 7" 3" 1 3/4"

16 1/2"

ARCHES WITHOUT A COMPASS

If you've taken a moment to try and figure out the radius necessary to make the arch on either the side or front rails, you'll know you're looking for a compass with about a 20 foot beam. Since this is a little silly, here's an easier way:

Find a piece of hardwood fall-off measuring about ¼" × 1" × 72". Tap a couple of brad nails into the rail at the extreme ends of the arch. Then bend the strip from the center up 1" and clamp it in place. Take a pencil and trace the inside of the strip, and there's your arch. Obviously a shorter strip will work just as well for the side rails.

and rigidity to the rails and allows the grain of the top rail to run the width of the cabinet without interruption. Also, the top back corner of each partition requires a ½" × 3" notch for the top rear rail to attach.

Join the three drawer rails to the cabinet with biscuits — the two short rails between the two partitions, and the long one between the two side panels. When cutting the biscuits in the side panels, remember that the drawers, partitions and drawer rails are set back ⅜" from the legs.

Next mark the bottom piece and the front and back lower rails for biscuits, attaching the rails flush to the top surface of the bottom piece. Then glue the rails in place to the bottom. Pay careful attention to the length of the bottom at the rail tenons.

Now clamp the center drawer section together and mark the partition locations on the bottom piece. Then drill clearance holes through the bottom for the screws to attach the partitions to the bottom.

The next step requires a little juggling and an extra pair of hands. Glue the rails between the two partitions, then screw the partitions to the bottom. Now put the front rail

in place in the partition's bridle joint and glue and tap the bottom tenons in place in the side panel mortises. Leave the top splayed open to glue the biscuits and tenons for the rear top rail and the long drawer rail. Tap it all into place, check for square and clamp it up.

DOORS AND DRAWERS
I used half-blind dovetail joinery for the drawers, using poplar as a secondary wood for the sides and backs of the drawers, and ¼" birch ply for the bottoms. The drawer bottoms slide into ¼" × ¼" grooves cut ½" up on the sides and drawer front. The backs are cut ½" shorter than the sides to allow the bottom to slide into place.

I went with a traditional drawer slide method and cut ⅝"-wide × ⁵⁄₁₆"-deep grooves in the drawer sides before assembly. Once the drawer was assembled, I notched the drawer backs to continue the groove the length of the drawer. I then mounted oak drawer runners to the inside of the cabinet. The captured drawer runners (with a little paraffin) proved to be fine drawer slides and will keep the drawers from drooping when opened to full length. The

The sides are where everything comes together with the three mortises, the back slot and finally the biscuit joint for the long drawer rail.

For the half-blind dovetails, I used the $20 jig method outlined in Troy Sexton's article in the September 1999 issue of *Popular Woodworking*. It seemed like a clever idea when we ran the article, so I had to try it for myself. The scrap-wood templates and router template guide worked great. There's a different template for each row of drawers, but the templates are quick and easy to make.

To mount the drawer runners, start with the top three drawers. Measure the opening space, subtract the height of the drawer, split the difference then add that number to the distance from the top of the drawer groove to the top of the drawer. In locating the front of the runner, remember that the legs extend ³⁄₈" beyond the drawer section.

size and location of your runners is critical and should be checked carefully before mounting.

The doors are built pretty much the same way as the cabinet's side panels, though I used a ³⁄₄"-deep groove and tongue for extra strength. I mortised the hinges into the doors only (half the thickness of the hinge) and it provided good spacing for the door in the opening.

TOP AND PLATE RAIL

I've included a plate rail on my sideboard that is a traditional touch. However you may opt to leave it off. The

plate rail piece is biscuited between the two posts, while the front rail is nailed in place to the front of the posts (see diagram). I used a 23-gauge air pinner that left almost no hole to putty.

The two post tops are beveled on four sides to a 20-degree angle to form a "point." I did this on the table saw with a stop mounted on the miter gauge. Four quick cuts and you're done. With the plate rail assembled, mark the drilling location on the top and drill the dowel holes in the top, but leave the rail loose until after applying the finish.

Attach the top using figure-eight fasteners. They require very little space, and allow the top to move during changes in humidity. The last pieces to cut are the backs and the shelves for the door sections.

HARDWARE AND FINISH

Now mount the hardware. The pulls shown are impressive, and they should be. The pulls are Stickley reproductions and priced at about $30 each. While they're worth the money, you may choose to use more affordable pulls.

Finishing an Arts & Crafts piece is always a challenge. The trick is to get the right color and still get the ray flake to "pop" from the wood. Start by applying an alcohol-soluble aniline dye. There are many available, but chose one with a reddish-brown cast, such as a brown mahogany. Because it's alcohol based, this dye will dry quickly and can soon be recoated with a warm brown glaze. While wiping the excess glaze from the piece you can control how dark the finish will be. After allowing the glaze to dry overnight, the final step is a couple of coats of satin lacquer. If you use shellac or varnish, be careful as the alcohol carrier can allow the stain to run.

This is an impressive piece, and I'm pleased with its scaled-down proportions. There's only one drawback to building your own Arts & Crafts sideboard — the next logical step is a dining table and chairs. Maybe next year.

With everything ready to finish, there's something satisfying in seeing the drawer dovetails surrounded by great hardware. If you want to keep the dovetails highly visible, carefully tape off the sides of the drawers before staining.

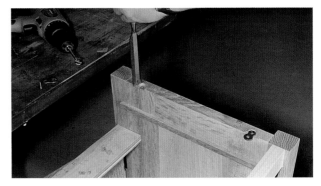

Use a Forstner bit to recess the smaller end of the fasteners into the top edgee of the partitions and side panels. Then take a chisel and notch the inner half of the recess to form a "V" which will allow the fastener to swivel front-to-back. This allows for wood movement and will keep the solid top from pulling the cabinet apart.

WRIGHT STYLE PRINT STAND

The celebrated architect designed a very similar print stand in 1908, but it was never built during his lifetime.

By Christopher Schwarz

For the last seven years, every time I opened the book *In the Arts & Crafts Style* it fell open to the same page. There, perched on a broad-armed settle, is a print stand that was originally designed by architect Frank Lloyd Wright in 1908 but never built during his lifetime.

The print stand shown in the book was built in 1990 by a company owned by Thomas A. Heinz, a Chicago-area architect and the author of more than 15 books about Wright. Apparently Wright designed the stand to display Asian prints, of which he was an avid collector. However, the stand in the book displays only a single rose, no prints. Even stranger, over the years I've noticed this design appear in several different forms. In one, the proportions of the stand have been altered and the space above the spindles houses an 8×10 photo. Other companies have built the stand in a much bigger form and turned it into a floor lamp.

As I set out to build my own version, I wanted it to look as "Wrightian" as possible, and be functional as a print stand. So I added the stubby stops on the table to prevent prints from sliding off the stand. I also made the top cap (above the spindles) a little longer to lock into the mitered frame. Finally, I pushed the legs out toward the edges of the table just a bit. The first prototype I mocked up seemed a bit wobbly to me.

You can build this print stand using thin pieces, shorts and offcuts that are hiding in your scrap pile. And here's the amusing part. Versions of this project sell for about $500 these days. Some days it feels great to be a woodworker.

BUILD THE MITERED FRAME

All of the parts of this project are wedged inside the mitered frame, so the frame is a good place to begin construction. Cut your pieces to rough size and then head to your miter saw or table saw.

If you're new to cutting miters, here's a piece of good advice: let geometry be your guide. Most beginning woodworkers will cut the first miter with their saw or miter gauge set 45° in one direction,

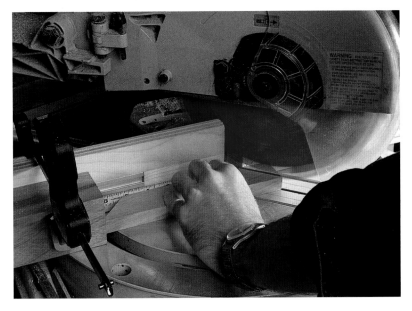

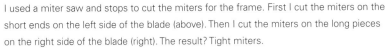
I used a miter saw and stops to cut the miters for the frame. First I cut the miters on the short ends on the left side of the blade (above). Then I cut the miters on the long pieces on the right side of the blade (right). The result? Tight miters.

and then turn the gauge or saw to 45° the other way to cut the adjoining miters. This is a mistake.

Your equipment probably isn't precise enough. You'll end up sanding your miters to fit, cutting them over and over or learning to live with your mistakes. Instead, let complementary angles help you out. Set your miter gauge or saw to 45° and cut one-half of the joint on the left side of the blade and one-half on the right side of the blade. If you are off by a degree or so it won't matter because the piece cut on the other side of the blade will cancel out the error. (If you do this with your table saw's miter gauge, you're going to need to screw a long accessory wooden fence to your gauge.) When your miters are complete, cut biscuit slots, dowel holes or a spline to reinforce these joints. Glue the frame together using a band clamp or miter clamps.

TABLE AND TOP CAP
The spindles are attached to the table and the top cap using mortise-and-tenon joinery. Lay out the location of the $\frac{1}{4}$"-wide × $\frac{1}{2}$"-deep × 1"-long mortises on the table and top cap using the full-size drawing on the next page. Cut your mortises using a mortiser, drill press or chisel. When done, go ahead and cut the tenons to match on the spindles. I cut mine on the table saw.

Dry-fit the spindles and make sure everything lines up. Take the assembly apart and set everything aside.

LEGS AND NOTCHES
Attach the legs to the table using No.20 biscuits. Cut the slots using a biscuit joiner and set the parts aside.

Now it's time to make the most critical cut in the whole project: the notches in the table and top cap. These notches allow the table and top cap to squeeze inside the frame. You want the fit between these pieces to be nice and tight because it's a highly visible area.

I cut the $\frac{5}{8}$" × $\frac{1}{2}$" notches using a dado stack in my table saw. Make several test cuts and shim the dado stack until you get just the right fit on the frame. Then, to make sure the height of the dado stack is correct, cut notches on a piece of scrap the same size as the table and see if it all fits.

Cut the notches on the sides, then cut the same size notches on the ends of the table to hold the two stops, which you'll glue in later.

REFERENCE	QUANTITY	PART	STOCK	THICKNESS	(mm)	WIDTH	(mm)	LENGTH	(mm)	COMMENTS
A	2	frame, long parts	white oak	5/8	(16)	1½	(38)	36	(914)	
B	2	frame, short parts	white oak	5/8	(16)	1½	(38)	8	(203)	
C	2	legs	white oak	3/4	(19)	5	(127)	5	(127)	
D	1	table	white oak	3/4	(19)	6	(152)	10	(254)	
E	5	spindles	white oak	3/4	(19)	1½	(38)	17	(432)	½" TBE
F	1	top cap	white oak	3/4	(19)	2½	(64)	6	(152)	
G	2	stops	white oak	5/8	(16)	3/4	(19)	5	(127)	

TBE = tenons both ends

SANDING AND FINISHING

It's best to sand all the parts, finish them and then assemble the project. Getting finish between the spindles would be no fun. Begin sanding with 100-grit paper and sand up to 180 grit. Now glue the stops into their notches, clamp and allow the glue to dry.

To prepare for finishing, cover all the tenons with masking tape and stuff packing peanuts into the mortises to keep finish off them.

A varnish, wiping varnish or oil/varnish blend will give the bare oak a nice warm tone that was typical of many of Wright's pieces. Add as many coats as you need to get a nice sheen.

ASSEMBLY

Begin assembly by gluing the feet to the table. Clamp and allow the glue to dry. Now place this assembly inside the frame, and glue the spindles between the table and top cap.

When the glue is dry, nail the table and top cap to the frame. Nail at an angle on the underside of the table and top cap. If any of your nail heads are sticking out when you are done, cut them off or sink them with a nail set.

Completing this project didn't solve the historical mystery of what Wright's print stand would actually have looked like, but it does solve the problem of where I can display my own collection of Asian prints.

When you sand the spindles, you will save yourself a world of headaches by clamping them all together and sanding them at once. Not only will you save time, you'll also ensure that all the edges are crisp and line up perfectly when glued in place.

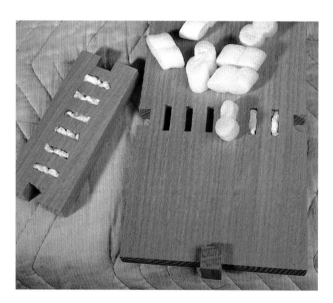

Around Christmas everything seems to come packed in foam peanuts. I kept a few handfuls of them for just this purpose. Before finishing the individual parts, stuff peanuts into your mortises to keep finish off the sides of the mortise.

After the glue is dry, remove the clamps from the print stand and nail the table and top cap to the frame. I used Accuset's micro-pinner to do the job because the brads are tiny. Any small diameter brads will do, however.

After finishing, it's time to assemble the print stand. Carefully place the table assembly between the sides of the frame (left). If you are cautious you can avoid scratching the finish. Now glue the spindles in place. After the glue is dry, remove the clamps from the print stand and nail the table and top cap to the frame (above). I used Accuset's micropinner to do the job because the brads are tiny. Any small-diameter brads will do, however.

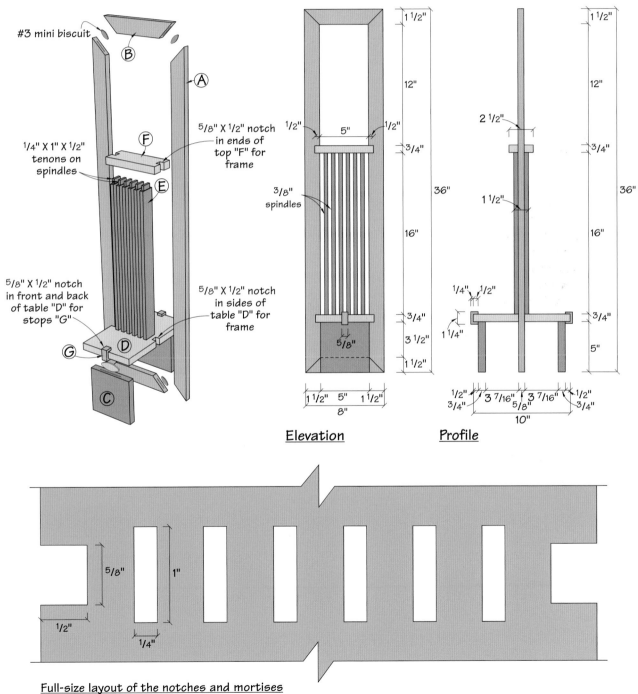

#3 mini biscuit

$\frac{5}{8}$" X $\frac{1}{2}$" notch in ends of top "F" for frame

$\frac{1}{4}$" X 1" X $\frac{1}{2}$" tenons on spindles

$\frac{3}{8}$" spindles

$\frac{5}{8}$" X $\frac{1}{2}$" notch in front and back of table "D" for stops "G"

$\frac{5}{8}$" X $\frac{1}{2}$" notch in sides of table "D" for frame

Elevation

1 $\frac{1}{2}$"
12"
$\frac{1}{2}$"   5" $\frac{1}{2}$"
$\frac{3}{4}$"
36"
16"
$\frac{3}{4}$"
3 $\frac{1}{2}$"
$\frac{5}{8}$"
1 $\frac{1}{2}$"
1 $\frac{1}{2}$"   5"   1 $\frac{1}{2}$"
8"

Profile

1 $\frac{1}{2}$"
12"
2 $\frac{1}{2}$"
$\frac{3}{4}$"
36"
1 $\frac{1}{2}$"
16"
$\frac{1}{4}$" $\frac{1}{2}$"
$\frac{3}{4}$"
1 $\frac{1}{4}$"
5"
$\frac{1}{2}$"   3 $\frac{7}{16}$"   3 $\frac{7}{16}$" $\frac{1}{2}$"
$\frac{3}{4}$" $\frac{5}{8}$" $\frac{3}{4}$"
10"

$\frac{5}{8}$"
1"
$\frac{1}{2}$"
$\frac{1}{4}$"

Full-size layout of the notches and mortises

ALL-WEATHER MORRIS CHAIR

Morris chairs are pretty darn comfortable,
but they aren't the type of furniture you
drag out onto the porch — until now.

By David Thiel

A morris chair is a great place to settle in and do lots of things, including reading a book, enjoying a drink, chatting with friends and watching a good rain storm. During at least half of the year in the Midwest these things are nice to do outside, as well as inside, but dragging a white oak mortise-and-tenoned Morris chair onto your deck isn't the easiest thing. Not one to be put out of a comfortable position, I decided painted pine could work for a Morris chair as well, and so I headed for the home center store.

The chair invitingly posed on my deck at left is made entirely from 1×4 and 1×6 pine from the home center store, about $50 worth. The hardest joint on this chair is a butt joint, and if you've got a jigsaw, drill and a hammer you can knock one out in a day. With the help of a couple extra tools, my personal best time is just under four hours. Your hardest work will be picking through the lumber racks to find the straightest and most knot-free lumber from the store.

The chair is designed to have a cushion (also available from many home center stores), but you don't have to add one. If you don't use a cushion the chair may feel a little deep when you sit in it. Because of this, I'd suggest taking 2" off the lengths for the side rails, arms, seat slats and side cleats. Readjust the spacing of the side slats to fit the shorter seat.

Start your building by cutting out the pieces to form the front and rear legs. Traditional Morris chairs typically have very stout legs, and I didn't want to lose that look or stability, so I edge-glued and nailed two pieces together to form a "T." Face-on or from the side the sturdy leg is still visible. With the legs formed, the rear (shorter) legs need

to have the top end cut at a 5° angle from front to back. Remember that the back on these legs is the top of the "T". A miter box made quick work of this step.

The next step is to get your box of 1¼" deck screws out and attach the lower side rails to the inside of the legs with the top edge 8" off the floor. With those rails attached, slip the top rails into place, flush with the front leg, and mark and cut the bevel on the rail to allow the arms of the chair to slope back. Then screw these rails in place, also on the inside of the legs. With the side frames complete, cut the pieces for the side slats using the sides themselves to determine the angle to cut on the top of the slats. I spaced them evenly and used a pneumatic brad nailer to attach the slats as they're more decorative than structural — and it was a lot faster.

With the legs assembled, attach both lower side stretchers. Then place an upper stretcher in position and draw a line from the top of the angle on the back leg to the front leg. Cut the stretcher on the mark, then attach the upper stretchers, completing the two side frames.

■ ■ all-weather morris chair
■ ■ INCHES (MILLIMETERS)

REFERENCE	QUANTITY	PART	STOCK	THICKNESS	(mm)	WIDTH	(mm)	LENGTH	(mm)	COMMENTS
A	2	legs (front)	pine	¾	(19)	3½	(89)	22	(559)	
B	2	legs (front)	pine	¾	(19)	2¾	(70)	22	(559)	
C	2	legs (rear)	pine	¾	(19)	3½	(89)	21	(533)	bevel to fit
D	2	legs (rear)	pine	¾	(19)	2¾	(70)	21	(533)	miter to fit
E	6	stretchers	pine	¾	(19)	3½	(89)	27	(686)	miter 2 to fit
F	2	arms	pine	¾	(19)	5½	(140)	37	(940)	trim to length
G	10	side slats	pine	¾	(19)	3½	(89)	17½	(450)	miter to fit
H	2	back stiles	pine	¾	(19)	1½	(38)	30	(762)	
I	2	back stiles	pine	¾	(19)	2	(51)	30	(762)	
J	2	back rails	pine	¾	(19)	3½	(89)	21	(533)	
K	1	back rail	pine	¾	(19)	1½	(38)	17	(432)	
L	5	back slats	pine	¾	(19)	1½	(38)	27	(686)	
M	1	back support	pine	¾	(19)	2	(51)	28	(711)	bevel to fit
N	4	seat cleats	pine	¾	(19)	1½	(38)	27	(686)	bevel 2 to fit
O	3	seat slats	pine	¾	(19)	3½	(89)	26½	(673)	trim to fit
P	4	seat slats	pine	¾	(19)	1½	(38)	26½	(673)	trim to fit
Q	2	dowels	pine			½	(13)	2	(51)	
R	1	hinge	pine			1½	(38)	20	(508)	
S	4	foot rest legs	pine	¾	(19)	1¼	(32)	13½	(343)	
T	4	foot rest legs	pine	¾	(19)	2	(51)	13½	(343)	
U	2	foot rest sides	pine	¾	(19)	3½	(89)	22½	(572)	
V	2	foot rest sides	pine	¾	(19)	3½	(89)	16	(406)	
W	4	foot rest slats	pine	¾	(19)	2½	(64)	16	(406)	
X	2	cleats	pine	¾	(19)	¾	(19)	17	(432)	

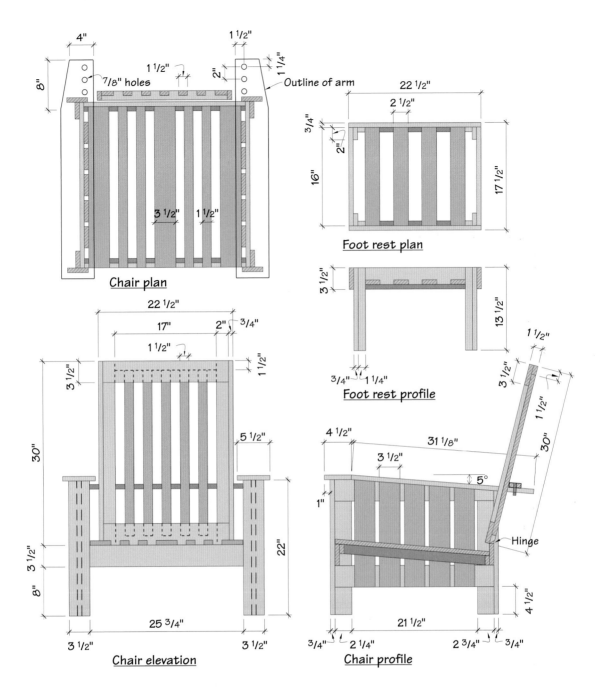

The two arms are cut from 37"-long pieces. Measure 4½" in from the front edge of each then crosscut the pieces at this point at a 2½° angle. By flipping over the shorter piece, a 5° angle is formed, and the arms can be attached to the legs and top rails. Cut the slight bevel (shown in the diagrams) on the back of the arms to add a little more grace to the piece, then center the arms on the front legs and nail in place.

The seat of the chair is formed by simply adding nailing cleats to the inside of the chair frame. Screw the rear cleat in place with the bottom edge flush to the bottom of the rear seat rail. Then lay a straightedge on the rear cleat, stretching across the front rail of the chair. This is the angle the seat will take. Mount the front cleat to the front

rail so that it fits under the straightedge. The two side cleats are mounted following the angle of the straightedge. Mounting the seat slats is simple from here. Cut the slats and use a router to round over at least the front edges of the boards. If you like, go ahead and round over the top edges as well. Then simply lay the two outside slats tight against the sides and back and nail them in place. Put the center slat in place next, then fill in with the four thinner slats, spacing them evenly.

The back is constructed by forming L-shaped sides, screwing a top and bottom rail between them, then nail the slats evenly spaced across the back. To allow the back to fold both forward and back, the continuous hinge needs to be mounted to the inside of the back chair rail and to the outside of the lower back rail. Mounted this way the two sides will keep the back from reclining. To solve this I cut a bevel on the back rails using a hand saw. Then mount the back and fold it forward for now.

To make the chair an adjustable recliner, cut a support bar as shown in the schedule and run a chamfer along one edge. Then mark the bar as shown in the diagrams and drill two ¾" holes through the piece. Put a little glue on the two 2"-long sections of dowel and insert them into the holes until they are flush with the top edge of the piece. The glue should hold, but to add a little extra strength I tagged a brad nail through the back of the piece into each dowel.

Next mark the ⅞" hole locations on the arms and drill the holes using a spade bit. To avoid tear-out, drill through the top of the arm until the tip of the bit pokes through the bottom of the arm, then drill the rest of the hole coming up from the underside of the arm.

It's not a decent Morris chair unless it's got a foot rest. This one is fairly simple, with the four legs again using the strength formed by an L-shaped glue-up. Four stretchers screwed between give the foot-stool its shape, and cleats and some evenly spaced slats finish the job. Again, this is designed for a cushion, so if you aren't

Simply screw the front and rear stretcher between the side frames and it starts to look like a chair.

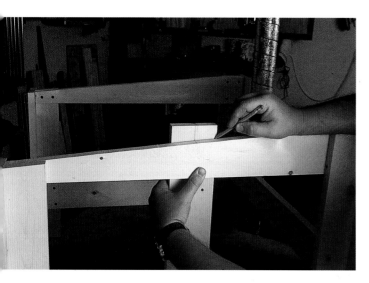

The side slats are mounted flush to the bottom of the lower side rail and cut to match the angle of the top rail. Simply hold the piece in place, make a mark, and choose your toothed tool of choice to make the cut.

The arms are cut to the front and rear lengths at a 2½° angle and then the front piece is flipped upside-down. This gives you a 5° angle at the joint. While the inner part of the arm is well supported by the legs and stretchers, the outer part of the arm needs some extra support. With a little variation on the Arts & Crafts exposed joinery theme I used a through-biscuit, cutting the biscuit slot at the mating point of the arm, then inserting the biscuit and later cutting and sanding it flush.

As you can see on the end, the back stiles are glued together to form "L"-shaped sides, then the back rails are screwed in place between the two sides. The 1½" rail is attached to the upper rail to make a more solid looking and feeling back.

using a cushion, adjust your dimensions and mount the slats to the top of the stretchers.

You're ready to finish. Do a little sanding to knock off the sharp edges and make a nice surface on the arms. The best outdoor finish is one that blocks light and seals the wood. Around my neighborhood that's a good description of paint. I picked a nice kelly green and used about seven cans of Krylon spray paint.

You may have noticed the reference to my "best time" at the beginning of this story. Since building the first of these chairs I've built a second for myself, and there have been orders pouring in from family, friends and neighbors. So why don't some of you entrepreneurs out there take these plans and start up a summer business. Please, take some pressure off me!

With the back slats in place, the ends of the back sides need to be beveled back to allow the back to recline to a comfortable position. I'm beveling the pieces here with a pull saw at more of an angle than necessary, but it won't hurt anything.

The completed back is screwed in place against the back seat rail with a continuous hinge. You can also see the three holes in the back edge of the arms that the back support drops into.

MANTLE CLOCK

A variation on a number of originals will quickly be one of your favorites.

By David Thiel

You might not be ready to build your own sideboard, but you can start your Arts and Crafts collection with this simple clock. The only tough part of the project is finding a great piece of quarter- sawn white oak (1" × 6" × 96").

FIRST THINGS FIRST
Cut the pieces according to the pats list. Resaw and book match the front for an impressive appearance. Taper the front to an 8" width at the top. Then, crosscut a 4° bevel on the top and bottom edges of both sides, parallel to one another.

CUT THE FRONT
Cut the dial hole (match the hole to the dial face you are using for your clock) and pendulum slots in the front. Use a chamfer bit to cut the beveled profile in the dial hole.

CUT THE TOP AND BOTTOM
To cut the top and bottom chamfer details (including the ⅛" bead), use your table saw. Start by making a ⅛"-deep cut 1" in on the ends and front edges. Cut the bevel by running the pieces on edge (use a zero-clearance throat plate) with the blade set to 23°. Set the blade height to

mantle clock
INCHES (MILLIMETERS)

REFERENCE	QUANTITY	PART	STOCK	THICKNESS	(mm)	WIDTH	(mm)	LENGTH	(mm)	COMMENTS
A	1	front	white oak	½	(13)	9	(229)	14	(356)	trim to fit
B	1	bottom	white oak	¾	(19)	5	(127)	12	(305)	edges beveled/3 sides
C	1	top	white oak	¾	(19)	5	(127)	10	(254)	edges beveled/3 sides
D	2	sides	white oak	½	(13)	3¹⁵⁄₁₆	(100)	14⅛	(359)	beveled top and bottom
E	1	back	oak ply	¼	(6)	9⅞	(251)	14⁹⁄₁₆	(370)	trim to fit
F	1	dial support	pine	¾	(19)	5½	(140)	6	(152)	
G	4	fake tenons	white oak	¼	(6)	½	(13)	1½	(38)	beveled all edges
H	8	fake pins	white oak	⅛	(3)	¼	(6)	¼	(6)	beveled all edges

intersect with the bead cut and set the fence to leave the $^3/_{16}$" flat shown in the diagram. To inset the front $^1/_4$" back from the sides, lay it on a $^1/_4$" piece of Masonite as a spacer; glue the two sides to the face. The fall-off pieces from the front taper make perfect clamping cauls to exert equal pressure on the sides. Pilot-drill, then nail the bottom and top to the sides, leaving a $^1/_{16}$" setback. Set the nails.

THROUGH-TENONS

Cut, chamfer, then glue the applied through-tenons as located on the diagrams. Cut, chamfer and glue the fake square pegs to cover the nail holes. Rout a $^1/_4$" by $^3/_8$"-deep rabbet in the clock's back edges. Then fit the back into the rabbet.

THE CLOCK AND FACE

Cut the dial support block and glue the clock face to the block, centered and 2-$^1/_2$" down from the top of the block. Apply two coats of clear finish to the block and face, which is typically paper.

ATTACH THE HANDS

Drill a hole in the center of the clock face for attaching the hands to the clock mechanism and attach the movement to the back of the support block.

APPLY GLAZE AND FINISH

To finish, first apply warm brown glaze (used as a stain) to the clock case. Apply a few coats of clear finish.

LAST THINGS LAST

Screw the dial support block to the inside of the face. Shorten and attach the pendulum, then pilot-drill the back and attach using no. 4 × $^3/_4$" brass screws.

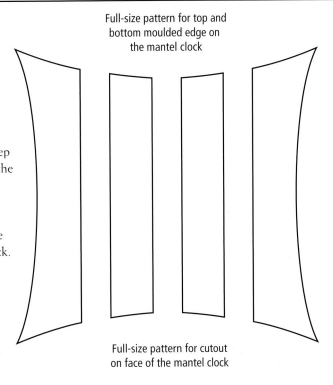

Full-size pattern for top and bottom moulded edge on the mantel clock

Full-size pattern for cutout on face of the mantel clock

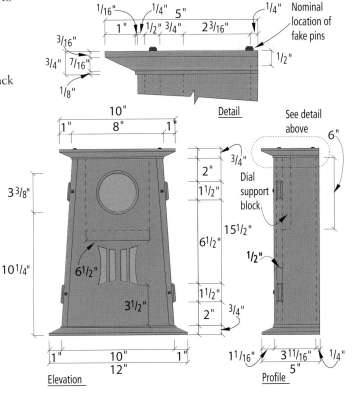

Elevation

Profile

Detail

Dial support block

SUPPLIERS

**ADAMS & KENNEDY —
THE WOOD SOURCE**
6178 Mitch Owen Rd.
P.O. Box 700
Manotick, ON
Canada K4M 1A6
613-822-6800
www.wood-source.com
Wood supply

ADJUSTABLE CLAMP COMPANY
404 N. Armour St.
Chicago, IL 60622
312-666-0640
www.adjustableclamp.com
Clamps and woodworking tools

B&Q
Portswood House
1 Hampshire Corporate Park
Chandlers Ford
Eastleigh
Hampshire, England SO53 3YX
0845 609 6688
www.diy.com
*Woodworking tools, supplies and
hardware*

BUSY BEE TOOLS
130 Great Gulf Dr.
Concord, ON
Canada L4K 5W1
1-800-461-2879
www.busybeetools.com
Woodworking tools and supplies

CRAFTSMAN PLANS
P.O. Box 325
Loveland, OH 45140
craftsmanplans.com
Plans, books, tools, hardware

**CONSTANTINE'S WOOD CENTER
OF FLORIDA**
1040 E. Oakland Park Blvd.
Fort Lauderdale, FL 33334
800-443-9667
www.constantines.com
Tools, woods, veneers, hardware

**FRANK PAXTON LUMBER
COMPANY**
5701 W. 66th St.
Chicago, IL 60638
800-323-2203
www.paxtonwood.com
Wood, hardware, tools, books

THE HOME DEPOT
2455 Paces Ferry Rd. NW
Atlanta, GA 30339
800-430-3376 (U.S.)
800-628-0525 (Canada)
www.homedepot.com
*Woodworking tools, supplies and
hardware*

KLINGSPOR ABRASIVES INC.
2555 Tate Blvd. SE
Hickory, N.C. 28602
800-645-5555
www.klingspor.com
Sandpaper of all kinds

LEE VALLEY TOOLS LTD.
P.O. Box 1780
Ogdensburg, NY 13669-6780
800-871-8158 (U.S.)
800-267-8767 (Canada)
www.leevalley.com
Woodworking tools and hardware

LEIGH INDUSTRIES LTD.
P.O. Box 357
104-1585 Broadway St.
Port Coquitlam, BC, Canada
V3C 4K6
800-663-8932
leighjigs.com
Tools and jigs

LIE-NIELSEN TOOLWORKS
Lie-Nielsen Toolworks
P.O. Box 9
Warren, ME 04864-0009
800-327-2520
lie-nielsen.com
handtools

LOWE'S COMPANIES, INC.
P.O. Box 1111
North Wilkesboro, NC 28656
800-445-6937
www.lowes.com
*Woodworking tools, supplies and
hardware*

**ROCKLER WOODWORKING AND
HARDWARE**
4365 Willow Dr.
Medina, MN 55340
800-279-4441
www.rockler.com
*Woodworking tools, hardware and
books*

TOOL TREND LTD.
140 Snow Blvd. Unit 1
Concord, ON
Canada L4K 4C1
416-663-8665
Woodworking tools and hardware

**TREND MACHINERY & CUTTING
TOOLS LTD.**
Odhams Trading Estate
St. Albans Rd.
Watford
Hertfordshire, U.K.
WD24 7TR
01923 224657
www.trendmachinery.co.uk
Woodworking tools and hardware

WATERLOX COATINGS
908 Meech Ave.
Cleveland, OH 44105
800-321-0377
www.waterlox.com
Finishing supplies

WHITECHAPEL LTD.
P.O. Box 11719
Jackson, WY 83002
800-468-5534
www.whitechapel-ltd.com
Fine quality hardware

WOODCRAFT SUPPLY LLC
1177 Rosemar Rd.
P.O. Box 1686
Parkersburg, WV 26102
800-535-4482
www.woodcraft.com
Woodworking hardware

WOODWORKER'S HARDWARE
P.O. Box 180
Sauk Rapids, MN 56379-0180
800-383-0130
www.wwhardware.com
Woodworking hardware

WOODWORKER'S SUPPLY
1108 N. Glenn Rd.
Casper, WY 82601
800-645-9292
http://woodworker.com
*Woodworking tools and accessories,
finishing supplies, books and plans*

INDEX

More great titles from Popular Woodworking!

Measure Twice, Cut Once
By Jim Tolpin

From design and layout to developing a cutting list, Jim Tolpin's easy-to-follow style introduces a variety of tools (new and old) used to transfer measurements accurately to the wood. You'll learn the best cutting techniques, how to prevent mistakes before they happen, and for those unavoidable mistakes, you'll learn how to fix them so no one will know!

ISBN 13: 978-1-55870-809-9
ISBN 10: 1-55870-809-X
paperback, 128 p., #Z0835

Pleasant Hill Shaker Furniture
By Kerry Pierce

Take a virtual tour through one of the remaining Shaker communities. Study the history, the lifestyle and delve deeply into the furniture created by these gifted craftsmen. Includes painstakingly detailed measured drawings of the original furniture pieces and hundreds of beautiful photos. Learn the secrets of Shaker construction while learning about the Shaker's themselves.

ISBN 13: 978-1-55870-795-5
ISBN 10: 1-55870-795-6
hardcover, 176 p., #Z0564

I Can Do That! Woodworking Projects
Edited by David Thiel

Beginning or experienced woodworkers can build these top-quality projects quickly and efficiently.
• Each project requires a minimum of tools.
• The projects need only inexpensive materials that are readily available at your local home improvement center.
• This book includes a training manual for using each tool.

ISBN 13: 978-1-55870-816-7
ISBN 10: 1-55870-816-2
paperback, 128 p., #Z0991

These and other great woodworking books are available at your local bookstore, woodworking stores or from online suppliers.

www.popularwoodworking.com

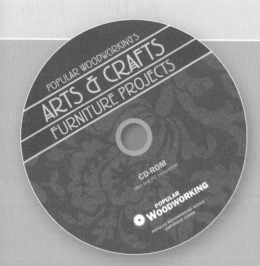

Easy to Use
Compatible with both Mac and PC, the bonus disc has twenty PDFs' (download a free Adobe Acrobat Reader from www.adobe.com) of project and technique articles from *Popular Woodworking*. Browse the articles, or print them out for use in the shop.

POPULAR WOODWORKING'S ARTS & CRAFTS FURNITURE PROJECTS
BONUS DISC TABLE OF CONTENTS

Projects
1. Arts & Crafts Cellarette
2. Byrdcliffe Wall Cabinet
3. Greene & Greene Garden Bench
4. Greene & Greene Garden Table
5. Wright Hall Tree
6. Knock-down Bookcase
7. Limbert Waste Basket
8. Magazine Stand
9. Stickley Side Table
10. Wright-style Table Lamp

Techniques
11. 3-D Mortising Upgrade
12. Arts & Crafts Finish
13. Greene & Greene Drawers
14. Mortise & Tenon Basics
15. Mortise & Tenon Joinery
16. Mortising Manual
17. Router Jig
18. Practical Mortise & Tenon Joinery
19. Recreating Greene & Greene
20. Tenoning Fixture